Short Term Forecasting

Short Term Forecasting

An Introduction to the Box-Jenkins Approach

Thomas M. O'Donovan

Department of Statistics
University College
Cork

JOHN WILEY & SONS

Chichester · New York · Brisbane · Toronto · Singapore

Library of Congress Cataloging in Publication Data:

O'Donovan, Thomas M.
  Short term forecasting.

  Includes index.
  1. Business forecasting. 2. Time-series analysis.
  I. Title. II. Title: Box–Jenkins approach.
  HD30.27.036 1983 338.5'442 82-11187
  ISBN 0 471 90013 3

British Library Cataloguing in Publication Data:

O'Donovan, Thomas M.
  Short term forecasting.
  i. Time-series analysis
  I. Title
  519.5'5 QA280
  ISBN 0 471 90013 3

Typeset by Unicus Graphics Ltd, Horsham, West Sussex
Printed and bound at the Pitman Press, Bath

For Bill Meeker,

whose computer program TSERIES

inspired this book

Contents

Preface ix

Chapter 1. An overview of forecasting 1
1.1 The growth of forecasting and some of its applications 1
1.2 Forecasting and decision making 2
1.3 Forecasting methods 3
1.4 Choosing a forecasting method 5
1.5 Another look at forecasting methods 10
1.6 The role of forecasting in management 12

Chapter 2. Characteristics of a time series 15
2.1 Definition of a time series 15
2.2 Visual examination of a time series 16
2.3 Some statistical concepts 19
2.4 Mean and standard deviation of a time series 23
2.5 Further statistical concepts 26
2.6 The sample autocorrelation function 31
2.7 The sample partial autocorrelation function 37
2.8 Exercises 40

Chapter 3. Forecasting for models of stationary time series 47
3.1 Minimum mean square error forecasts 47
3.2 The white noise model 49
3.3 The first order autoregressive model 53
3.4 The second order autoregressive model 59
3.5 The first order moving average model 62
3.6 The second order moving average model 70
3.7 The first order autoregressive moving average model 70
3.8 Autoregressive moving average models 71
3.9 Exercises 76

Chapter 4. Forecasting stationary time series 77
4.1 Stages in the Box–Jenkins approach to forecasting 77

4.2   Identification of a tentative model   79
4.3   Estimation of model parameters   83
4.4   Diagnostic checks of the tentative model   86
4.5   Example 4.1   92
4.6   Example 4.2   105
4.7   Example 4.3   114
4.8   Exercises   122

Chapter 5. Forecasting non-stationary time series   129
5.1   Transforming a time series to achieve stationarity   129
5.2   Differencing a time series to achieve stationarity   131
5.3   The random walk model   136
5.4   Autoregressive integrated moving average models   138
5.5   Example 5.1   142
5.6   Example 5.2   148
5.7   Example 5.3   154
5.8   Exercises   160

Chapter 6. Forecasting seasonal time series   179
6.1   Differencing a seasonal time series to achieve stationarity . . .   179
6.2   Seasonal autoregressive and moving average models   182
6.3   Multiplicative seasonal models   185
6.4   Example 6.1   190
6.5   Example 6.2   196
6.6   Example 6.3   202
6.7   Review of the Box–Jenkins approach to forecasting time series .   212
6.8   Exercises   213
6.9   Revision exercises   237

Appendix A.1 References   239

Appendix A.2 Statistical tables   241

Appendix A.3 Collection of time series   245

Appendix A.4 Table of fitted models for time series used in examples and exercises   267

Appendix A.5 TSERIES – a user-oriented computer program for time series analysis   269

Appendix A.6 Some computer packages for time series analysis using the Box–Jenkins approach   275

Index   279

Preface

The analysis and forecasting of time series data are techniques which are of vital importance to business managers and economists. One approach to forecasting time series is known as the Box–Jenkins method and was suggested by George E. P. Box and Gwilym M. Jenkins in their book *Time Series Analysis: Forecasting and Control*, which was first published in 1970. Since then, this approach has become widely used and many of the computer packages for time series analysis that are available today are based on this approach. The main advantage of this method is that short term forecasts produced by this method are usually more accurate than those produced by any other method. Its main disadvantage is that it is rather difficult to understand. This has inhibited its use in business management. In fact, some firms have discontinued using this method simply because it was too difficult for the ultimate users of the forecasts to understand the conceptual basis for the method and to feel confident that it was being correctly applied. However, it is to be expected that as management becomes more sophisticated, the Box–Jenkins method will be more widely used for short term forecasting because of its high accuracy.

The aim of this book is to provide an elementary introduction to the Box–Jenkins approach to short term forecasting. No previous knowledge of statistics is required to read this book. The statistical concepts underlying the Box–Jenkins method are introduced as they are needed and illustrated by simple examples. Mathematical proofs are omitted, as these are available in other textbooks. A complete description is given of all the stages of the Box–Jenkins approach to short term forecasting for a single time series. The most difficult stage of this approach is the identification of an appropriate model for a time series. Skill at model identification is only acquired by experience and so numerous worked examples and exercises are provided based on real time series data to give the reader plenty of practice at model identification. For each time series studied, all the characteristics of that time series that are needed for model identification are provided, so that readers who do not have access to a computer package for time series analysis can still obtain practice at model identification.

The plan of this book is evident from the Table of Contents. In Chapter 1, an overview of forecasting is given. The Box–Jenkins method is compared with other forecasting methods and its advantages and disadvantages are outlined. Chapter 2 deals with the characteristics of a time series that are used to identify an appro-

ix

priate model. Chapter 3 is devoted to describing a class of models for time series which are stationary, i.e. whose underlying probabilistic mechanism does not change over time. In Chapter 4, we see how to fit a model from this class to a stationary time series and how to use the model to forecast future values of the time series. Chapter 5 deals with non-stationary time series and Chapter 6 describes the Box–Jenkins approach to forecasting seasonal time series.

Many computer packages for time series analysis based on the Box–Jenkins approach are available today. However, the items included in the computer printout from these packages are very similar. In this book, the time series studied were analysed using the TSERIES package, which was developed by Professor William Q. Meeker of the Statistical Laboratory at Iowa State University. The aim of this book is to help the reader to make an intelligent interpretation of the computer printout from this package. Because of the similarity between computer printouts from different computer packages using the Box–Jenkins approach, the reader should then be able to interpret the computer printout from any such package.

This book was written while the author was on a sabbatical visit to the Statistics Department, Iowa State University. The author would like to thank Professor H. A. David for making this visit possible and all the staff of the Statistics Department, the Statistical Laboratory, the Computation Center, and the Library at Iowa State University for their helpfulness during my visit. I am particularly grateful to Mrs Phyllis Carr who typed the manuscript. I owe a special debt of gratitude to Professor William Q. Meeker, the author of the TSERIES package, who read the manuscript and made many helpful suggestions, as well as answering all my questions about the TSERIES package with unfailing patience.

THOMAS M. O'DONOVAN

Chapter 1

An overview of forecasting

1.1 THE GROWTH OF FORECASTING AND SOME OF ITS APPLICATIONS

Forecasting is widely used today by business managers and economists. Many scientists and engineers are also involved in forecasting in a technical capacity. Forecasts have always been made in business planning, but until recently they were all too often purely subjective managerial guesses. Management today has a wide variety of quantitative techniques which can be incorporated into a formal forecasting system. This rapid expansion in the application of quantitative forecasting is the result of a number of factors:

1. The growth in forecasting techniques which are available for different problem situations and the growth in expert personnel to handle them.
2. The development and adoption of computers. The computer can be used not only to make the many computations that these forecasting techniques require, but also to store historical data and then retrieve that data rapidly and efficiently when it is needed for a new forecast.
3. The increasing size and complexity of business operations in which no one man can now adequately deal with decision making. The resulting formalized management structures have in turn encouraged the adoption of sophisticated forecasting methods.
4. Forecasting techniques have developed a record of accuracy. Thus managers have placed increased confidence in them as an aid to decision making.
5. The resources that must be devoted to research and development and to capital expenditure have risen enormously in recent years so that any mistakes in evaluating the level of product sales can lead to heavy losses and business failure. This increase in the riskiness of business has encouraged the use of quantitative forecasting methods in order to reduce uncertainty to acceptable levels.

Business firms require forecasts of many events and conditions in all phases of their operations. Some examples of situations in which business forecasts are required are given below:

1

In *marketing*, reliable forecasts of demand must be available so that sales strategies can be planned. For example, total demand for products must be forecasted in order to plan total promotional effort.

In *finance*, interest rates must be predicted so that new capital acquisitions can be planned and financed.

In *personnel management*, forecasts of the number of workers required in different job categories are required in order to plan job recruiting and training programmes.

In *production scheduling and inventory control*, predictions of demand for each product line are needed. These forecasts allow the firm to plan production schedules and inventory maintenance.

In *process control*, forecasts of the behaviour of an industrial process are needed. If the process is becoming less efficient as hours of continuous operation increase, forecasts of future behaviour can be used to plan the shutdown time and overhaul schedule.

1.2 FORECASTING AND DECISION MAKING

It is important to understand the role that forecasting plays in management. Management is concerned with decision making in the face of uncertainty. The aim of forecasting is to reduce the risk in decision making by accurately predicting the future values of important variables. The nature of the decisions being made will dictate many of the desired characteristics of the forecasting method to be used. In particular, it will determine the answers to the following questions:

What variable is to be predicted?
This will depend largely on the needs of the management and the availability of historical information.

What form of forecast is required?
There are two types of forecasts: *point forecasts* and *prediction interval forecasts*. An example of the former is 'Forecast sales for next month is 40 000 units'. An example of the latter is 'A 95% prediction interval forecast for next month's sales is [38 000 units, 42 000 units]', meaning that the firm is 95% sure that sales for next month will be between 38 000 and 42 000 units. Prediction interval forecasts are often very useful in decision making. For example, if it is known that sales will not be more than 42 000 units next month, this can be used to determine the level of inventory it should carry next month.

How far into the future are forecasts required?
Depending on the decisions being made, forecasts may be required for points in time that are a number of days, weeks, months, quarters, or years in the future. This length of time is called the *forecast lead time*, *time horizon*, or *time frame*. Different forecasting methods are appropriate for different lead times.

How many items must be forecast?

In some situations, it may be satisfactory to forecast total sales for the company as a whole. However, in another situation forecasts may be required of the sales of each product produced by the company. When forecasts of many items are required, simple forecasting methods are often appropriate because they are quick and cheap, whereas if forecasts are required for only a few items, more sophisticated forecasting methods can be considered.

What accuracy is required?

By the *accuracy* of a forecasting method is meant the extent to which forecast values generated by that method approximate to the actual future values that emerge in time. The factors that determine the most suitable level of accuracy are the importance of the management decision being made and the role of the forecast in affecting that decision. In some cases, a forecast may be peripheral to the decision being made and so a low level of accuracy may be adequate, even though the decision may be an important one. On the other hand, a decision of only minimum importance could use as a basis for decision making the forecast for a single variable. In this situation, a high level of accuracy in the forecast would be desired. Some forecasting methods are more accurate than others, but invariably this increased accuracy is accompanied by increased cost, so that it is important to determine in advance the minimum level of forecasting accuracy that will be acceptable in any situation. In practice, forecast accuracy is generally limited by the inherent variability in the variable being forecasted.

1.3 FORECASTING METHODS

Forecasting methods can be divided into two basic types: *qualitative methods* and *quantitative methods. Qualitative forecasting methods* generally use the opinion of experts to predict future events subjectively. Such methods are described in the references in Appendix A.1, but will not be discussed here. *Quantitative forecasting methods* involve the analysis of historical data in an attempt to predict future values of a variable of interest.

All quantitative forecasting methods make use of the following basic strategy. Past data are analysed in order to identify a pattern that can be used to describe them. Then this pattern is extrapolated, or extended, into the future in order to make forecasts. This strategy rests on the assumption that the pattern that has been identified will continue into the future. A forecasting technique cannot be expected to give good predictions unless this assumption is valid. This assumption is more likely to be valid in the short term than in the long term and so it is not surprising that, in general, short term forecasts are more accurate than long term forecasts.

Quantitative forecasting methods can be grouped into two kinds: *time series* and *causal*. In *time series* models, historical data on the variable to be forecast are analysed in an attempt to identify a data pattern. Then, assuming that it will continue in the future, this pattern is extrapolated in order to produce forecasts.

Note that time series models generate predictions that are based solely on the historical pattern of the variable to be forecast. Thus any decisions management might implement will not alter the predictions generated by a time series model. Time series forecasting models are, therefore, most useful when conditions are expected to remain the same; they are not very useful in forecasting the impact of changes in management policies.

The most widely used types of time series models are outlined below. More detailed descriptions are given in the references in Appendix A.1.

Simple exponential smoothing
A weighted average of the recently observed values of the variable under study is used as a forecast. An exponentially decreasing set of weights is assigned to these values so that the more recent values receive more weight than older values.

Holt-Winters
This is a more sophisticated version of exponential smoothing in which allowance is made for trend and seasonal patterns in the data. (These patterns are described in the next section.)

Decomposition
A time series is regarded as having a number of components: trend, seasonality, cyclicality, and randomness. The first three of these components are estimated and used to forecast future values. One decomposition method which is widely used is the Census X.11 method.

Box-Jenkins
A class of models known as Autoregressive Moving Average (or just ARMA) is studied. From a study of the data, an appropriate model is selected from this class and used to make forecasts.

Bayesian forecasting
This method allows one to specify a range of models for the data, rather than a single model, with associated probabilities which are updated as more data become available. Estimates of the model parameters are also updated, using a technique known as *Kalman filtering*. The method potentially includes both exponential smoothing and ARMA models, though in practice it is limited to a selection of a small number of models which are in some ways equivalent to ARMA models and which have been found to cover many of the practically occurring situations.

Besides time series models, the other main type of quantitative forecasting method is *causal models*. These models involve the identification of other variables related to the variable to be predicted. Then a model is developed that describes the relationship between these variables and the variable to be predicted. This model is then used to forecast the variable of interest. For example, the sales of a product might be related to the price of the product, advertising expenditures to promote the product, and competitors' prices charged for similar products. In such a case, sales would be referred to as the *dependent variable*, while the other variables are referred to as the *independent variables*. The forecaster's job is to estimate the relationship between sales and the independent variables. The forecaster then uses predicted future values of the independent variables (price of the product, advertising expenditures, competitors' prices) to predict future values of sales (the dependent variable).

The main types of causal models are outlined below.

Multiple regression
The relationship between the dependent and independent variables is known as the *regression equation*. Multiple regression is the technique by which estimates are found for the coefficients of the independent variables in the regression equation. The regression equation is then used to forecast future values of the dependent variable.

Econometrics
Econometrics involves systems of interrelated regression equations. Regression analysis is used to estimate the coefficients of the variables in these equations.

Multivariate Box-Jenkins
The Box-Jenkins method outlined above could more accurately be described as the *univariate* Box-Jenkins method, since the method uses only past values of a single variable (e.g. sales of a product) to forecast future values of that variable. Suppose that independent variables exist (e.g. price of the product, advertising expenditures) that are related to the dependent variable which is to be forecasted. The Multivariate Box-Jenkins method is an extension of the univariate Box-Jenkins method which attempts to relate these independent variables to the dependent variable by means of *transfer functions*.

1.4 CHOOSING A FORECASTING METHOD

In this section, we consider the main factors governing the choice of a forecasting method for use in a given situation. Some of these factors arise from the nature of the associated decision problem, as discussed in the previous section. The factors we will consider are:

1. Lead time
2. Time to prepare forecast
3. Pattern of data
4. Data requirements
5. Ease of understanding
6. Cost
7. Accuracy

These factors are considered in turn and in each case the forecasting methods are compared in the light of that factor. This discussion is summarized in Table 1.1. In this table, an 'X' is used to indicate that a forecasting method is appropriate for that situation.

Table 1.1 Comparison of forecasting methods

Factor	Forecasting method						
	Simple exponential smoothing	Holt–Winters	De-composition	Box–Jenkins	Multiple regression	Econometrics	Multivariate Box–Jenkins
Lead time							
Immediate	X	X	X	X	–	–	–
Short term	X	X	X	X	X	X	X
Medium term	–	–	–	–	X	X	X
Long term	–	–	–	–	X	X	X
Time to prepare forecast (1 – shortest; 7 – longest)	1	2	3	5	4	7	6
Pattern of data							
Horizontal	X	–	X	X	–	–	X
Trend	–	X	X	X	X	X	X
Seasonal	–	X	X	X	X	X	X
Cyclical	–	–	X	–	X	X	–
Date requirements (S: period of seasonality)	10	15 2(S)	30 6(S)	30 6(S)	30 6(S)	Few 100	60 8(S)
Ease of understanding (1 – easiest; 7 – hardest)	1	2	3	4	5	7	6
Cost (1 – least costly; 7 – most costly)	1	2	3	5	4	7	6

Lead time

The lead time has already been defined as the length of time into the future for which forecasts are required. The length of the lead time is usually categorized as follows:

Immediate: less than one month
Short term: one to three months
Medium term: more than three months to less than two years
Long term: two years or more

It has been found that because of the other factors considered below, certain forecasting methods are more suitable for a short lead time and other methods for a long lead time.

For immediate forecasts, simple exponential smoothing, Holt–Winters, decomposition, and Box–Jenkins are used. For short term forecasts, all seven methods have been used. For medium and long term forecasts, multiple regression, econometric methods, and multivariate Box–Jenkins are used. However, for very long term forecasts, qualitative methods are more useful than quantitative methods.

Time to prepare forecast

By this is meant the total time needed to collect the necessary data, analyse them, and prepare the forecast. The various forecasting methods differ in the total time that this process takes. In any situation, forecasts must be ready before a certain time; otherwise they are useless for decision making. This makes some of the forecasting methods inappropriate when forecasts are urgently needed. In this case, simple forecasting methods are used simply because they are the only methods that would produce forecasts in time. Better a good forecast when needed than a superb forecast three months too late. When there are many items to be forecasted, the problem of preparing forecasts on time is even more crucial.

In Table 1.1, the methods are ranked from those that take the shortest time to prepare a forecast to those that take the longest time. The order is: simple exponential smoothing, Holt–Winters, decomposition, multiple regression, Box–Jenkins, multivariate Box–Jenkins, and econometric methods.

Pattern of data

There are four basic subpatterns, some combination of which usually exists in any business or economic series of data. These are (a) *trend*, (b) *horizontal*, (c) *seasonal*, and (d) *cyclical*. A *trend* exists when there is a pattern of growth or decline in the data over the time span being studied. A *horizontal* subpattern exists when the data are evenly distributed over time, that is, when there is no apparent growth or decline over time. A *seasonal* subpattern is a periodic regular pattern with a constant period, such as a day, a week, a month, or a year. Finally, a *cyclical* subpattern exists when the data are influenced by longer term economic fluctuations related to the general business cycle.

Knowledge of the types of subpatterns included in the data can be very useful in selecting the most appropriate forecasting method, since different methods vary in their ability to cope with different types of patterns. Simple exponential smoothing can deal only with horizontal subpatterns in the data. Higher forms of exponential smoothing, such as the Holt–Winters method, can deal with both trend and seasonal subpatterns in the data. Decomposition can handle all combinations of horizontal, trend, seasonal, and cyclical components. Box–Jenkins and multivariate Box–Jenkins can deal with horizontal, trend, and seasonal subpatterns. Finally, multiple regression and econometric methods are not appropriate when the subpattern is horizontal, but can deal with trend, seasonal, and cyclical components.

Data requirements

Since various forecasting methods require different amounts of historical data, the quantity of data available is important in determining the feasibility of using alternative methods. If the needed historical data are not available, special data-collecting procedures may have to be implemented. When immediate or short term forecasts are required, there is rarely enough time to collect new data. Causal models typically require more data than time series models and this is one reason why such models are more appropriate for medium and long term forecasting. The minimum data requirements for the various forecasting methods are shown in Table 1.1. It is seen that simple exponential smoothing requires at least 10 observations, and that for non-seasonal data, the Holt–Winters method requires 15 observations, the decomposition, Box–Jenkins, and multiple regression methods require at least 30 observations, and multivariate Box–Jenkins requires at least 60. For seasonal data, the Holt–Winters method requires at least 2 seasons' data (e.g. 24 observations for monthly data), decomposition, Box–Jenkins, and multiple regression methods require at least 6 seasons' data, and multivariate Box–Jenkins requires at least 8 seasons' data. Econometric methods typically require several hundred observations.

Ease of understanding

The ease with which a forecasting method is understood is very important. Managers are held responsible for the decisions they make and if they are to be expected to base their decisions on predictions generated by forecasting techniques, they must be able to understand these techniques. A manager simply will not have confidence in the predictions obtained from a forecasting technique he or she does not understand, and if the manager does not have confidence in these predictions, they will not be used in the decision making process. This is the main reason why sophisticated forecasting methods, such as the Box–Jenkins methods, are not more widely used. Although the Box–Jenkins method produces very accurate forecasts, some firms have discontinued using this method simply because it was too difficult for the ultimate users of the forecasts to understand the conceptual basis for the method and to feel confident that it was being correctly applied.

As shown in Table 1.1, the forecasting methods are ranked from the easiest to understand to the most difficult. The order is: simple exponential smoothing, Holt-Winters, decomposition, Box-Jenkins, multiple regression, multivariate Box-Jenkins, and econometric methods. It is seen that, of the time series models, the Box-Jenkins method is the most difficult to understand.

Cost

When choosing a forecasting technique, several costs are relevant. First, the cost of developing the model must be considered. The complexity, and hence the cost, of this process varies from technique to technique. Secondly, the cost of storing the necessary data must be considered. Some forecasting methods require the storage of relatively small amounts of data, while other methods require the storage of large amounts of data. Lastly, the cost of the actual operation of the forecasting technique is obviously very important. When there are many items to be forecasted, consideration of the cost of a forecasting method becomes crucial.

Taking costs in each of the above categories into account, the methods ranked from least costly to most costly are as follows: simple exponential smoothing, Holt-Winters, decomposition, multiple regression, Box-Jenkins, multivariate Box-Jenkins, and econometric methods. It is seen that the Box-Jenkins method is the most costly of the time series models.

Accuracy

In Section 1.2 the accuracy of a method was defined as the extent to which forecast values generated by that method approximate to the actual future values that emerge in time. It was mentioned there that the level of accuracy needed in a given situation will depend on the importance of the decision being made and the role of the forecast in influencing that decision.

It is difficult to rank the forecasting methods in order of accuracy, as the accuracy of the methods will be different in different situations. Studies have been made to compare the accuracy of some of these methods and the results of these studies can be summarized as follows. For immediate and short term forecasts, Box-Jenkins is more accurate than Holt-Winters, though this advantage decreases as the lead time increases. Comparisons of decomposition methods and other methods have not been reported in the literature, but it is known that decomposition methods give reasonably accurate forecasts. In summary, it would be safe to say that for immediate and short term forecasts, the Box-Jenkins method is probably the most accurate of the time series models.

In comparing Box-Jenkins and econometric models, there is some conflict of evidence. While some studies suggest that econometric models are more accurate than Box-Jenkins models, the overall impression is that for immediate and short term forecasts, Box-Jenkins models give more accurate forecasts than econometric models. Not many applications of the multivariate Box-Jenkins method have been reported in the literature, so there is not enough evidence to suggest that this method is appreciably more accurate than the univariate Box–Jenkins method.

In general, the selection of a forecasting method using the criteria described in this section might proceed as follows. First, a number of feasible forecasting methods are selected on the basis of the following factors: the lead time, the time to prepare a forecast, the pattern of the data, the data requirements, and the ease of understanding the methods. A final choice of forecasting method will be made on the basis of the cost and accuracy of the selected methods. This will depend on the use that will be made of the forecast. When the risks associated with forecasting errors are high, highly accurate forecasts are required and so the high cost of a sophisticated forecasting method, such as the Box–Jenkins method, may be justified. When the risks associated with forecasting errors are low, less accurate forecasts may be adequate and so a simple and inexpensive forecasting method may be appropriate.

1.5 ANOTHER LOOK AT FORECASTING METHODS

Having studied the factors governing the choice of a forecasting method, we now review the forecasting methods, pointing out the advantages and disadvantages of each and in what circumstances it is most appropriate to use them.

Simple exponential smoothing

This method has the advantages of being quick to prepare, having minimal data requirements, and being easily understood by managers. Since the cost of storing the data and computing the forecast is so small, it is often the only acceptable method when forecasts are needed for thousands of items, as in the case of many inventory systems. The method is fully automatic, so there is no need to use skilled manpower in its operation. In spite of its low accuracy, it is very widely used for immediate and short term forecasting, because to use a more accurate method may not be feasible or justifiable in terms of cost. Its main disadvantage is its inability to cope with trend and seasonal patterns in the data, but this does not apply to the Holt–Winters method which is considered next.

Holt–Winters

This method has all the advantages of exponential smoothing, but its accuracy is much greater. In fact, for immediate and short-term forecasts, the accuracy of the Holt–Winters method is sometimes comparable to that of the Box–Jenkins method. Holt–Winters is often used for immediate and short term forecasts in preference to the Box–Jenkins method, since it is quicker to prepare, has lower data requirements, is easier to understand, and is less costly. It is also completely automatic, whereas the Box–Jenkins method requires interaction on the part of the forecaster in the choice of an appropriate model.

Decomposition

The main advantages of decomposition are that it is easy to understand, easy to use, and easy to interpret. Unlike the Box-Jenkins method, it provides measures of the seasonal component in the form of seasonal indices, which can be used to deseasonalize data. Decomposition is the strongest available method for dealing with cyclical components. For immediate and short term forecasts, it is reasonably accurate and for these reasons it is often used in preference to the Box–Jenkins method.

The main disadvantages of decomposition are that it is arbitrary in nature and requires some interaction on the part of the forecaster in predicting the trend and cyclical components.

Box–Jenkins

The main advantage of the Box-Jenkins method is that in immediate and short term forecasting it provides the most accurate forecasts. It allows for a wide range of possible models for the data and provides a strategy for selecting a model from that class which best represents the data. This contrasts with the exponential smoothing approach, in which the form of the model for the data is effectively assumed *a priori*.

The main disadvantage of the Box-Jenkins approach is that the process of identifying the correct model from the class of possible models is difficult to understand, is slow, and is costly in terms of computer time. The process is not fully automatic, like the Holt-Winters method, but requires skilled intervention on the part of the forecaster. Because of the freedom to choose between different models, different forecasters may arrive at different models for the same data. However, it is unlikely that this will produce widely different forecasts.

As already mentioned, the fact that the Box-Jenkins method is so difficult to understand has inhibited its use in business management. It is to be expected that as management becomes more sophisticated, the highly accurate Box–Jenkins method will be more widely used for immediate and short term forecasts when the high risks associated with forecasting errors justify the high cost of using the method. It is hoped that this book will assist in this education process, by providing managers with an elementary introduction to the Box–Jenkins method.

Bayesian forecasting was not included in the comparison in Table 1.1. This method has only recently been developed and very little information is available on its performance compared with other forecasting methods. Its advantages include its great flexibility, since it includes both exponential smoothing and ARMA models. It is also able to cope with changes in the model over time. Its accuracy appears to be comparable to that of the Box-Jenkins method, but it is cheaper to use in terms of computer time. Its main disadvantage appears to be that it is computationally complex and difficult to understand.

Multiple regression, econometric methods, and multivariate Box–Jenkins

The main advantage that these causal models have over time series models has already been mentioned. With time series models, the forecasts are based solely on the historical pattern of the variable to be forecast. These forecasts are based on the assumption that conditions remain the same. Thus time series models cannot be used to predict the impact of changes in management policies, e.g. to predict the effect that a price increase will have on the sales of a product. Causal models are designed to do just this, by relating the dependent variable (sales of product) to a number of independent variables (price of the product, advertising expenditure, competitors' prices, etc.).

The main disadvantages of econometric models are that they are more difficult to understand and more costly than time series models. These high costs are incurred in developing a model and collecting and analysing data. Running the model to calculate forecasts is relatively inexpensive. Also, it has been found that for immediate and short term forecasts, the Box–Jenkins method is often more accurate than complex econometric methods, which are far more costly. Another disadvantage of econometric models is that they require forecasts of future values of the independent variables in the regression equations.

The multivariate Box–Jenkins method should produce more accurate forecasts than the univariate Box–Jenkins method, since it uses information about other variables related to the variable being forecasted. However, it is more difficult to understand than univariate Box–Jenkins and more costly to use. Not many applications of multivariate Box–Jenkins have been reported in the literature, so it is not proven that this method is appreciably more accurate than the univariate Box–Jenkins method for immediate and short term forecasts.

In summary, it may be said that for immediate and short term forecasting, causal models are not appropriate because of the large amounts of data required and the high costs involved. For medium and long term forecasts, however, causal models come into their own. This is especially true when management has control over various independent variables, so that the impact of changes in management policy can be estimated.

1.6 THE ROLE OF FORECASTING IN MANAGEMENT

The important part that forecasting plays in management decision making has already been outlined. Whatever quantitative forecasting method is used to produce the forecast, these forecasts are almost always subjectively evaluated by management. This is because the quantitative forecasts are based on the assumption that the future will behave like the past. If a manager expects that future events are likely to be different from past events because of the appearance of some new factor (e.g. a major new customer is expected in the next year), he can use his expert opinion to modify the quantitative forecast accordingly.

Quantitative forecasts give management estimates of the future effects of their present policies. If these are acceptable, then management has no reason to change its present policies. However, having seen a preliminary forecast indicating that sales can be expected to be low at some future period, management may adopt new policies so as to stimulate sales by cutting prices or increasing advertising expenditure. Forecasts generated by time series models will be misleading in predicting sales under these new conditions, but causal models can produce revised forecasts to estimate the effects of various combinations of price changes and advertising expenditures. Whatever combination is decided on, then it is the corresponding revised forecast of sales that must be used in measuring the accuracy of the forecasting method, not the original forecast that caused the change of policy.

Whatever forecasting method is being used, it is essential that management monitor the forecasts and compare them with actual future values as they emerge in time. This is known as *forecast control*. When the forecast errors are larger than would be expected on a statistical basis, corrective action should be taken to modify the forecasting model to produce more accurate forecasts. The measurement of forecasting errors is discussed in a later chapter.

Chapter 2

Characteristics of a time series

2.1 DEFINITION OF A TIME SERIES

In the previous chapter, we surveyed quantitative forecasting methods and concluded that the Box-Jenkins method was the most accurate method available for immediate and short term forecasts. In this and subsequent chapters, an elementary introduction is provided to the Box-Jenkins method. In the present chapter, we begin by defining a time series. We then describe the characteristics of a time series and look at some examples of the types of time series that arise in practice. The Box-Jenkins method involves picking an appropriate model for the data and, in this chapter, we consider certain characteristics of a time series which are used to decide which model is appropriate. Finding an appropriate model for the data is the most difficult and time-consuming part of the Box-Jenkins method. Once an appropriate model has been found, forecasting future values of the time series is relatively easy.

A *time series* is a time-ordered sequence of observations of a variable. By a *time-ordered* sequence is meant one in which the observations are arranged in the order in which they were observed. An example of a time series is given in Table 2.1, which shows the yields of seventy consecutive batches from a chemical process. This time series also appears as time series 2.1 in Appendix A.3 at the end of this book.

For some time series, it is possible to observe the value of the variable being studied at every moment of time. Such a series is said to form a *continuous time series.* Examples of continuous time series are: temperature, prices, and interest rates. However, most available time series consist of observations of the variable made at predetermined, equal-interval time points, so that one might get hourly, daily, monthly, quarterly, or yearly observations. Such data form a *discrete time series.*

Discrete time series can arise in several ways. Even if the basic time series being studied is continuous, one can still imbed a discrete series by reading off the value of the variable at equally spaced time points. Such a time series is called a *sampled time series.* An example is stock market prices. Although the price of a stock

15

Table 2.1 A time series of 70 consecutive yields from a batch chemical process. (From Box, G. E. P., and Jenkins, G. M. (1976). *Time Series Analysis: Forecasting and Control.* Reproduced by permission of Holden-Day Inc.)

1–15	16–30	31–45	46–60	61–70
47	44	50	62	68
64	80	71	44	38
23	55	56	64	50
71	37	74	43	60
38	74	50	52	39
64	51	58	38	59
55	57	45	59	40
41	50	54	55	57
59	60	36	41	54
48	45	54	53	23
71	57	48	49	
35	50	55	34	
57	45	45	35	
40	25	57	54	
58	59	50	45	

fluctuates more or less continuously during the trading day, stock market prices are usually reported as daily closing prices, i.e. the price of the stock at the end of the trading day. Another type of discrete time series arises when the variable being studied cannot be measured at every moment of time, but we can still accumulate the values over equal intervals of time. Such a time series is called an *accumulated time series* or an *aggregated time series*. Examples are exports measured monthly or rainfall measured daily. In this book we are concerned with discrete time series, where the observations are taken at equal intervals. Occasionally the convenient interval between observations is not quite constant, for instance the calendar month. This will make little difference in the case of a sampled series, but an adjustment will generally be necessary for an accumulated series.

2.2 VISUAL EXAMINATION OF A TIME SERIES

The first step in analysing a time series is to plot the observations against time. This will often show up the most important properties of a time series. Features such as trend, seasonality, and discontinuities will usually be visible if present in the series. Plots of the time series 2.1 in Table 2.1 and of four other time series (time series 2.2 to 2.5 in Appendix A.3) are shown in Figures 2.1 to 2.5. Descriptions of all these time series are given in Appendix A.3.

The data in Figure 2.1 follow a *horizontal* pattern, as defined in the previous chapter, because the data appear to fluctuate about a constant average. There is apparently no upward or downward trend in the average over time. Although there is considerable variability about the average, this variability appears to stay fairly constant over time. In Figure 2.2, there is a pronounced upward trend in the

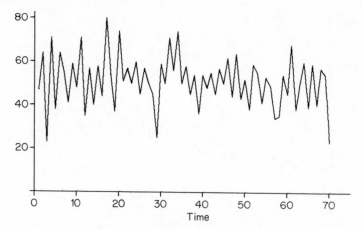

Figure 2.1 Plot of time series 2.1

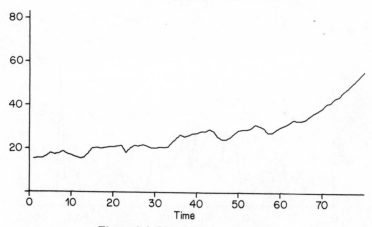

Figure 2.2 Plot of time series 2.2

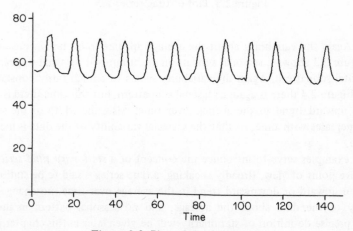

Figure 2.3 Plot of time series 2.3

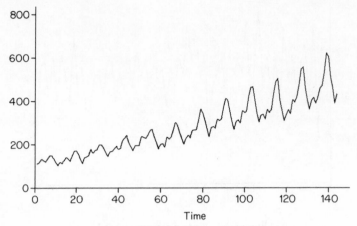

Figure 2.4 Plot of time series 2.4

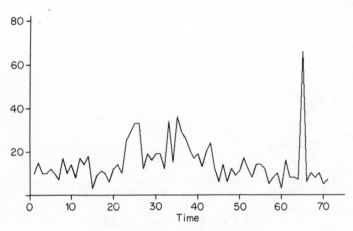

Figure 2.5 Plot of time series 2.5

average. Again the variability about the average appears to be fairly constant over time. Figure 2.3 shows a seasonal subpattern superimposed on what appears to be a horizontal subpattern. Again the variability seems to remain fairly constant over time. In Figure 2.4 there is again a seasonal subpattern, but this time there is also an apparent upward trend in the average over time. Also, the width of the seasonal pattern increases with time, so that the seasonal variability of the data is increasing with time.

These examples serve to introduce the concept of a *stationary time series* from an intuitive point of view. Broadly speaking, a time series is said to be stationary if there is no upward or downward trend in the average over time, no change in the variability of the data about the average, and no seasonal pattern in the data. (A more precise definition of stationarity will be given later in this chapter.) Using this broad definition of stationarity, we see that only the time series 2.1 in Figure

2.1 is apparently stationary. The time series 2.2 in Figure 2.2 is non-stationary because of the upward trend. The time series 2.3 in Figure 2.3 is non-stationary because of the seasonal pattern, and the time series 2.4 in Figure 2.4 is non-stationary because of the upward trend, the seasonal pattern, and the increase in seasonal variability over time. The importance of the concept of stationarity stems from the fact that the Box–Jenkins method provides a class of models of stationary time series. Hence, if a series is stationary, we can immediately proceed to look for an appropriate model from this class. However, if a time series is non-stationary, we must first attempt to transform it to a stationary series and then fit a model to the transformed series. This is easily accomplished for the examples of non-stationary series considered above.

The time series 2.5 which is plotted in Figure 2.5 contains an *outlier*. An outlier is an observation which does not appear to be consistent with the rest of the data. Here the 65th observation is approximately five times larger than adjacent observations. An outlier may be a perfectly valid observation, in which case the model for the time series will need to take it into account. The extension of the Box–Jenkins method described here to cover such changes in the underlying model is known as *intervention analysis*. Bayesian forecasting is also capable of handling such outliers. Alternatively, an outlier may be a freak observation arising, for example, when a recording device goes wrong. In such cases, the outlier needs to be adjusted to its expected value under normal circumstances before further analysis of the time series.

Visual examination of a time plot of the data has been stressed as an important first step in the analysis of a time series. However, we must always be wary of reading something into the data that is not there. An apparent upward trend in the data, as in Figure 2.2, may be only a random fluctuation away from the average and this will emerge as further observed values of the time series are obtained. If the time series fluctuates considerably, seasonal peaks and troughs may not be distinguishable from the other fluctuations and so we have to fall back on measurements of the time series to determine whether a seasonal pattern is present or not. Thus, in general, visual examination of the time series will not be enough to decide whether the time series is stationary or not. This decision is based on certain measurements that we make of the time series. These measurements are described in the remaining sections in this chapter.

2.3 SOME STATISTICAL CONCEPTS

In order to give a more precise definition of stationarity, some statistical concepts are introduced in the present section and illustrated by simple examples. In the next section, these concepts will be applied to a time series.

Probability

A *random experiment* is an experiment having two or more possible outcomes, with uncertainty in advance as to which outcome will occur. *Elementary outcomes* of an experiment are the simplest units in which the results of the experiment are expressed. The set of all elementary outcomes of a random experiment is called the *sample space*. An event, A, is a subset of the sample space. The *probability $P(A)$* of an event A is a measure of the likelihood that the event A will occur when the random experiment is performed. The probability $P(A)$ is a number lying between 0 and 1. The nearer $P(A)$ is to 0, the more unlikely it is that the event A will occur. The nearer $P(A)$ is to 1, the more certain it is that the event A will occur.

Example

If a fair die is rolled, then any one of the numbers 1, 2, 3, 4, 5, and 6 is equally likely to turn up, but it is not known in advance which number will turn up. Rolling the die is a random experiment, since the outcome is uncertain. The elementary outcomes here consist of getting a one, denoted by {1}, getting a two, denoted by {2}, etc., and the set of these six elementary outcomes is the sample space. If A is the event of getting an even number, then A will occur if any of the three elementary outcomes {2}, {4}, or {6} occur. The probability $P(A)$ is defined to be 3/6, which is the ratio of the number of elementary outcomes favourable to the event A, to the total number of elementary outcomes. Each elementary outcome has probability 1/6.

Random variable

A *random variable* is a variable whose numerical value is determined by the outcome of a random experiment. We use an upper case letter, such as X, to denote the random variable and the corresponding lower case letter, x, to denote a particular value assumed by this random variable. A random variable that takes on a finite or infinite set of values x_1, x_2, ..., x_n, ..., is called a *discrete* random variable. A random variable that can take on any value x on a continuum is called a *continuous* random variable.

Example

Let X be ten times the number that turns up when a fair die is rolled. Since the only possible values of X are 10, 20, 30, 40, 50, and 60, then X is a discrete random variable. The probability that X assumes the value 10 is the probability of the elementary event {1} occurring and this probability is 1/6. The other possible values of X all have the same probability of occurrence. In Table 2.2 are shown the possible values x of the variable X, along with the probability $f(x)$ attached to that value. This array of values x and corresponding probabilities $f(x)$ is called the *probability distribution* of the random variable X. The function $f(x)$ is called the *probability mass function* of X.

For a continuous random variable, X, the probability distribution is defined in terms of its *probability density function*, $f(x)$. This is a function with the property that, if plotted as a curve against x, the area under the curve corresponding to any

Table 2.2 Probability distribution of a
discrete random variable X

Possible value x	Probability $f(x)$
10	1/6
20	1/6
30	1/6
40	1/6
50	1/6
60	1/6

interval is equal to the probability that the random variable X will take on a value in that interval. There are many different types of probability density functions. One very important type of probability density function is shown in Figure 2.6. It is a symmetric, bell-shaped curve, known as the *normal curve*. The value of x about which the curve is symmetrical is denoted by the symbol μ (pronounced mu). The curve has turning points at either side of μ and equidistant from it and the distance from μ to the turning points is denoted by σ (sigma). If X has such a probability density curve, it is said to have a *normal probability* distribution with parameters μ and σ.

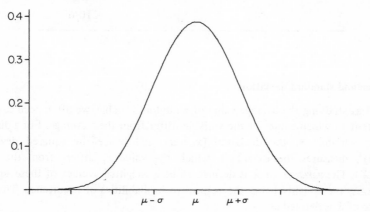

Figure 2.6 The normal curve

Expected value

Often we are interested in the 'expected value' or the 'average value' of a random variable. If X is a discrete random variable with values $x_1, x_2, \ldots, x_n$, then the expected value of X is defined as

$$\mu = E(X) = \sum_{i=1} x_i f(x_i).$$

It is seen that $E(X)$ is just a *weighing average* of the possible values of X, with the probabilities used as weights. For this reason, $E(X)$ is often called the *mean* of the variable X. Table 2.3 illustrates the calculation of the expected value of a discrete random variable X. It is seen that the expected value of X is $210/6 = 35$. The expected value of a continuous random variable X is defined in an analogous way as follows:

$$\mu = E(X) = \int_{-\infty}^{\infty} xf(x)\,dx.$$

The only difference is that integration has replaced summation in the definition.

Table 2.3 Expected value of a discrete random variable X

Possible value x	Probability $f(x)$	$xf(x)$
10	1/6	10/6
20	1/6	20/6
30	1/6	30/6
40	1/6	40/6
50	1/6	50/6
60	1/6	60/6
		210/6

Variance and standard deviation

As well as studying the average value of a random variable, we often need to study the extent to which values of the variable differ from their average. For a discrete random variable X, the deviation $(x_i - \mu)$, and hence the squared deviation $(x_i - \mu)^2$, measures the extent to which the value x_i differs from the mean $\mu = E(X)$. The *variance* of X is defined to be a weighted average of these squared deviations, the weights being the respective probabilities of occurrence. Thus the variance of X is defined as

$$\sigma^2(X) = \sum_{i=1} (x_i - \mu)^2 f(x_i).$$

Table 2.4 illustrates the calculation of the variance of a discrete random variable X. It is seen that $\sigma^2(X) = 1750/6 = 291.7$. The variance of a continuous random variable X is analogously defined as

$$\sigma^2(X) = \int_{-\infty}^{\infty} (x - \mu)^2 f(x)\,dx.$$

Table 2.4 Variance and standard deviation of a discrete random variable X

Possible value x	Probability $f(x)$	$x - \mu$	$(x - \mu)^2$	$(x - \mu)^2 f(x)$
10	1/6	−25	625	625/6
20	1/6	−15	225	225/6
30	1/6	−5	25	25/6
40	1/6	5	25	25/6
50	1/6	15	225	225/6
60	1/6	25	625	625/6
				1750/6

The *standard deviation* of X is defined as the positive square root of the variance of X and is denoted by $\sigma(X)$. Thus

$$\sigma(X) = \sqrt{\sigma^2(X)}.$$

For the example in Table 2.4, $\sigma(X) = \sqrt{291.7} = 17.1$. Like the variance, the standard deviation of X is a measure of the variability of the random variable X about its average value. If X has a normal probability distribution with parameters μ and σ, it may be shown that these parameters can be interpreted as the mean and standard deviation, respectively, of the random variable X.

2.4 MEAN AND STANDARD DEVIATION OF A TIME SERIES

In this section, we apply the statistical concepts introduced in the last section to the problem of forecasting future values of a time series. We consider only discrete time series where observations are made at some fixed time interval h. When we have N successive values of such a time series available for analysis, we write $z_1, z_2, \ldots, z_N$ to denote observations made at equidistant time points $\tau_0 + h$, $\tau_0 + 2h, \ldots, \tau_0 + th, \ldots, \tau_0 + Nh$ (τ is pronounced tau). For many purposes, the values τ_0 and h are unimportant, but if the observation times need to be defined exactly, these two values must be specified. If we adopt τ_0 as the time origin and h as the unit of time, we can regard z_t as the observation at time t. Thus, for time series 2.1, we have $z_1 = 47, z_2 = 64, \ldots, z_{70} = 23$. We wish to use these values to predict future values of the time series.

We regard these values $z_1, z_2, \ldots, z_N$ as being generated by some *underlying process*, which is currently unknown to us. If this process is such that future values are exactly determined by some mathematical function, and once we have identified this function we can exactly predict future values of the time series, then the underlying process is said to be a *deterministic process*. If, on the other hand, the process is such that a future value of the process must be regarded as a random variable and identifying the underlying process only enables us to identify the probability distribution of this random variable, then the underlying process is said to be a *stochastic process*. The word stochastic means random, indicating that the mechanism generating the values of the time series involves probability. Thus a stochastic process can be thought of as a phenomenon that evolves in time according to certain laws of probability.

We now consider the relationship between the observed values of the time series, $z_1, z_2, \ldots, z_N$, and the underlying stochastic process, which we cannot currently identify. Since this generating mechanism involves probability, the value that it will generate at time 1 can be regarded as a random variable denoted by Z_1 and z_1 can be regarded as an observed value or *realization* of this random variable. Thus z_1 is only one of perhaps an infinite number of possible values of the variable Z_1, but this is the value that happened to be observed at time 1. Similarly z_2 is regarded as a realization of a variable random variable Z_2, z_3 is a realization of Z_3, etc. In this way, the observed time series, $z_1, z_2, \ldots, z_N$ is regarded as a realization of the values of N random variables $Z_1, Z_2, \ldots, Z_N$. There are an infinite number of other possible realizations of these same variables and the observed time series is only one of these. This is what is meant by saying that the observed time series is a *realization* of a stochastic process. The value that the underlying stochastic process will generate at the next time point in the future must also be regarded as a random variable and is denoted by Z_{N+1}. The problem now is to use the observed time series to make inferences about the underlying stochastic process, i.e. about the random variables $Z_1, Z_2, \ldots, Z_N$ representing values of the time series already observed and the random variables $Z_{N+1}, Z_{N+2}, \ldots$, representing future values of the time series.

Each of the random variables Z_t has its own probability distribution with its own probability mass function $f(z_t)$ or its own probability density function $f(z_t)$, depending on whether the variable being forecasted is discrete or continuous. Each random variable Z_t has a mean

$$\mu_t = E(Z_t)$$

and a variance

$$\sigma_t^2 = \sigma^2(Z_t).$$

In general, the underlying probabilistic mechanism will vary with time and so all these probability distributions, means, and variances will be different. A great simplification will be introduced if we can assume that the underlying probabilistic mechanism does not vary with time, so that all the variables Z_t have the same mean μ and the same variance σ_z^2. When this happens, we say that the stochastic process is *stationary in the mean and variance*. This agrees with the intuitive concept of *stationarity* presented earlier in this chapter, according to which a time series is said to be stationary if there is no upward or downward trend in the average over time, no change in the variability about the average over time, and no seasonal pattern in the data. A more complete definition of a stationary stochastic process will be given later in this chapter.

If we can assume that a stochastic process is stationary in the mean and variance, the next step is to estimate the unknown mean μ and the unknown variance σ_z^2 of the process using the observed values $z_1, z_2, \ldots, z_N$. An obvious estimate of μ is provided by the *mean* of the time series

$$\bar{z} = \frac{1}{N} \sum_{t=1}^{N} z_t.$$

Similarly, an estimate of the variance σ_z^2 of the stochastic process is provided by the *variance* of the time series:

$$\hat{\sigma}_z^2 = \frac{1}{N-1} \sum_{t=1}^{N} (z_t - \bar{z})^2.$$

The deviation $(z_t - \bar{z})$ measures the extent to which the observation z_t differs from the mean $\bar{z}$ of the time series and thus the variance of the time series is a measure of the overall variability of the time series about its mean. An obvious estimate of the standard deviation σ_z of the stochastic process is provided by the positive square root of the variance of the time series:

$$\hat{\sigma}_z = \sqrt{\frac{1}{N-1} \sum_{t=1}^{N} (z_t - \bar{z})^2}.$$

Table 2.5 illustrates the calculation of the mean, variance, and standard deviation for the first ten values of the time series 2.1 in Table 2.1. It is seen that the mean is $510/10 = 51$, the variance is $1896/9 = 210.7$, and the standard deviation is $\sqrt{210.7} = 14.5$.

Table 2.5   Mean and variance of the first ten
values of the time series 2.1 in Table 2.1

z_t	$z_t - \bar{z}$	$(z_t - \bar{z})^2$
47	−4	16
64	13	169
23	−28	784
71	20	400
38	−13	169
64	13	169
55	4	16
41	−10	100
59	8	64
48	−3	9
510	0	1896

As outlined earlier, the importance of the concept of stationarity stems from the fact that the Box-Jenkins method provides a class of models of stationary stochastic processes. Hence, if the observed time series appears to have been generated by a stationary stochastic process, we can immediately proceed to look for an appropriate model from this class. It is important, therefore, to develop techniques for deciding whether or not the observed time series was generated by a stationary stochastic process. Visual examination of a plot of the time series provides some help in this direction, but it has already been noted that this evidence is not conclusive.

To check that the underlying stochastic process is stationary in the mean and variance, the following simple procedure should be followed. Divide the observed time series into subsets and calculate the mean and standard deviation for each subset. If the underlying stochastic process is stationary, all these means should have approximately the same value and so should all the standard deviations. Subsets of between 4 and 12 observations are useful for this purpose and the size of the subsets should ideally be related to the size of the seasonal period. These calculations were performed for the time series 2.1 to 2.4 and the results are tabulated in Table 2.6. For the time series 2.1, the means of the subsets are approximately the same and so are the standard deviations, indicating that the underlying stochastic process is stationary in the mean and variance. For the time series 2.2, the means of the subsets increase steadily, indicating an upward trend in the average, and the standard deviations also increase, especially for the last three subsets. For the time series 2.3, the means of the subsets are approximately the same and so are the standard deviations. However, we know that this time series is non-stationary because of the seasonal pattern in the data which is evident from Figure 2.3. For the time series 2.4, the means of the subsets increase steadily and so do the standard deviations and at approximately the same rate, indicating that this time series is non-stationary in the variance as well as non-stationary in the mean.

Non-stationarity in the mean due to a trend in the data is indicated by an upward or downward trend in the means of the subsets. When there is an upward trend in the data, as in time series 2.2 and 2.4, it often happens that the standard deviations also increase over time. This is best illustrated by plotting the means and standard deviations of the subsets of each time series, as in Figures 2.7 to 2.10. If the standard deviation is independent of the mean, the relationship between the means and standard deviations of the subsets should be a random scatter about a horizontal line, as in Figures 2.7 and 2.9. If the standard deviation increases with the mean, the relationship between the means and standard deviation of the subsets should be a random scatter about an upward-sloping straight line, as in Figures 2.8 and 2.10. Thus series 2.2 and 2.4 are non-stationary in the variance and so each of these time series must be transformed into another time series which is stationary in the variance before we look for an appropriate model. The plot in Figure 2.10 suggests an appropriate transformation, the logarithmic transformation in this case, as the standard deviation is proportional to the mean. This will be discussed in a later chapter.

2.5 FURTHER STATISTICAL CONCEPTS

In the discussion of stationarity in the previous section, nothing was said about the relationship between the variables $Z_1, Z_2, \ldots, Z_N, \ldots$. This will be discussed in the next section. Some further statistical concepts are needed for this and these are presented in the present section. Again these concepts are illustrated by simple examples.

Table 2.6 Mean and standard deviations of subsets of the time series 2.1 to 2.4

| | Time series 2.1 | | | Time series 2.2 | | | Time series 2.3 | | | Time series 2.4 | |
Subset	Mean	Standard deviation	Subset	Mean	Standard deviation	Subset	Mean	Standard deviation	Subset	Mean	Standard deviation
1–7	51.7	16.9	1–8	17.0	1.3	1–12	61.1	6.9	1–12	126.7	13.7
8–14	50.1	12.8	9–16	17.6	1.9	13–24	59.4	6.6	13–24	139.7	19.1
15–21	57.0	15.4	17–24	20.4	1.0	25–36	58.6	6.9	25–36	170.2	18.4
22–28	52.0	6.1	25–32	21.0	0.5	37–48	58.0	6.6	37–48	197.0	23.0
29–35	55.0	16.2	33–40	25.2	2.2	49–60	58.3	6.6	49–60	225.0	28.5
36–42	50.0	7.6	41–48	26.7	1.9	61–72	58.6	6.6	61–72	238.9	34.9
43–49	52.1	8.8	49–56	29.4	1.3	73–84	58.5	5.9	73–82	284.0	42.1
50–56	49.6	7.6	57–64	30.6	2.3	85–96	58.3	7.2	85–96	328.3	47.9
57–63	46.3	12.2	65–72	37.4	3.1	97–108	57.6	6.4	97–108	368.4	57.9
65–70	47.4	13.8	73–80	49.4	4.5	109–120	57.7	6.3	109–120	381.0	64.5
						121–132	57.2	6.7	121–132	428.3	69.8
						133–144	57.3	6.6	133–144	476.2	77.7
						145–156	58.8	6.4			
						157–168	61.0	7.8			
1–70	51.1	11.9	1–80	27.5	9.8	1–178	58.8	6.7	1–144	280.3	120.0

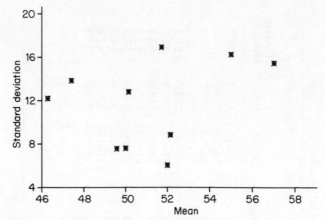

Figure 2.7 Plot of means and standard deviations of subsets
of time series 2.1

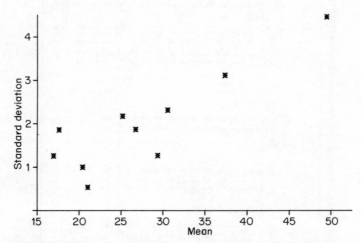

Figure 2.8 Plot of means and standard deviations of subsets of
time series 2.2

Independent events

Two events A and B are said to be *statistically independent* if the probability that
A occurs is unaffected by whether or not B occurs. Alternatively, if AB denotes the
event that both A and B occur together, then A and B are independent if

$$P(AB) = P(A)P(B).$$

Otherwise, A and B are said to be *dependent* events.

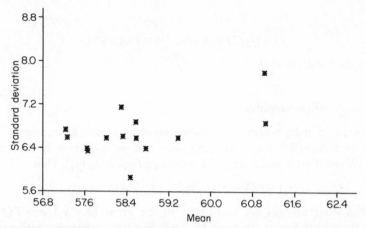

Figure 2.9 Plot of means and standard deviations of subsets of time series 2.3

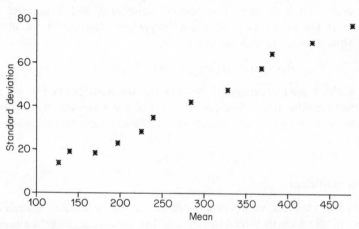

Figure 2.10 Plot of means and standard deviations of subsets of time series 2.4

Example

Two fair dice are rolled. Let A be the event of getting a six with the first die and B the event of getting a six with the second. Then AB is the event of getting two sixes. Since there are 36 equally likely outcomes when the two dice are rolled, we have

$$P(AB) = 1/36,$$

but

$$P(AB) = 1/36 = 1/6 \cdot 1/6 = P(A)P(B),$$

so A and B are independent.

Independent random variables

The concept of independence of random variables is just an extension of the concept of independence of events. Suppose that we have two discrete random variables X and Y with probability mass functions $f(x_i)$ and $g(y_j)$. Thus

$$f(x_i) = P(X = x_i) \quad \text{and} \quad g(y_j) = P(Y = y_j)$$

where $P(X = x_i)$ denotes the probability of the event $\{X = x_i\}$ and $P(Y = y_j)$ denotes the probability of the event $\{Y = y_j\}$. The *joint probability mass function* of X and Y is defined to be the function

$$h(x_i, y_j) = P(X = x_i, Y = y_j),$$

where $P(X = x_i, Y = y_j)$ denotes the probability that the events $\{X = x_i\}$ and $\{Y = y_j\}$ occur simultaneously. The random variables X and Y are said to be *independent* if the events $\{X = x_i\}$ and $\{Y = y_j\}$ are independent for all values x_i and y_j. Thus X and Y are independent if

$$h(x_i, y_j) = f(x_i)g(y_j) \quad \text{for all } x_i \text{ and } y_j.$$

Basically X and Y are independent if the value that one variable has does not affect the value that the other has. If this is not the case, X and Y are said to be *dependent* random variables. Independence of continuous random variables is defined in an analogous way.

Correlation coefficient

In studying two variables, we are often interested in the association between them, i.e. the extent to which they tend to vary together. One measure of the association between two variables X and Y is the *correlation coefficient* $\rho(XY)$ defined as follows:

$$\rho(XY) = \frac{E(XY) - E(X)E(Y)}{\sigma(X)\sigma(Y)} \quad (\rho \text{ is pronounced rho}).$$

Here $E(XY)$ is just the mean of the random variable XY, the product of X and Y; $E(X)$ and $\sigma(X)$ are the mean and standard deviation of the variable X; $E(Y)$ and $\sigma(Y)$ are the mean and standard deviation of the variable Y. It may be shown that the correlation coefficient $\rho(XY)$ has a number of properties. Firstly, it is dimensionless, that is, its value does not depend on the scales of measurement of X and Y. Also,

$$-1 \leqslant \rho(X, Y) \leqslant 1.$$

If high values of X tend to occur with high values of Y, then $\rho(X, Y)$ will be near 1. If high values of X tend to occur with low values of Y, then $\rho(X, Y)$ will be near -1. If X and Y are independent, then $\rho(X, Y)$ will be 0.

2.6 THE SAMPLE AUTOCORRELATION FUNCTION

Now we apply the concepts discussed in the previous section to the analysis of a time series. Recall that the observed time series values $z_1, z_2, \ldots, z_N$ are regarded as realizations of the random variables $Z_1, Z_2, \ldots, Z_N$. Now the distinctive feature of stochastic processes is that the variables $Z_1, Z_2, \ldots, Z_N$ are *dependent* rather than *independent*. While this complicates the analysis of such processes, it is this dependence that makes it possible to make useful forecasts of future values of the time series. Because the variables $Z_{N+1}, Z_{N+2}, \ldots,$ representing future values of the time series, are dependent on the variables $Z_1, Z_2, \ldots, Z_N$, then if we can identify the form of this dependence, we can use it to make forecasts of future values of the time series. Consider the correlation coefficient between the variables Z_t and Z_{t+k}, which are separated by k intervals of time. Thus

$$\rho(Z_t, Z_{t+k}) = \frac{E(Z_t Z_{t+k}) - E(Z_t)E(Z_{t+k})}{\sigma(Z_t)\,\sigma(Z_{t+k})}.$$

In general, the correlation coefficient $\rho(Z_t, Z_{t+k})$ will depend on the time t as well as on k. A stochastic process is said to be *stationary* if in addition to having a mean and variance that do not change with time, the correlation coefficient between values of the process at two time points depends only on the distance between these time points and not on the time itself. For a stationary process, the correlation coefficient between Z_t and Z_{t+k} is called the *autocorrelation* at lag k and is given by

$$\rho_k = \frac{E(Z_t Z_{t+k}) - \mu^2}{\sigma_z^2},$$

since $E(Z_t) = E(Z_{t+k}) = \mu$ and $\sigma(Z_t) = \sigma(Z_{t+k}) = \sigma_z$. We have

$$\rho_0 = 1,$$

since it may be shown that $E(Z_t^2) - \mu^2 = \sigma_z^2$.

The properties of the autocorrelation ρ_k we may infer from those of an ordinary correlation coefficient $\rho(X, Y)$. Thus ρ_k is dimensionless, that is, it does not depend on the scale of measurement of the variable being forecasted. When observations k lags apart are close together in value, we would expect to find ρ_k close to $+1$. When a large observation at time t is followed by a small observation at time $t + k$, we would find ρ_k close to -1. If there is little relationship between observations k lags apart, we would expect to find ρ_k approximately zero. We have

$$\rho_{-k} = \rho_k,$$

so that it is necessary to consider only positive lags. The sequence $\{\rho_1, \rho_2, \ldots\}$

indicates the extent to which one value of the process is correlated with previous values.

A listing or graphical display of ρ_k versus the lag k for $k = 1, 2, \ldots$ is called the *theoretical autocorrelation function* (ACF) or the theoretical *correlogram* of the stochastic process. The autocorrelations contained in the autocorrelation function are the characteristics of the stochastic process that are of most interest to us because they enable us to decide if the stochastic process is stationary and, if so, to select an appropriate model from a class of models of stationary stochastic processes. However, all these autocorrelations are currently unknown to us and have to be estimated from the observed time series.

An obvious estimate of ρ_k is given by the *sample autocorrelation of lag k* defined by

$$
r_k = \frac{\displaystyle\sum_{t=1}^{N-k} (z_t - \bar{z})(z_{t+k} - \bar{z})}{\displaystyle\sum_{t=1}^{N} (z_t - \bar{z})^2}.
$$

Table 2.7 illustrates the calculation of the sample autocorrelation r_1 for the first ten values of the time series 2.1 in Table 2.1.

Table 2.7 The autocorrelation r_1 for the first ten values of the time series 2.1 in Table 2.1

z_t	$z_t - \bar{z}$	$z_{t+1} - \bar{z}$	$(z_t - \bar{z})(z_{t+1} - \bar{z})$	$(z_t - \bar{z})^2$
47	−4	13	−52	16
64	13	−28	−364	169
23	−28	20	−560	784
71	20	−13	−260	400
38	−13	13	−169	169
64	13	4	52	169
55	4	−10	−40	16
41	−10	8	−80	100
59	8	−3	−24	64
48	−3			9
510	0		−1497	1896

It is seen that $r_1 = -1497/1896 = -0.79$. The above calculations are made for illustration only. In practice, to obtain useful values of sample autocorrelations, we would need at least fifty observations and the sample autocorrelations would only be calculated for $k = 1, \ldots, K$ where K was not larger than, say, $N/4$. Although it was stated in the previous chapter that a minimum of 30 observations are needed for the Box-Jenkins method, we now see that at least 50 observations are in fact needed to obtain useful values of sample autocorrelations which are the fundamental tools of the Box-Jenkins method.

For the complete set of 70 observations in the time series 2.1 in Table 2.1, plots of pairs of observations (z_t, z_{t+1}) and (z_t, z_{t+2}) are presented as scatter diagrams in Figures 2.11 and 2.12. Thus the first two observations provide the point (47, 64) in Figure 2.11 and the first and third observations provide the point (47, 23) in Figure 2.12. Figure 2.11 indicates that adjacent observations tend to move together in a linear fashion with large values of z_t associated with small values of z_{t+1} and small values of z_t associated with large values of z_{t+1}. On the other hand, observations two time periods apart tend to move together in a linear fashion with large values of z_t associated with large values of z_{t+2} and small values of z_t associated

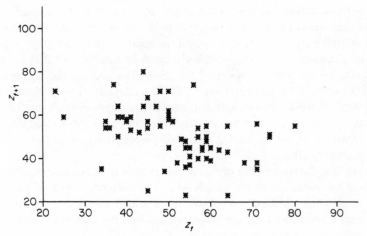

Figure 2.11 Plot of pairs of observations (z_t, z_{t+1}) for time series 2.1

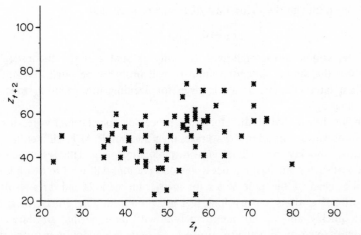

Figure 2.12 Plot of pairs of observations (z_t, z_{t+2}) for time series 2.1

with small values of z_{t+2}. Hence we would expect r_1 to be negative and r_2 to be positive. Sample autocorrelations like these are not uncommon in production data and can arise because of 'carry over' effects. In this particular example, a high yielding batch tended to produce tarry residues which were not entirely removed from the vessel and adversely affected the yield of the next batch. The signs of r_1 and r_2 have implications in forecasting future values of the time series. Since the last observed value of the time series ($z_{70} = 23$) is below average and r_1 is negative, we would predict that the future value z_{71} will be above average. Similarly since r_2 is positive, we would predict that the future value z_{72} will be below average.

A listing or graphical display of r_k versus k for $k = 1, 2, \ldots$ is called the *sample autocorrelation function* (ACF) or the *sample correlogram* for the time series. The sample autocorrelation function is the single most important characteristic of the observed time series because it enables us to decide if the underlying stochastic process is stationary and, if so, to select an appropriate model from a class of models of stationary stochastic processes. It must be remembered that the sample autocorrelations are only estimates of the theoretical autocorrelations and, for a short time series, these estimates may differ considerably from their theoretical counterparts. However, the sample autocorrelation function tends to follow the same pattern as the theoretical autocorrelation function, so that we can infer many of the properties of the underlying stochastic process from a study of the sample autocorrelation function.

In particular, the stationarity or non-stationarity of the stochastic process can be determined by inspection of the sample ACF. The theoretical ACF of a stationary process tends either to *die down quickly towards zero* with increasing lag k or to *cut off* after a particular lag $k = q$. When we say that the theoretical ACF *cuts off* after a particular lag $k = q$, we mean that

$$\rho_k = 0, \quad \text{for } k > q.$$

We can determine when the theoretical ACF cuts off by using the sample ACF. However, even though the theoretical ACF may be such that

$$\rho_k = 0, \quad \text{for } k > q,$$

because the sample autocorrelations are only estimates of the theoretical autocorrelations, the sample autocorrelation r_k will probably be small, but not 0, for $k > q$. In a later chapter, a rule is given for deciding how small r_k must be to conclude that $\rho_k = 0$.

It can be shown that if the stochastic process is non-stationary because of an upward or downward trend in the average, then the sample ACF will neither cut off nor die down quickly, but will *die down extremely slowly*. This is because in any realization of such a stochastic process, the observations will tend to be on the same side of the mean of the time series for many time periods and, as a result, large sample autocorrelations at very long lags are produced. The precise meanings of 'die down quickly' and 'die down extremely slowly' are somewhat arbitrary and can best be determined by experience. However, if there is any doubt as to the stationarity of the original time series, this time series can be 'differenced' and the sample

ACF of the differenced time series examined for stationary behaviour. This procedure is explained in a later chapter.

Seasonal peaks and troughs are often easy to spot simply by visual examination of a plot of the time series. On many occasions, however, if the time series fluctuates considerably or if trend is present, seasonal peaks and troughs are not always easy to identify. Fortunately, recognition of seasonality is made easier using the sample ACF. If a monthly time series exhibits an annual seasonal pattern, e.g. high in winter and low in summer, then we would expect to find a high positive correlation between observations that are 12 time periods apart. Thus we would expect the sample autocorrelation r_{12} to have a large positive value. Since there is a high correlation between Z_t and Z_{t+12}, and between Z_{t+12} and Z_{t+24}, we would expect to find some correlation between Z_t and Z_{t+24}. Thus we would expect the sample autocorrelation r_{24} to have a fairly large positive value, but not as large as r_{12}. In summary, if there is a seasonal pattern in the data, we would expect to find that the sample ACF will exhibit 'peaks' at the seasonal lags 12, 24, 36, etc. By this is meant that these sample autocorrelations are larger in value than the sample autocorrelations at other lags. The stronger the trend in the time series, the less obvious this seasonal pattern in the sample ACF will be, as it will be swamped by the fact that the sample ACF will tend to die down extremely slowly. Thus if the sample ACF suggests that trend is present, the time series should be 'differenced' before looking for a seasonal pattern in the sample ACF.

While the sample ACF is useful in detecting non-stationarity due to a trend in the average or a seasonal pattern, it will not detect non-stationarity due to changes in the variance of the stochastic process. This can only be detected by visual examination of a plot of the time series, or by calculating and plotting the standard deviations of subsets of the time series, as described in the previous section.

As an illustration of the usefulness of these properties of the sample ACF in detecting non-stationarity, consider the sample ACF of the time series 2.1 to 2.4 which are given in Figures 2.13 to 2.16. Thus from Figure 2.13 we see that for time series 2.1 we have $r_1 = -0.390$ and $r_2 = 0.304$. It is seen that the sample ACF in Figure 2.13 dies away quickly, indicating a stationary process, which agrees with our initial assessment of the time series plot in Figure 2.1. Note that in Figure 2.13 moderately large sample autocorrelations occur for a few large lags after the sample ACF has died away. This often happens and is due to the fact that the sample autocorrelations can have rather large variances and can be highly autocorrelated with each other. Thus apparent trends and ripples can occur in the sample ACF which have no basis in the theoretical ACF. The sample ACF in Figure 2.14 dies down extremely slowly, indicating non-stationarity due to a trend in the data. We have already remarked on the obvious upward trend in the time series plot in Figure 2.2. The sample ACF in Figure 2.15 has peaks at the seasonal lags 12 and 24, which is not surprising as there is an obvious seasonal pattern in the time series plot in Figure 2.3. Note that the sample ACF has 'troughs' at the seasonal lags 6 and 18. By this is meant that the seasonal sample autocorrelations r_6 and r_{18} are negative and larger in absolute value than the sample autocorrelations at other lags. The reason for this is obvious from the time series plot in Figure 2.3, in which a high

36

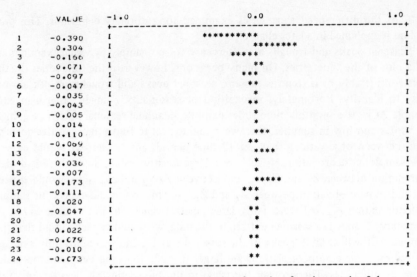

```
        VALUE   -1.0                   0.0                        1.0
                +-------------------------------------------------+
  1    -0.390   I              **********                         I
  2     0.304   I                      ********                   I
  3    -0.166   I                 *****                           I
  4     0.071   I                      **                         I
  5    -0.097   I                   ***                           I
  6    -0.047   I                    **                           I
  7     0.035   I                     *                           I
  8    -0.043   I                    **                           I
  9    -0.005   I                     *                           I
 10     0.014   I                     *                           I
 11     0.110   I                     ***                         I
 12    -0.069   I                    **                           I
 13     0.148   I                     ****                        I
 14     0.036   I                     *                           I
 15    -0.007   I                     *                           I
 16     0.173   I                     *****                       I
 17    -0.111   I                   ***                           I
 18     0.020   I                     *                           I
 19    -0.047   I                    **                           I
 20     0.016   I                     *                           I
 21     0.022   I                     *                           I
 22    -0.079   I                    **                           I
 23    -0.010   I                     *                           I
 24    -0.073   I                    **                           I
                +-------------------------------------------------+
```

Figure 2.13 Sample autocorrelation function for time series 2.1

```
        VALUE   -1.0                   0.0                        1.0
                +-------------------------------------------------+
  1     0.929   I                     ***************************** I
  2     0.858   I                     **************************   I
  3     0.790   I                     ***********************      I
  4     0.726   I                     *********************        I
  5     0.674   I                     *******************          I
  6     0.622   I                     ******************           I
  7     0.578   I                     ****************             I
  8     0.534   I                     ***************              I
  9     0.494   I                     **************               I
 10     0.453   I                     *************                I
 11     0.414   I                     ***********                  I
 12     0.375   I                     **********                   I
 13     0.338   I                     *********                    I
 14     0.307   I                     ********                     I
 15     0.285   I                     ********                     I
 16     0.264   I                     *******                      I
 17     0.242   I                     *******                      I
 18     0.216   I                     ******                       I
 19     0.196   I                     *****                        I
 20     0.177   I                     *****                        I
 21     0.158   I                     *****                        I
 22     0.145   I                     ****                         I
 23     0.132   I                     ****                         I
 24     0.122   I                     ****                         I
                +-------------------------------------------------+
```

Figure 2.14 Sample autocorrelation function for time series 2.2

point in the seasonal pattern is followed by a low point six months later. The sample ACF in Figure 2.16 dies down extremely slowly, indicating a trend in the data, and has peaks at the seasonal lags 12 and 24, indicating a seasonal pattern. Both of these patterns are obvious from the time series plots in Figure 2.4. However, there is no way of telling from the sample ACF in Figure 2.16 that the time series 2.4 is non-stationary in the variance.

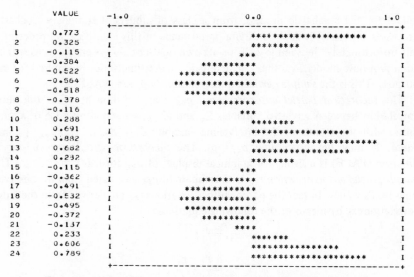

Figure 2.15 Sample autocorrelation function for time series 2.3

Figure 2.16 Sample autocorrelation function for time series 2.4

2.7 THE SAMPLE PARTIAL AUTOCORRELATION FUNCTION

We have seen that a study of the sample ACF determines if the original time series is stationary, i.e. was generated by a stationary stochastic process. If the original time series is not stationary, it is usually possible to 'difference' or transform the original time series in order to obtain a stationary time series. Once a stationary time series has been obtained, the problem becomes one of finding an appropriate model for the stochastic process, from a class of models of stationary stochastic processes. The sample ACF is of vital importance in this identification procedure, but unfortunately the sample ACF on its own does not always enable us to specify an appropriate model. Another characteristic of the time series is required for this purpose. This is the *sample partial autocorrelation function* (PACF).

The *theoretical partial autocorrelation* ρ_{kk} may be thought of as the auto-correlation between any two variables Z_t and Z_{t+k}, separated by a lag of k time units, with the effects of the intervening variables $Z_{t+1}, Z_{t+2}, \ldots, Z_{t+k-1}$ elimi-nated. It may be shown that $\rho_{11} = \rho_1$. The *theoretical partial autocorrelation function* (PACF) is a listing, or graphical display, of ρ_{kk} for lags $k = 1, 2, \ldots$. The *sample partial autocorrelation* r_{kk} is an estimate of ρ_{kk} calculated from the observed time series values. In fact the partial autocorrelations r_{kk} are derived from the auto-correlations r_k by means of the following equations:

$$r_{11} = r_1,$$

$$r_{22} = \frac{r_2 - r_1^2}{1 - r_1^2},$$

with more complicated equations for $r_{33}, r_{44}, \ldots$. For the time series 2.1 in Table 2.1, we know from Figure 2.13 that $r_1 = -0.390$ and $r_2 = 0.304$. Hence the first two partial autocorrelations are $r_{11} = -0.390$ and

$$r_{22} = \frac{0.303 - (-0.390)^2}{1 - (-0.390)^2} = 0.180.$$

The *sample partial autocorrelation function* (PACF) is a listing or graphical display of r_{kk} for lags $k = 1, 2, \ldots$. Again, the sample partial autocorrelations are only

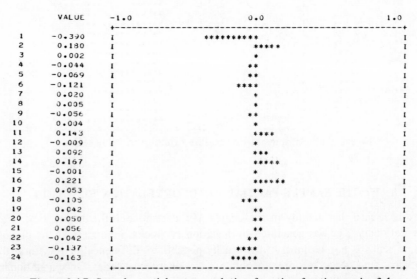

Figure 2.17 Sample partial autocorrelation function for time series 2.1

Table 2.8 Means and standard deviations of subsets of the time series used in the exercises in this chapter

	Time series 4.2			Time series 5.1			Time series 6.3			Time series 6.4	
Subset	Mean	Standard deviation	Subset	Mean	Standard deviation	Subset	Mean	Standard deviation	Subset	Mean	Standard deviation
1–10	−0.2	1.1	1–10	299.2	4.8	1–12	244.7	6.7	1–12	146.8	92.7
11–20	0.0	0.8	11–20	282.3	3.7	13–24	246.4	8.2	13–24	183.8	104.1
21–30	0.1	0.9	21–30	275.3	4.3	25–36	251.3	8.6	25–36	220.7	148.1
31–40	0.3	0.9	31–40	279.6	3.8	37–48	260.5	9.8	37–48	320.3	164.4
41–50	−0.1	1.5	41–50	276.1	4.1	49–60	272.6	10.9	49–60	405.8	190.0
51–60	0.3	1.1	51–60	272.5	1.2	61–72	288.0	10.9	61–72	489.0	242.1
61–70	0.3	1.1	61–70	281.4	9.3	73–84	298.0	10.9			
71–80	0.2	1.3	71–80	290.2	2.1	85–96	308.6	9.8	1–77	298.4	198.4
81–90	0.2	1.2	81–90	289.3	2.7	97–108	321.6	11.2			
91–100	0.0	1.1	91–100	284.9	2.0	109–120	327.4	7.2			
						121–132	332.1	9.1			
						133–144	346.9	13.6			
						145–156	364.4	12.9			
						157–168	376.6	13.7			
1–100	0.1	1.1	1–100	283.6	8.7	1–178	307.5	46.8			

estimates of the corresponding theoretical correlations and, for short series, may differ considerably from their theoretical counterparts. However, the sample PACF tends to follow the same pattern as the theoretical PACF, so that we can use the sample PACF to identify an appropriate model for the underlying stochastic process. The theoretical PACF of a stationary series tends either to die down quickly towards zero with increasing lag k or to cut off after a particular lag k. We can determine when the theoretical PACF cuts off by using the sample PACF. This is very useful in identifying an appropriate model for the stochastic process.

The sample PACF for the time series 2.1 in Table 2.1 is given in Figure 2.17. We see that $r_{11} = -0.390$ and $r_2 = 0.180$, as has already been calculated above. It is seen that for this time series the sample ACF appears to cut off after the first few lags. The sample PACF's for the time series 2.2 to 2.4 will not be given here, as these time series have been determined to be non-stationary for one reason or another.

In summary, it may be said that the main characteristics of a time series that are used to identify an appropriate model are the time series plot, the mean and standard deviation of the time series (and of subsets of the time series), the sample ACF, and the sample PACF. Computer programs for time series analysis invariably calculate these characteristics. The figures in the present chapter were produced using the TSERIES package which is described in Appendix A.5. The short computer program needed for the calculation of these characteristics for time series 2.1 is given as Program A.5.1 in that Appendix.

2.8 EXERCISES

2.8.1 The plots of time series 4.2, 5.1, 6.3, and 6.4 are given in Figure 2.18, 2.21, 2.24, and 2.27. Means and standard deviations of subsets of these time series are given in Table 2.8 and plotted in Figures 2.19, 2.22, 2.25, and 2.28. The sample ACF's for these time series are given in Figures 2.20, 2.23, 2.26 and 2.29.

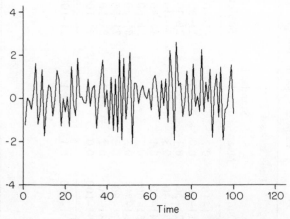

Figure 2.18 Plot of time series 4.2

41

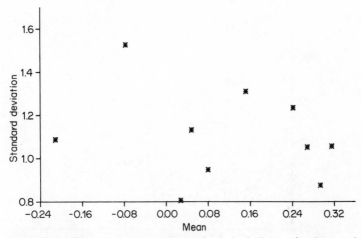

Figure 2.19 Plot of means and standard deviations of subsets of
time series 4.2

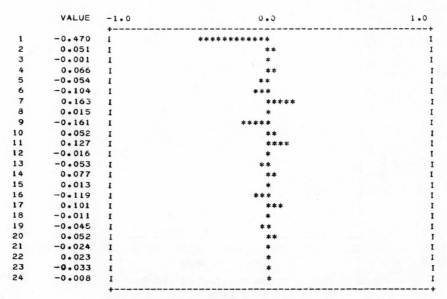

Figure 2.20 Sample ACF for time series 4.2

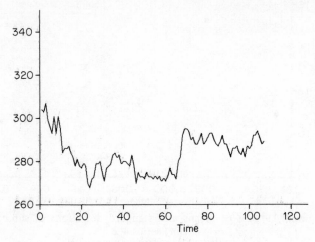

Figure 2.21 Plot of time series 5.1

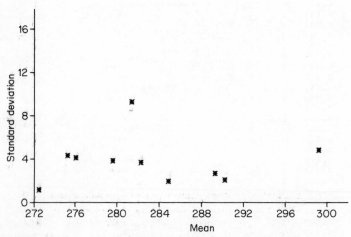

Figure 22 Plot of means and standard deviations of subsets of time series 5.1

43

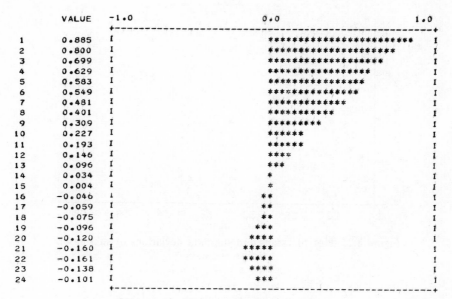

Figure 2.23 Sample ACF for time series 5.1

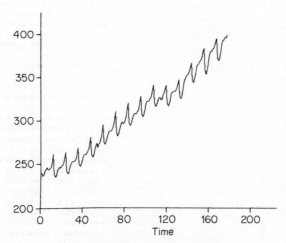

Figure 2.24 Plot of time series 6.3

44

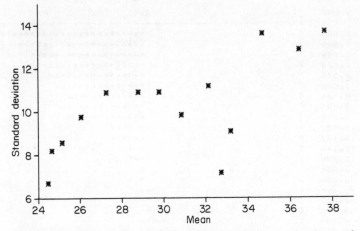

Figure 2.25 Plot of means and standard deviations of subsets of
time series 6.3

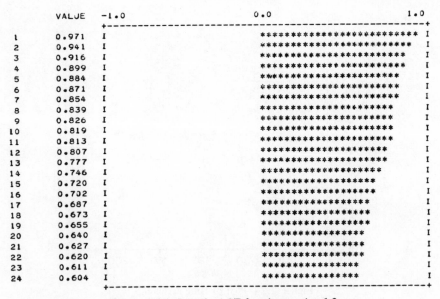

Figure 2.26 Sample ACF for time series 6.3

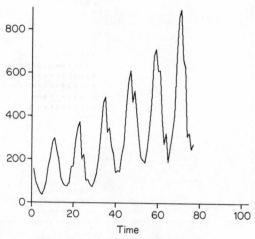

Figure 2.27 Plot of time series 6.4

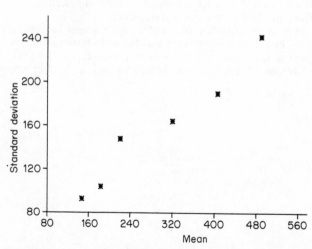

Figure 2.28 Plot of means and standard deviations of
subsets of time series 6.4

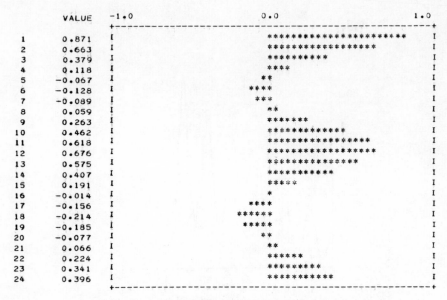

Figure 2.29 Sample ACF for time series 6.4

(a) Which of these time series is non-stationary in the variance?
(b) Which of these time series is non-stationary in the mean?
(c) Which of these time series exhibits a seasonal pattern?
(d) Which of these time series is stationary?

2.8.2 (This exercise is intended for readers with access to computer packages using the Box–Jenkins approach and the only information provided about each time series is the time series itself.) Answer questions (a), (b), (c), and (d) in Exercise 2.8.1 for time series 6.5, 6.6, 6.7, and 6.8 in Appendix A.3.

Chapter 3

Forecasting for models of stationary time series

3.1 MINIMUM MEAN SQUARE ERROR FORECASTS

In this chapter, we study a class of stationary stochastic processes which can be used as models for stationary time series. The characteristic properties of these models are described in turn and summarized in Table 3.3 at the end of the chapter. These characteristic properties will be used in the next chapter when we come to select an appropriate model from this class of models for fitting to an observed time series. If an observed time series is a realization of one of the models described in this chapter, then forecasting future values of the time series involves very simple calculations. In the present section, we describe the general principles underlying the calculation of forecasts using the Box–Jenkins method. In subsequent sections, the calculation of these forecasts is described in turn for each model and these calculations are summarized in Table 3.5 at the end of the chapter. In the next chapter, once we have decided on an appropriate model for a stationary time series, we will use the results in this table for calculating forecasts of future values of the observed time series.

Suppose that we have a time series of t observations, denoted by $z_1, z_2, \ldots, z_t$. These are regarded as observed values of the random variables $Z_1, Z_2, \ldots, Z_t$. We wish to forecast the value of the time series l time periods into the future. This value is denoted by z_{t+l} and is a random value of the variable Z_{t+l}. Of course, z_{t+l} is currently unknown, but a forecast of z_{t+l}, based on the observed values $z_1, z_2, \ldots, z_t$, is denoted by $\hat{z}_t(l)$. This forecast is said to have *origin t and lead time l*. The set of forecasts $\hat{z}_t(l)$ for $l = 1, 2, \ldots$, is called the *forecast function at origin t* or the *forecast profile at origin t*.

Suppose that the observed time series is stationary so that the variables $Z_1, Z_2, \ldots$, have a common mean μ. Then an obvious forecast of z_{t+l} is just μ, the expected value of the variable Z_{t+l}. This forecast is a trivial one since it takes no account of the observed values $z_1, z_2, \ldots, z_t$. However, it is an optimal forecast in the following sense. Let f be any forecast of z_{t+l}. Then the *forecast error* in using this forecast is the random variable $(Z_{t+l} - f)$. The expected value of the square of

47

this variable is called the *mean square error of the forecast*

$$E(Z_{t+l} - f)^2.$$

It may be shown that of all the forecasts f, the forecast $\hat{z}_t(l) = \mu$ has the smallest mean square error. It is said to be a *minimum mean square error* forecast.

In general, we can get a better forecast of z_{t+l} by using the observed values $z_1, z_2, \ldots, z_t$. Instead of studying the ordinary or unconditional probability distribution of the variable Z_{t+l}, we need to consider the probability distribution of the variable Z_{t+l} conditional on the information that the values of $Z_1, Z_2, \ldots, Z_t$ are known. This information will be referred to as *the information at origin t*. As before, let f be any forecast of z_{t+l}. Then the mean square error of this forecast, conditional on the information that $Z_1 = z_1, Z_2 = z_2, \ldots, Z_t = z_t$, is denoted by

$$E((Z_{t+l} - f)^2 | Z_1 = z_1, Z_2 = z_2, \ldots, Z_t = z_t).$$

By an extension of the argument used above, it may be shown that the forecast of z_{t+l} which has smallest mean square error conditional on the information at origin t is the expected value of the variable Z_{t+l}, conditional on this information. This expected value is denoted by

$$E(Z_{t+l} | Z_1 = z_1, Z_2 = z_2, \ldots, Z_t = z_t)$$

or, more briefly, by

$$\underset{t}{E}[Z_{t+l}]. \tag{3.1}$$

Thus $\hat{z}_t(l) = E_t[Z_{t+l}]$ is the minimum mean square error (MMSE) forecast of z_{t+l}, conditional on the information at origin t. In future, the notation $\hat{z}_t(l)$ will be reserved for this MMSE forecast $\hat{z}_t(l) = E_t[Z_{t+l}]$.

While it might seem that the forecast $\hat{z}_t(l) = E_t[Z_{t+l}]$ will be difficult to evaluate, since it is the mean of the conditional distribution of a random variable, it will be seen that in fact it is very easily calculated for the time series models discussed here. The *forecast error* for the forecast $\hat{z}_t(l)$, conditional on the information at origin t, is denoted by $e_t(l)$. Thus

$$e_t(l) = Z_{t+l} - \hat{z}_t(l).$$

Note that we are using a lower case letter, e, to denote this forecast error, in spite of the fact that this forecast error is a random variable. This is an exception to our usual convention, and is necessary because we are using the upper case letter, E, to denote expected value. The expected value of this forecast error, conditional on the information at origin t, is denoted by $\underset{t}{E}[e_t(l)]$. Since

$$\hat{z}_t(l) = \underset{t}{E}[Z_{t+l}],$$

it follows that

$$\underset{t}{E}[e_t(l)] = \underset{t}{E}[Z_{t+l}] - \underset{t}{E}[Z_{t+l}] = 0,$$

so that the forecast error has mean zero conditional on the information at origin t. The *variance of the forecast error*, again conditional on the information at origin t, is denoted by

$$\sigma^2 [e_t(l)].$$

In general, the value of $\sigma^2 [e_t(l)]$ will depend on the particular time series model that is being used, but $\sigma^2 [e_t(l)]$ will invariably increase with the lead time l. This implies that the width of prediction intervals for z_{t+l} also increases with the lead time l. This is intuitively satisfying, as the further we forecast into the future, the less accurate we expect our forecasts to be.

These prediction interval forecasts are derived as follows. From the assumptions that we will make in the time series models discussed here, we can assume that the conditional distribution of Z_{t+l}, given the information at origin t, is a normal probability distribution. Now the mean of this conditional distribution is

$$\hat{z}_t(l) = \mathop{E}_{t} [Z_{t+l}]$$

and since

$$e_t(l) = Z_{t+l} - \hat{z}_t(l),$$

the variance of this conditional distribution is $\sigma^2 [e_t(l)]$, the variance of the forecast error $e_t(l)$. Hence this conditional distribution is normal with known mean and variance. Now if the random variable X is normal with known mean μ and variance σ^2, the probability that a random value of X lies between any given limits can be found using a normal probability table (Table A.2.1 in Appendix A.2). In particular, the probability that X lies between the limits $\mu \pm (1.96)\sigma$ is 0.95 or 95%. Applying this result to the conditional distribution of Z_{t+l}, we can say that, conditional on the information available at origin t, the probability is 0.95 that the future value z_{t+l} will lie between the limits

$$\hat{z}_t(l) \pm (1.96)(\sigma^2 [e_t(l)])^{1/2}. \tag{3.2}$$

These limits are said to be 95% prediction limits for z_{t+l}. The interval between these limits is said to be a 95% prediction interval for z_{t+l}.

In practice, both the forecast and the variance of the forecast error will depend on the unknown parameters of the time series model and these will have to be estimated from the observed time series values $z_1, z_2, \ldots, z_t$. However, the accuracy of the point forecasts and of the prediction interval forecasts will not be greatly affected by having to estimate these unknown parameters, provided these estimates are optimal and there are at least 50 observations in the time series.

3.2 THE WHITE NOISE MODEL

By saying that the observed time series is stationary, we are assuming that the underlying variables $Z_1, Z_2, \ldots$ have the same mean μ and variance σ_z^2. The simplest possible model for a stationary time series is one in which the variables Z_t are independent and have the same probability distribution for each t. In order to apply statistical theory to develop tests of significance and prediction intervals, we need to assume that this common probability distribution is the normal probability distribution. Thus we assume that the variables Z_t are independent and normally distributed with mean μ and variance σ_z^2. To express the fact that the variables Z_t are independent and normal with mean μ and variance σ_z^2, we use the notation $Z_t \sim \text{IN}(\mu, \sigma_z^2)$. It is more usual to write the model in a different form by introducing a sequence of variables A_t as follows:

$$Z_t = \theta_0 + A_t, \tag{3.3}$$

where

$$A_t \sim \text{IN}(0, \sigma_A^2).$$

The parameter θ_0 is known as the *constant term* in the model. (θ is pronounced theta.) Thus the variables A_t are independent and normally distributed with mean 0 and variance σ_A^2. When a sequence of variables A_t with these properties arises in engineering, it is said to form a *white noise process* and hence the model (3.3) is called the *white noise model*. From the form of the model in (3.3) it may be deduced that the variables Z_t are independent; that μ (the mean of the variables Z_t) equals θ_0 (the parameter in model (3.3)); and that σ_z^2 (the variance of the variables Z_t) equals σ_A^2 (the variance of the variables A_t). An alternative form for the model is obtained by considering the deviations of the variables Z_t from their mean μ. Thus if $\tilde{Z}_t = Z_t - \mu$, then the model can be written in the form

$$\tilde{Z}_t = A_t,$$

where

$$A_t \sim \text{IN}(0, \sigma_A^2).$$

Thus the deviations $\tilde{Z}_t$ form a white noise process.

The variable A_t may be interpreted as the 'random shock' or 'noise' that enters the system at time t causing the process to deviate from its overall level θ_0. The outstanding feature of the white noise model (3.3) is that the variables Z_t are independent and so what happens at time t is not influenced by what occurred in the past nor will it influence what will happen in the future. For this reason, the white noise model is sometimes called the *purely random* model. Since the variables Z_t are independent, all the autocorrelations ρ_k ($k = 1, 2, \ldots$) in the theoretical ACF will be zero, and hence it may be shown that all the partial autocorrelations ρ_{kk} ($k = 1, 2, \ldots$) in the theoretical PACF are also zero. This is the characteristic property of the white noise model. Thus the theoretical ACF and the theoretical PACF are as shown in Figures 3.1 and 3.2. Of course, the sample ACF and sample PACF of any realization of this model will not be identical with Figures 3.1 and 3.2, respectively, because the sample autocorrelations and partial autocorrelations are only estimates of their theoretical counterparts, but most of these sample autocorrelations and partial autocorrelations should be near zero.

The model (3.3) involves two unknown parameters, θ_0 and σ_A^2. Estimation of these parameters is straightforward, because of their relationship with the mean μ

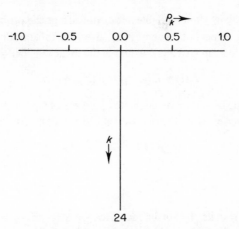

Figure 3.1 ACF for white noise model or
white noise process

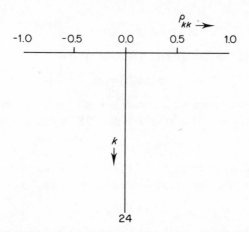

Figure 3.2 PACF for white noise model or
white noise process

and variance σ_z^2 of the variables Z_t. Henceforth we will refer to μ and σ_z^2 as the *process mean* and the *process variance*, respectively. We have from (3.3),

$$\theta_0 = \mu$$

and

$$\sigma_A^2 = \sigma_z^2.$$

Thus obvious estimates of θ_0 and σ_A^2 are $\bar{z}$ and $\hat{\sigma}_z^2$, respectively, the mean and variance of the observed time series.

If an observed time series is a realization of a white noise model, then forecasting future values of the time series is trivial. Since Z_{t+l} is independent of $Z_1, Z_2, \ldots, Z_t$, being told the values of these variables does not affect the probability distribution of Z_{t+l}, so that the expected value of Z_{t+l}, given the information at origin t, is just the ordinary expected value of Z_{t+l}, which is the mean $\mu = E(Z_{t+l})$. Thus we have

$$\hat{z}_t(l) = \underset{t}{E}[Z_{t+l}] = E(Z_{t+l}) = \mu.$$

The parameter μ, or rather its estimate $\bar{z}$, is used as a point forecast of all future values of the time series. Now the one step ahead forecast error is

$$\begin{aligned} e_t(1) &= Z_{t+1} - \hat{z}_t(1) \\ &= Z_{t+1} - \mu \\ &= A_{t+1}. \end{aligned}$$

Thus the random shocks A_t are in fact the one step ahead forecast errors. This holds, not only for the white noise model, but for all the members of the class of models considered in this chapter. What is unique about the white noise model is that for each lead time l, the forecast error for lead time l is also equal to a random shock:

$$e_t(l) = Z_{t+1} - \hat{z}_t(l) = A_{t+l}.$$

Thus the variance of the forecast errors is given by

$$\sigma^2[e_t(l)] = \sigma_A^2,$$

the variance of the variables A_t, which in turn is equal to the process variance σ_z^2. Substituting for $\hat{z}_t(l)$ and $\sigma^2[e_t(l)]$ in (3.2) gives 95% prediction limits for z_{t+l}:

$$\mu \pm (1.96)\sigma_z.$$

Replacing μ and σ_z by their estimates $\bar{z}$ and $\hat{\sigma}_z$, the mean and standard deviation of the observed time series, gives approximate 95% prediction limits for z_{t+l}:

$$\bar{z} \pm (1.96)\hat{\sigma}_z.$$

Time series which appear to be realizations of a white noise model do not occur widely in practice, because of the assumption that successive observations are independent. For the majority of time series encountered in practice, successive observations are dependent. However, the white noise model provides a convenient starting point for introducing the class of models to be considered here, because the sequence of variables A_t, forming a white noise process, is an essential component of all the models of this class. Note that the white noise process can be regarded as a particular case of a white noise model with $\theta_0 = 0$, so that the theoretical ACF and PACF of a white noise process are as shown in Figures 3.1 and 3.2 and most of the sample autocorrelations and partial autocorrelations of any realization of a white noise process should be near zero. Whenever we fit a model to an observed time series, we will make use of this fact in testing the fit of the proposed model to the observed time series.

In summary, it may be said that the white noise model does not occur frequently in practice, but that the white noise process is important in testing the fit of other models to an observed time series, as will be described in the next chapter. Both the white noise model and the white noise process are characterized by the fact that the autocorrelations in the ACF and the partial autocorrelations in the PACF are all zero.

3.3 THE FIRST ORDER AUTOREGRESSIVE MODEL

The simplest generalization of the white noise model discussed in the previous section is obtained by assuming that the variable Z_t, instead of being independent of the variables $Z_1, Z_2, \ldots, Z_{t-1}$, does depend on the variable Z_{t-1} immediately preceding it, but only on this variable. Such a sequence of variables is called a *Markov process*. More precisely, we will assume that the variable Z_t is a linear function of the preceding variable Z_{t-1}, plus a random shock A_t. Thus one form of our model is

$$Z_t = \theta_0 + \phi_1 Z_{t-1} + A_t, \tag{3.4}$$

where

$$A_t \sim \text{IN}(0, \sigma_A^2).$$

This model is a particular case of a linear regression model between two variables X and Y, which has the form

$$E(Y) = \alpha + \beta X \quad (\alpha \text{ and } \beta \text{ are pronounced alpha and beta}).$$

In our case, the variable Z_t is related to Z_{t-1}, the preceding member of the same sequence of variables, and so the model (3.4) is called an *autoregressive model*. The coefficient ϕ_1 is called a *first order autoregression coefficient*. (ϕ is pronounced phi.) Since Z_t is related to only one preceding member of the same sequence, the model (3.4) is said to be an *autoregressive model of order 1* or, more briefly, an AR(1) model. An alternative form for the model in terms of the deviations $\tilde{Z}_t = Z_t - \mu$ is

$$\tilde{Z}_t = \phi_1 \tilde{Z}_{t-1} + A_t. \tag{3.5}$$

Thus the current deviation from the mean, $\tilde{Z}_t$, is a proportion $\phi_1 \tilde{Z}_{t-1}$ of the previous deviation, plus a random shock, A_t. Substituting for $\tilde{Z}_t$ in (3.5) gives

$$Z_t = \mu(1 - \phi_1) + \phi_1 Z_{t-1} + Z_t. \tag{3.6}$$

Thus from (3.4) and (3.6) the relationship between the mean μ of the variable Z_t and the parameters θ_0 and ϕ_1 in model (3.4) is

$$\theta_0 = \mu(1 - \phi_1)$$

or

$$\mu = \theta_0/(1 - \phi_1). \tag{3.7}$$

Since A_t is independent of Z_{t-1}, it may be deduced from (3.4) that

$$\sigma_z^2 = \phi_1^2 \sigma_z^2 + \sigma_A^2$$

and hence

$$\sigma_z^2 = \sigma_A^2/(1 - \phi_1^2). \tag{3.8}$$

Thus for σ_z^2 to be finite and non-negative, we must have

$$-1 < \phi_1 < 1. \tag{3.9}$$

It may be shown that if this condition is satisfied, the model (3.4) is a stationary stochastic process and so condition (3.9) is called the *condition for stationarity* for an AR(1) model.

It may be shown that the autocorrelations ρ_k for an AR(1) model are given by

$$\rho_k = \phi_1^k \quad (k \geqslant 1)$$

and hence

$$\rho_k = \phi_1 \rho_{k-1} \quad (k \geqslant 1). \tag{3.10}$$

Thus the autocorrelations decline geometrically towards zero with the lag k. If ϕ_1 is positive, the autocorrelations will decline smoothly towards zero, as shown in the theoretical ACF in Figure 3.3. In this case, the plot of the time series itself will also be smooth, since a high observation will tend to be followed by another high observation, not only in the next period, but in the next few periods. If ϕ_1 is negative, ρ_k will be positive for even lags and negative for odd lags and so the auto-correlations will alternate in sign as they decline towards zero, as shown in Figure 3.5. In this case, the plot of the time series itself will also tend to oscillate, since a high observation will tend to be followed by a low observation in the next period. If ϕ_1 is near ± 1, the theoretical autocorrelations die away fairly slowly, but if ϕ_1 is near 0, the theoretical autocorrelations die away rapidly towards zero, because the variable $\tilde{Z}_t$ is very nearly equal to A_t, i.e. the model is very nearly a white noise model. Comparing equations (3.5) and (3.10), we see that apart from the noise, the autocorrelations ρ_k bear exactly the same relationship to one another as do the

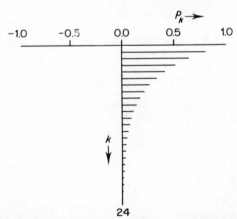

Figure 3.3 ACF for AR(1) model with $\phi_1 > 0$

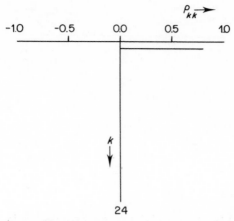

Figure 3.4 PACF for AR(1) model with
$\phi_1 > 0$

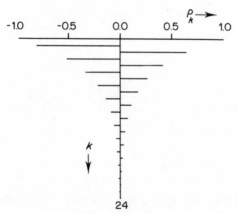

Figure 3.5 ACF for AR(1) model with
$\phi_1 < 0$

deviations $\tilde{Z}_t$. Hence we would expect the autocorrelations to follow the same pattern as the plot of the time series itself and this pattern depends on the value of ϕ_1.

It may be shown that the theoretical partial autocorrelations for an AR(1) model are given by

$$\rho_{11} = \phi_1, \quad \rho_{kk} = 0 \quad (k > 1).$$

Thus the theoretical PACF cuts off after lag 1 as shown in Figures 3.4 and 3.6. This is easily explained when we recall that

$$\rho_{11} = \rho_1$$

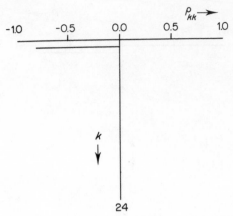

Figure 3.6 PACF for AR(1) model with
$\phi_1 < 0$

and hence

$$\rho_{11} = \phi_1.$$

We also have

$$\rho_{22} = \frac{\rho_2 - \rho_1^2}{1 - \rho_1^2}.$$

Substituting for ρ_2, we find that

$$\rho_{22} = \frac{\rho_1^2 - \rho_1^2}{1 - \rho_1^2} = 0.$$

In the same way, it may be shown that all the theoretical partial autocorrelations ρ_{kk} are zero, except for $\rho_{11} = \phi_1$. It will be recalled that ρ_{kk} was defined as the autocorrelation between Z_t and Z_{t-k}, with the effects of the intervening variables eliminated. Thus if ρ_{22} is zero, then the autocorrelation between Z_t and Z_{t-2}, with the effect of the variable Z_{t-1} eliminated, is zero. This is what is meant by saying that Z_t only depends on the variable Z_{t-1} and not on the variable Z_{t-2}. Similarly it may be shown that Z_t does not depend on any of the variables $Z_{t-3}, \ldots, Z_1$, but only on Z_{t-1}.

If an observed time series is a realization of an AR(1) model, then forecasting future values of the time series involves very simple calculations. Consider the one step ahead forecast:

$$\hat{z}_t(1) = \underset{t}{E}[Z_{t+1}].$$

However, from (3.4),

$$Z_{t+1} = \mu + \phi_1(Z_t - \mu) + A_{t+1}.$$

Since A_{t+1} is independent of $Z_1, Z_2, \ldots, Z_t$, we have

$$\underset{t}{E}[A_{t+1}] = 0$$

and since $E_t[Z_t]$ is just the observed value z_t, we have

$$\hat{z}_t(1) = \mu + \phi_1(z_t - \mu). \tag{3.11}$$

Thus the forecast of the next deviation from the mean, $\hat{z}_t(1) - \mu$, is a fraction, ϕ_1, of the current deviation from the mean, $z_t - \mu$. Similarly we have

$$Z_{t+2} = \mu + \phi_1(Z_{t+1} - \mu) + A_{t+2} \tag{3.12}$$

and hence

$$\hat{z}_t(2) = \mu + \phi_1(\underset{t}{E}[Z_{t+1}] - \mu)$$
$$= \mu + \phi_1(\hat{z}_t(1) - \mu). \tag{3.13}$$

Substituting for $\hat{z}_t(1)$ from (3.11) gives

$$\hat{z}_t(2) = \mu + \phi_1^2(z_t - \mu). \tag{3.14}$$

In general, the forecast for lead time l is given by the recursive relationship

$$\hat{z}_t(l) = \mu + \phi_1(\hat{z}_t(l-1) - \mu)$$

or alternatively by

$$\hat{z}_t(l) = \mu + \phi_1^l(z_t - \mu). \tag{3.15}$$

This shows that all future forecasts are determined by the current deviation $(z_t - \mu)$. However, as the lead time l increases, it is obvious from (3.15) that the forecast $\hat{z}_t(l)$ tends to the mean μ, since $-1 < \phi_1 < 1$. Thus although initial forecasts may fluctuate about the mean μ in a manner determined by ϕ_1 and the last observation z_t, as the lead time l increases, the information contained in the last observation becomes less relevant and the best that we can do is to predict future values using the mean μ.

We now evaluate $\sigma^2[e_t(l)]$, the variance of the forecast error conditional on the information at origin t. For $l = 1$, the one step ahead forecast error, conditional on the information at origin t, is

$$e_t(1) = Z_{t+1} - \hat{z}_t(1).$$

Now from (3.4),

$$Z_{t+1} = \mu + \phi_1(Z_t - \mu) + A_{t+1},$$

so that, conditional on the information at origin t, the only unknown component of Z_{t+1} is the random shock A_{t+1}, since the value of Z_t is known to be z_t. Thus we have

$$e_t(1) = \mu + \phi_1(z_t - \mu) + A_{t+1} - \hat{z}_t(1),$$

but from (3.11),

$$\hat{z}_t(1) = \mu + \phi_1(z_t - \mu),$$

so that

$$e_t(1) = A_{t+1}.$$

Thus the one step ahead forecast error is just the random shock A_{t+1} and hence the variance of this forecast error is

$$\sigma^2[e_t(1)] = \sigma_A^2.$$

For $l = 2$, from (3.12) and (3.13) we have

$$e_t(2) = A_{t+2} + \phi_1(Z_{t+1} - \hat{z}_t(1))$$
$$= A_{t+2} + \phi_1 A_{t+1}.$$

Hence since $A_t \sim \mathrm{IN}(0, \sigma_A^2)$, it follows that

$$\sigma^2[e_t(2)] = (1 + \phi_1^2)\sigma_A^2. \tag{3.16}$$

In general, it can be shown that

$$e_t(l) = A_{t+l} + \phi_1 A_{t+l-1} + \ldots + \phi_1^{l-1} A_{t+1}$$

and hence

$$\sigma^2[e_t(l)] = [1 + \phi_1^2 + \phi_1^4 + \ldots + \phi_1^{2l-2}]\sigma_A^2$$
$$= \frac{(1 - \phi_1^{2l})}{1 - \phi_1^2}\sigma_A^2. \tag{3.17}$$

The rate at which the variance of the forecast error increases with the lead time is determined by the value of ϕ_1. When ϕ_1 is small, the increase in this variance for an increase in lead time is small. When ϕ_1 is large, the increase in this variance for an increase in lead time is large. This has implications for the widths of prediction interval forecasts for z_{t+l}. It is obvious from (3.17) that as the lead time l increases, the variance of the forecast error increases to

$$\frac{\sigma_A^2}{1 - \phi_1^2},$$

which, from (3.8), is the process variance, σ_z^2.

As usual, 95% prediction limits for z_{t+l} are found by substituting for $\hat{z}_t(l)$ and $\sigma^2[e_t(l)]$ in the expression

$$\hat{z}_t(l) \pm (1.96)(\sigma^2[e_t(l)])^{1/2}.$$

Now $\hat{z}_t(l)$ and $\sigma^2[e_t(l)]$ depend on the unknown parameters θ_0, ϕ_1, and σ_A^2 and these have to be estimated from the observed time series. We will see in the next chapter how to calculate *least squares estimates* of these parameters.

To illustrate the results given here, suppose we have a time series of 70 observations which can be regarded as a realization of an AR(1) model with $\mu = 49.7$,

$\phi_1 = -0.59$, and $\sigma_A^2 = 55.7$. Suppose that the last observation is $z_{70} = 49$ and we wish to forecast two time periods into the future. Then from (3.14) we have

$$\hat{z}_{70}(2) = 49.7 + (-0.59)^2(49 - 49.7) = 49.6$$

and, from (3.16), 95% prediction limits for z_{72} are given by

$$49.5 \pm (1.96)((1 + (-0.59)^2)55.7)^{1/2} = 49.5 \pm 17.0.$$

In summary, it may be said that the AR(1) model is one of the simplest and most widely used models in time series analysis. By adjusting the parameter ϕ_1, this model is capable of representing a wide variety of stationary time series, from smooth time series to time series that tend to oscillate rapidly. It is characterized by the fact that the sample PACF cuts off after lag 1 and the sample ACF dies down towards zero. The model is easily interpreted. Thus if monthly sales are described by an AR(1) model, then the deviation of this month's sales from the overall average is a proportion of the deviation of last month's sales from the overall average, plus a random shock.

3.4 THE SECOND ORDER AUTOREGRESSIVE MODEL

An obvious generalization of the model in the previous section is to allow Z_t to depend on Z_{t-1} and Z_{t-2}, but only on these two of the preceding variables Z_{t-1}, $Z_{t-2}, \ldots, Z_1$. This gives the model

$$Z_t = \theta_0 + \phi_1 Z_{t-1} + \phi_2 Z_{t-2} + A_t \tag{3.18}$$

where

$$A_t \sim \text{IN}(0, \sigma_A^2).$$

This is called an *autoregressive model of order 2*, or, more briefly, an AR(2) model. The coefficient ϕ_2 is called a *second order autoregression coefficient*. An alternative form for the model in terms of the deviations $\tilde{Z}_t = Z_t - \mu$ is

$$\tilde{Z}_t = \phi_1 \tilde{Z}_{t-1} + \phi_2 \tilde{Z}_{t-2} + A_t. \tag{3.19}$$

Expressions for the process mean and variance in terms of the model parameters are given in Table 3.4 at the end of the chapter. The parameters ϕ_1 and ϕ_2 must satisfy a number of conditions for the model (3.18) to be a stationary stochastic process. These conditions for stationarity are:

$$\phi_2 + \phi_1 < 1,$$
$$\phi_2 - \phi_1 < 1,$$
$$-1 < \phi_2 < 1.$$

Graphically, these conditions imply that ϕ_1 and ϕ_2 lie within the triangle shown in Figure 3.7, with vertices at $(0, 1)$, $(2, -1)$, and $(-2, -1)$. The theoretical autocorrelations ρ_k for the AR(2) model die down towards zero, as shown in the ACF's in Figures 3.8, 3.10, 3.12, and 3.14. The exact pattern for the ACF depends on the

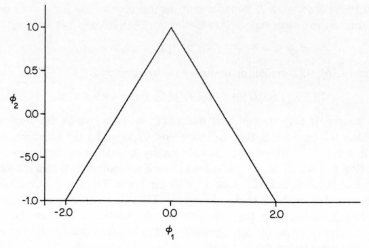

Figure 3.7 Stationarity conditions for AR(2) model

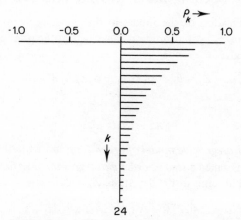

Figure 3.8 ACF for AR(2) model with
$\rho_{11} > 0$ and $\rho_{22} > 0$

values of the parameters ϕ_1 and ϕ_2. Expressions for the autocorrelations ρ_k in terms of the model parameters are given in Table 3.3.

The theoretical partial autocorrelations ρ_{kk} for the AR(2) model are given by

$$\rho_{11} = \frac{\phi_1}{1 - \phi_2},$$

$$\rho_{22} = \phi_2,$$

$$\rho_{kk} = 0, \quad k > 2,$$

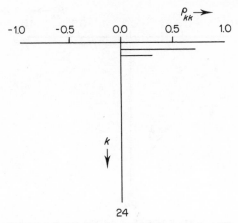

Figure 3.9 PACF for AR(2) model with
$\rho_{11} > 0$ and $\rho_{22} > 0$

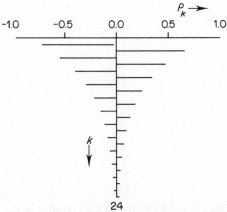

Figure 3.10 ACF for AR(2) model with
$\rho_{11} < 0$ and $\rho_{22} > 0$

so that the PACF cuts off after lag 2, as shown in Figures 3.9, 3.11, 3.13, and 3.15. This is the characteristic property of the AR(2) model. The exact pattern for the PACF depends on the signs of ϕ_1 and ϕ_2, which in turn determine the signs of ρ_{11} and ρ_{22}, as shown in these figures. Note that for the AR(2) model, we have

$$\rho_{22} = \phi_2,$$

while for the AR(1) model, we had

$$\rho_{11} = \phi_1.$$

Thus, in each case, the theoretical partial autocorrelation was equal to the highest

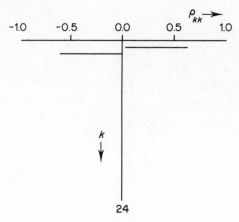

Figure 3.11 PACF for AR(2) model with
$\rho_{11} < 0$ and $\rho_{22} > 0$

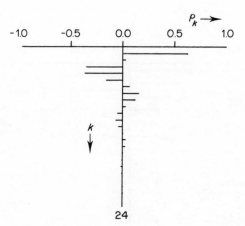

Figure 3.12 ACF for AR(2) model with
$\rho_{11} > 0$ and $\rho_{22} < 0$

order autoregression coefficient in the model. This is true in general for autoregressive models. Expressions for the forecast $\hat{z}_t(l)$ and the variance of the forecast errors $\sigma^2[e_t(l)]$ are given in Table 3.5 at the end of the chapter.

In summary, it can be said that although the AR(2) model often occurs in practice, it is less widely used than the AR(1) model. It is characterized by the fact that the PACF cuts off after the second lag and the ACF dies down towards zero.

3.5 THE FIRST ORDER MOVING AVERAGE MODEL

As well as the autoregressive models described in the previous two sections, another type of simple model of a stationary time series is also available. This is the *moving*

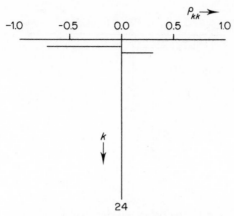

Figure 3.13 PACF for AR(2) model with $\rho_{11} > 0$ and $\rho_{22} < 0$

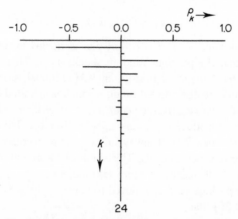

Figure 3.14 ACF for AR(2) model with $\rho_{11} < 0$ and $\rho_{22} < 0$

average model. Most time series observed in practice have a smoother time series plot than a realization of a white noise process, since in this process the successive observations are realizations of independent variables. For most time series observed in practice, successive observations are dependent. A standard way of smoothing a time series is to use a 'moving average', i.e. a weighted average of successive terms of the time series. This leads us to consider a process which is a moving average of successive terms of a white noise process.

The simplest such process is the following

$$Z_t = \theta_0 + A_t - \theta_1 A_{t-1}, \qquad (3.20)$$

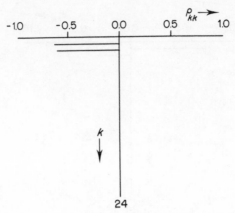

Figure 3.15 PACF for AR(2) model with
$\rho_{11} < 0$ and $\rho_{22} < 0$

where

$$A_t \sim \text{IN}(0, \sigma_A^2).$$

In this model, the variable Z_t is a constant plus a moving average of the current random shock, A_t, and the previous random shock, A_{t-1}. This is called a *moving average model of order 1* or, more briefly, an MA(1) model, since only one of the random shocks previous to the current random shock is included in the model. The parameter θ_1 is called a *moving average coefficient of order 1*. The minus sign for θ_1 is arbitrary and is introduced for convenience later on. The reader should be aware that other textbooks do not always adopt this convention, nor do all computer packages for time series analysis. This should be borne in mind in comparing results presented here with results in other textbooks or with results derived using a different computer package to that referred to here.

It follows from (3.20) that

$$\mu = E(Z_t) = \theta_0.$$

Thus the parameter θ_0 is just the mean process μ. We also have

$$\sigma_z^2 = (1 + \theta_1^2)\sigma_A^2.$$

From this, it would appear that no conditions need be imposed on the parameters θ_0 and θ_1 to ensure that the model (3.20) is stationary and it can be proved that this is indeed the case. This is true for all moving average models. However, certain conditions must be imposed on the parameters of moving average models to ensure *invertibility*. By invertibility is meant that it is possible to invert a moving average model and express it as an autoregressive model of infinite order, i.e. with an infinite number of autoregression coefficients. In practical terms, a moving average process is invertible if the deviation $(Z_t - \mu)$ does not depend overwhelmingly on deviations in the remote past. This is a sensible requirement in practice. For an

MA(1) model, the condition for invertibility is

$$-1 < \theta_1 < 1,$$

which is similar to the condition $-1 < \phi_1 < 1$ for stationarity for an AR(1) model.

For an MA(1) model, the autocorrelations ρ_k are given by

$$\rho_1 = \frac{-\theta_1}{1 + \theta_1^2},$$

$$\rho_k = 0, \quad k > 1.$$

Thus the ACF cuts off after lag 1, as shown in Figures 3.16 and 3.18. This is the characteristic property of an MA(1) model. This means that the 'memory' of an

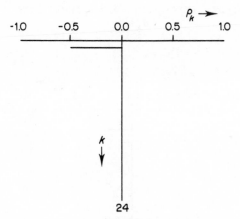

Figure 3.16 ACF for MA(1) model with
$\theta_1 > 0$

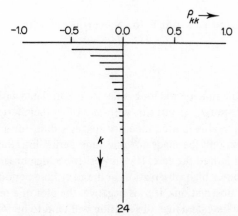

Figure 3.17 PACF for MA(1) model with
$\theta_1 > 0$

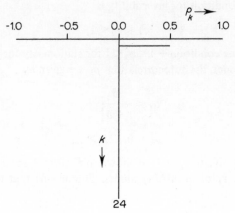

Figure 3.18 ACF for MA(1) model with
$\theta_1 < 0$

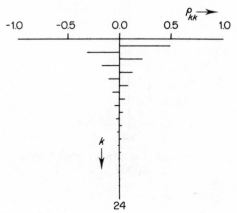

Figure 3.19 PACF for MA(1) model with
$\theta_1 < 0$

MA(1) model is only one time period long, since Z_t is correlated with its predecessor Z_{t-1} and with its successor Z_{t+1}, but not with any other members of the sequence of variables $Z_1, Z_2, \ldots$. This limited memory suggests that, for an MA(1) model, non-trivial forecasts can only be made for one time period into the future. We will shortly see that this is indeed the case. If ρ_1 is positive, a high observation will tend to be followed by another high observation in the next time period, but not neces- sarily by a run of high observations. If ρ_1 is negative, the plot of a realization of this model will tend to oscillate, as a high observation will tend to be followed by a low observation in the next time period. It can be shown that for the MA(1) model, the theoretical PACF dies down to zero, as shown in Figures 3.17 and 3.19. The exact pattern of the PACF depends on the value of the parameter θ_1, as shown in these figures. An expression for ρ_{kk} in terms of the parameter θ_1 is given in Table 3.4.

If an observed time series is a realization of an MA(1) model, then forecasting future values of the time series involves very simple calculations. From (3.20), we have

$$Z_{t+l} = \theta_0 + A_{t+l} - \theta_1 A_{t+l-1}.$$

Now for $l > 1$, the random shocks A_{t+l} and A_{t+l-1} have not yet occurred at time t and since they are independent of the random shocks $A_t, A_{t-1}, \ldots$ that have occurred at time t, their expected values, conditional on the information at origin t, is zero. Thus

$$\hat{z}_t(l) = E_t[Z_{t+l}] = \theta_0, \quad l > 1.$$

This was to be expected, as the MA(1) model has a memory of only one time period. Thus recent data are of no help in making a forecast two or more periods ahead and the best forecast is the process mean $\mu = \theta_0$.

For one step ahead forecasts, the situation is somewhat different. In this case, we have

$$Z_{t+1} = \theta_0 + A_{t+1} - \theta_1 A_t$$

and at time t the random shock A_t will have occurred, though the random shock A_{t+1} will not yet have occurred. Thus we have

$$\hat{z}_t(1) = E_t[Z_{t+1}] = \theta_0 - \theta_1 a_t, \tag{3.21}$$

where a_t is the realized value of the random shock at time t. Now the forecast error, conditional on the information at origin $(t-1)$, is

$$e_{t-1}(1) = Z_t - \hat{z}_{t-1}(1)$$

and from (3.20),

$$Z_t = \theta_0 + A_t - \theta_1 A_{t-1},$$

so that at time $(t-1)$, the unknown component of Z_t that has not yet occurred is the random shock A_t. Now from (3.21), we have

$$\hat{z}_{t-1}(1) = \theta_0 - \theta_1 a_{t-1}$$

so that

$$e_{t-1}(1) = A_t.$$

Thus for this model, as indeed for all the models in this chapter, the random shock A_t is just the one step ahead forecast error $e_{t-1}(1)$. Now while we cannot directly observe the realization of the random shock A_t at time t, we can observe the actual one step ahead forecast errors $z_t - \hat{z}_{t-1}(1)$. Now by what we have just established, this must be the realization of the random shock at time t. So by keeping track of the observed one step ahead forecast errors $z_t - \hat{z}_{t-1}(1)$, $z_{t-1} - \hat{z}_{t-2}(1)$, ...,

$z_1 - \hat{z}_0(1)$, we can calculate $\hat{z}_t(1)$ recursively from (3.21) as shown below. There is a *starting value problem* in that the first observed forecast error is

$$z_1 - \hat{z}_0(1)$$

but from (3.21),

$$\hat{z}_0(1) = \theta_0 - \theta_1 a_0,$$

and we have no way of estimating a_0, the realized value of the random shock A_0 at time 0. The concept of a random shock at time 0 may seem surprising at first but it is easily explained. It is conceivable that the stochastic process which generated the observed values $z_1, z_2, \ldots, z_t$ was also in operation before time 1, when the first observation was made. Let Z_0 be a random variable of which a realization z_0 occurred one time period before z_1 occurred, although we did not observe z_0. Similarly let Z_{-1} be a random variable of which a realization z_{-1} occurred two time periods before z_1, although again we did not observe z_{-1}. In this way, a sequence of random variables $Z_0, Z_{-1}, \ldots$ may be visualized corresponding to realizations of the process before our first observation at time 1. Now if the stochastic process consisting of the sequence of variables $\ldots, Z_{-1}, Z_0, Z_1, Z_2, \ldots$ is given by the model (3.20), we can visualize the random shocks $A_0, A_{-1}, \ldots$ occurring at times $0, -1, \ldots$, i.e. one or more time periods before the start of the observed time series $z_1, z_2, \ldots, z_t$.

To overcome the starting value problem, we initially estimate a_0, the realized value of A_0 which we did not observe, as zero, the unconditional mean of the random variable A_0. Then taking $\hat{a}_0 = 0$, we calculate $\hat{z}_t(1)$ recursively as follows:

$$\hat{z}_0(1) = \theta_0 - \theta_1(\hat{a}_0), \qquad (3.22)$$

$$\hat{z}_1(1) = \theta_0 - \theta_1(z_1 - \hat{z}_0(1)),$$

$$\vdots$$

$$\hat{z}_t(1) = \theta_0 - \theta_1(z_t - \hat{z}_{t-1}(1)),$$

where at every step after the first, the observed forecast errors are used in place of the realizations of the random shocks. This procedure is illustrated in Table 3.1.

Suppose that we have an observed time series of ten observations, as shown in the second column of Table 3.1, and that this time series is a realization of an MA(1) model with $\theta_0 = 0$ and $\theta_1 = 0.5$. Then taking $\hat{a}_0 = 0$ as an initial estimate of the realized value of A_0, we calculate $\hat{z}_{10}(1)$ recursively as follows. First, $\hat{z}_0(1)$ is calculated from (3.22) as

$$\hat{z}_0(1) = \theta_0 - \theta_1(\hat{a}_0)$$

$$= 0 - 0.5(0) = 0,$$

which gives the first entry in the third column of Table 3.1. Then we have

$$z_1 - \hat{z}_0(1) = 0.303 - 0 = 0.303,$$

Table 3.1 Calculation of $\hat{z}_t(1)$ for an MA(1) model with $\theta_0 = 0$, $\theta_1 = 0.5$, and $\hat{a}_0 = 0$

t	z_t	$\hat{z}_{t-1}(1)$	$z_t - \hat{z}_{t-1}(1)$	$\hat{z}_t(1)$
0				
1	0.303	0	0.303	0.1515
2	−0.887	−0.151	−0.736	0.368
3	−0.419	0.368	−0.787	0.393
4	0.798	0.393	0.405	−0.202
5	0.368	−0.202	0.570	−0.285
6	−0.661	−0.285	−0.376	0.188
7	−0.508	0.188	−0.696	0.348
8	−2.108	0.348	−2.456	1.228
9	1.638	1.228	0.410	−0.205
10	−0.430	−0.205	−0.225	0.112

which gives the first entry in the fourth column of Table 3.1. Next

$$\hat{z}_1(1) = \theta_0 - \theta_1(z_1 - \hat{z}_0(1))$$
$$= 0 - 0.5(0.303)$$
$$= -0.1515,$$

which gives the first entry in the fifth column of Table 3.1. Continuing in this way, we find that $\hat{z}_{10}(1) = 0.112$. Note that, in this example, the one step ahead forecasts differ considerably from the observed values, e.g. $\hat{z}_8(1) = 1.228$ while $z_9 = 1.638$. This is because the random shock term, which is the unforeseeable component of the value being forecast, is relatively important in this example. By using a technique known as *back forecasting*, which will be described in the next chapter, a new estimate of the realized value of a_0 may be obtained and substituted in (3.22). Using this estimate as a new starting value, a new forecast $\hat{z}_t(1)$ is calculated as above. This back forecasting procedure may be repeated as often as desired, but usually little is gained by repeating it more than once.

The variance of the forecasting error is given by

$$\sigma^2[e_t(1)] = \sigma_A^2,$$
$$\sigma^2[e_t(l)] = (1 + \theta_1^2)\sigma_A^2, \quad l \geqslant 2.$$

Note that for $l \geqslant 2$, the variance of the forecast error is the same for all lead times l. This implies that prediction intervals for z_{t+l} will have the same width for all such lead times. Note also that for $l \geqslant 2$, $\sigma^2[e_t(l)]$ is just the process variance σ_z^2.

In summary, it may be said that the MA(1) is a simple and useful time series model, though it is not as widely used as the AR(1) and AR(2) models. It is characterized by the fact that its ACF cuts off after lag 1 and its PACF dies away towards zero.

3.6 THE SECOND ORDER MOVING AVERAGE MODEL

An obvious generalization of the model described in the previous section is

$$Z_t = \theta_0 + A_t - \theta_1 A_{t-1} - \theta_2 A_{t-2}, \tag{3.23}$$

where

$$A_t \sim \text{IN}(0, \sigma_A^2).$$

Here the model includes two of the previous random shocks and is said to be a *moving average model of order 2* or, more briefly, an MA(2) model. The parameter θ_2 is called a *moving average coefficient of order 2*. Again the minus sign for θ_2 is arbitrary and is introduced for convenience later on. It follows from (3.23) that

$$\mu = \theta_0.$$

An expression for the process variance in terms of the model parameters is given in Table 3.3. No conditions need be imposed on the parameters in model (3.23) to ensure stationarity. Again the conditions for invertibility for an MA(2) model are similar to the conditions for stationarity for an AR(2) model:

$$\theta_2 + \theta_1 < 1,$$
$$\theta_2 - \theta_1 < 1,$$
$$-1 < \theta_2 < 1.$$

It may be shown that, for the MA(2) model, the autocorrelations ρ_k have the following properties: $\rho_1 \neq 0$ in general, $\rho_2 \neq 0$ in general, but

$$\rho_k = 0, \quad k > 2.$$

Thus the ACF cuts off after lag 2. This is the characteristic property of the MA(2) model. The exact pattern for the ACF depends on the values of θ_1 and θ_2. Expressions for ρ_1 and ρ_2 in terms of the model parameters are given in Table 3.4. It may be shown that for the MA(2) model the PACF dies away towards zero. Expressions for the forecasts $\hat{z}_t(l)$ and the variance of the forecast error $\sigma^2[e_t(l)]$ are given in Table 3.5. It transpires that for more than two periods ahead, the best forecast is just the process mean $\mu = \theta_0$. This was to be expected, as the MA(2) model has a memory of only two time periods.

In summary, it may be said that the MA(2) model occurs less frequently in practice than the MA(1) model. It is characterized by the fact that its ACF cuts off after lag 2 and its PACF dies away towards zero.

3.7 THE FIRST ORDER AUTOREGRESSIVE MOVING AVERAGE MODEL

A simple and important model is obtained by combining an AR(1) model with an MA(1) model to obtain a model which has both an autoregressive term and a moving average term. Such a model is given by

$$Z_t = \theta_0 + \phi_1 Z_{t-1} + A_t - \theta_1 A_{t-1}, \tag{3.24}$$

where

$$A_t \sim \text{IN}(0, \sigma_A^2).$$

This model is called a *first order autoregressive moving average* model or, more briefly, ARMA(1, 1) model. Note that if $\theta_1 = 0$ the ARMA(1, 1) model reduces to an AR(1) model and if $\phi_1 = 0$ the ARMA(1, 1) model reduces to an MA(1) model, while if $\phi_1 = \theta_1$ the ARMA(1, 1) model reduces to a white noise model. Thus we can regard these models as special cases of an ARMA(1, 1) model. If θ_1 is close to zero, an ARMA(1, 1) model will exhibit behaviour very similar to that of an AR(1) model. On the other hand, if θ_1 is close to zero, the ARMA(1, 1) model will exhibit the characteristics of an MA(1) model. When ϕ_1 is close to θ_1, an ARMA(1, 1) model will behave like a white noise model. In this case, the parameters ϕ_1 and θ_1 are said to be *redundant*, as the model will behave like one with fewer parameters. In practice, the simpler models, white noise, AR(1) and MA(1), should be considered first for fitting to an observed time series. Only when these are ruled out should we consider fitting the more complicated ARMA(1, 1) model. An alternative form for the model in terms of the deviations $\tilde{Z}_t = Z_t - \mu$ is

$$\tilde{Z}_t - \phi_1 \tilde{Z}_{t-1} = A_t - \theta_1 A_{t-1}. \tag{3.25}$$

Expressions for the process mean and variance in terms of the model parameters are given in Table 3.4. As the model is a mixture of an AR(1) model and an MA(1) model, it can be shown that the condition for stationarity is

$$-1 < \phi_1 < 1$$

and the condition for invertibility is

$$-1 < \theta_1 < 1.$$

It may be shown that the ACF for the ARMA(1, 1) model dies away towards zero. An expression for ρ_k in terms of the model parameters is given in Table 3.4. The PACF for this model also dies away towards zero. What distinguishes the ARMA(1, 1) model from the other models discussed in this chapter is that neither the ACF nor the PACF cut off after a certain number of lags, but both die away towards zero.

3.8 AUTOREGRESSIVE MOVING AVERAGE MODELS

The six models considered in this chapter are all particular cases of the following model:

$$Z_t = \theta_0 + \phi_1 Z_{t-1} + \ldots + \phi_p Z_{t-p} + A_t - \theta_1 A_{t-1} - \ldots - \theta_q A_{t-q} \tag{3.26}$$

where

$$A_t \sim \text{IN}(0, \sigma_A^2).$$

This model has p autoregression coefficients $\phi_1, \phi_2, \ldots, \phi_p$ and q moving average coefficients $\theta_1, \theta_2, \ldots, \theta_q$ as well as the constant term θ_0. It is said to be an *auto-*

regressive moving average model of order (p, q), or, more briefly, an ARMA(p, q)
model. The first five models we have studied may be described in this notation as
shown in Table 3.2. Thus the white noise model is an ARMA$(0, 0)$ model, a first
order autoregressive AR(1) model is an ARMA$(1, 0)$ model, etc. It has been found
that most of the stationary time series occurring in practice can be fitted by an
ARMA(p, q) model with $p + q \leqslant 2$. In other words, the six models that we have
studied are the only ARMA models that are usually needed in practice.

The definitions of these six models are given in Table 3.2 and their characteristic
properties are summarized in Table 3.3. These two tables should be committed to
memory as the information contained in them is essential for further reading. Since
for some models there are several possible patterns for the theoretical ACF and
theoretical PACF, the reader will find it easier to remember the general descriptions
of these patterns given in Table 3.3 rather than the numerous figures of these
patterns given previously. Detailed properties of the six models are given in Table
3.4, but this table is for reference only and need not be committed to memory.

For these six models, forecasting future values involves very simple calculations.
The results are summarized in Table 3.5, but again this table is for reference only
and need not be committed to memory. The method by which these forecasts are
calculated applies to all the models we will study from now on, as well as those
discussed in the present chapter. This method for calculating the forecast $\hat{z}_t(l)$
may be summarized in general terms as follows:

(1) Using the definition of the model under study, express Z_{t+l} in terms of the
variables $Z_t, Z_{t-1}, \ldots, Z_1$ (corresponding to the observations $z_t, z_{t-1}, \ldots, z_1$
that have occurred at time t), the variables $Z_{t+1}, Z_{t+2}, \ldots$ (corresponding to
the observations $z_{t+1}, z_{t+2}, \ldots$ that have not occurred at time t), the random
shocks $A_t, A_{t-1}, \ldots$ (which have occurred at time t), and the random shocks
$A_{t+1}, A_{t+2}, \ldots$ (which have not occurred at time t).

(2) Since

$$\hat{z}_t(l) = E_t[Z_{t+l}],$$

by taking the expected value of each of these components, conditional on the
information at origin t, we arrive at an expression for $\hat{z}_t(l)$ by making the
following substitutions in the original expression for Z_{t+l}:

    (a) Replace $Z_t, Z_{t-1}, \ldots$ by their observed values $z_t, z_{t-1}, \ldots$

    (b) Replace $Z_{t+1}, Z_{t+2}, \ldots$ by the forecasts $\hat{z}_t(1), \hat{z}_t(2), \ldots$

    (c) Replace $A_t, A_{t-1}, \ldots, A_1$ by the observed one step ahead forecast
errors

$$(z_t - \hat{z}_{t-1}(1)), (z_{t-1} - \hat{z}_{t-2}(1)), \ldots, (z_1 - \hat{z}_0(1)).$$

    (d) Replace $A_{t+1}, A_{t+2}, \ldots$ by zeros.

    (e) In starting the forecasting process, it may be necessary to assume that
$a_0, a_{-1}, \ldots$, the realizations of the random shocks $A_0, A_{-1}, \ldots$, are all
zero. Then the forecast $\hat{z}_t(l)$ is built up recursively from the forecasts
$\hat{z}_t(1), \hat{z}_t(2), \ldots, \hat{z}_t(l-1)$. The reader may verify that the forecast
functions given in Table 3.5 are all particular cases of this method.

The reader may also verify from Tables 3.4 and 3.5 that for the six ARMA models we have studied the forecasts $\hat{z}_t(l)$ tend to the process mean, μ, and the variance of the forecast error, $\sigma^2[e_t(l)]$, tends to the process variance, σ_z^2, as the lead time l increases. For all these models, $\hat{z}_t(l)$ converges to μ fairly quickly. This implies that only short term forecasts produced by these models will be non-trivial, but this is not a disadvantage as these models are invariably used for short term forecasting.

Table 3.2 Definitions of six ARMA models

Model	ARMA notation	Model definition ($A_t \sim \mathrm{IN}(0, \sigma_A^2)$ for all models)	Stationarity/ Invertibility conditions
White noise	ARMA(0, 0)	$Z_t = \theta_0 + A_t$	–
First order autoregressive AR(1)	ARMA(1, 0)	$Z_t = \theta_0 + \phi_1 Z_{t-1} + A_t$	$-1 < \phi_1 < 1$
Second order autoregressive AR(2)	ARMA(2, 0)	$Z_t = \theta_0 + \phi_1 Z_{t-1} + \phi_2 Z_{t-2} + A_t$	$\phi_2 + \phi_1 < 1$, $\phi_2 - \phi_1 < 1$, $-1 < \phi_2 < 1$
First order moving average MA(1)	ARMA(0, 1)	$Z_t = \theta_0 + A_t - \theta_1 A_{t-1}$	$-1 < \theta_1 < 1$
Second order moving average MA(2)	ARMA(0, 2)	$Z_t = \theta_0 + A_t - \theta_1 A_{t-1} - \theta_2 A_{t-2}$	$\theta_2 + \theta_1 < 1$, $\theta_2 - \theta_1 < 1$, $-1 < \theta_2 < 1$
First order autoregressive moving average	ARMA(1, 1)	$Z_t = \theta_0 + \phi_1 Z_{t-1} + A_t - \theta_1 A_{t-1}$	$-1 < \phi_1 < 1$, $-1 < \theta_1 < 1$

Table 3.3 Characteristic properties of six ARMA models

Model	Theoretical ACF	Theoretical PACF
White noise	All autocorrelations zero	All partial autocorrelations zero
AR(1)	Tails off towards zero	Cuts off after lag 1
AR(2)	Tails off towards zero	Cuts off after lag 2
MA(1)	Cuts off after lag 1	Tails off towards zero
MA(2)	Cuts off after lag 2	Tails off towards zero
ARMA(1, 1)	Tails off towards zero	Tails off towards zero

Table 3.4 Means, variances, autocorrelations, and partial autocorrelations of six ARMA models

Model	Mean μ	Variance σ_z^2	Autocorrelations ρ_k	Partial autocorrelations ρ_{kk}
ARMA(0, 0)	θ_0	σ_A^2	$\rho_k = 0, k \geqslant 1$	$\rho_{kk} = 0, k \geqslant 1$
ARMA(1, 0)	$\dfrac{\theta_0}{1-\phi_1}$	$\dfrac{\sigma_A^2}{1-\phi_1^2}$	$\rho_k = \phi_1^k, k \geqslant 1$	$\rho_{11} = \phi_1,$ $\rho_{kk} = 0, k > 1$
ARMA(2, 0)	$\dfrac{\theta_0}{1-\phi_1-\phi_2}$	$\dfrac{(1-\phi_2)\sigma_A^2}{(1+\phi_2)((1-\phi_2)^2-\phi_1^2)}$	$\rho_0 = 1, \rho_1 = \dfrac{\phi_1}{1-\phi_2},$ $\rho_k = \phi_1\rho_{k-1} + \phi_2\rho_{k-2}, k > 1$	$\rho_{11} = \dfrac{\phi_1}{1-\phi_2}, \rho_{22} = \phi_2,$ $\rho_{kk} = 0, k > 2$
ARMA(0, 1)	θ_0	$(1+\theta_1^2)\sigma_A^2$	$\rho_1 = \dfrac{-\theta_1}{1+\theta_1^2},$ $\rho_k = 0, k > 1$	$\rho_{kk} = \dfrac{-\theta_1^k(1-\theta_1^2)}{(1-\theta_1^{2k+2})}$
ARMA(0, 2)	θ_0	$(1+\theta_1^2+\theta_2^2)\sigma_A^2$	$\rho_1 = \dfrac{-\theta_1(1-\theta_2)}{1+\theta_1^2+\theta_2^2},$ $\rho_2 = \dfrac{-\theta_2}{1+\theta_1^2+\theta_2^2},$ $\rho_k = 0, k > 2$	Tails off towards zero
ARMA(1, 1)	$\dfrac{\theta_0}{1-\phi_1}$	$\dfrac{(1+\theta_1^2-2\phi_1\theta_1)\sigma_A^2}{1-\phi_1^2}$	$\rho_1 = \dfrac{(1-\phi_1\theta_1)(\phi_1-\theta_1)}{1-\theta_1^2-2\phi_1\theta_1},$ $\rho_k = \phi_1^{k-1}\rho_1, k > 1$	Tails off towards zero

Table 3.5 Forecast functions and forecast error variances for six ARMA models

Model	Forecast function $\hat{z}_t(l)$	Forecast error variance $\sigma^2[e_t(l)]$
ARMA(0, 0)	$\mu, l \geqslant 1$	σ_A^2
ARMA(1, 0)	$\mu + \phi_1^l(z_t - \mu), l \geqslant 1$	$\left(\dfrac{1-\phi_1^{2l}}{1-\phi_1^2}\right)\sigma_A^2$
ARMA(2, 0)	$\hat{z}_t(1) = \mu + \phi_1(z_t - \mu) + \phi_2(z_{t-1} - \mu)$	$\left(1 + \displaystyle\sum_{j=1}^{l-1}\psi_j^2\right)\sigma_A^2,$
	$\hat{z}_t(2) = \mu + \phi_1(\hat{z}_t(1) - \mu) + \phi_2(z_t - \mu)$	$\psi_0 = 1, \psi_1 = \phi_1,$
	$\hat{z}_t(l) = \mu + \phi_1(\hat{z}_t(l-1) - \mu) + \phi_2(\hat{z}_t(l-2) - \mu), l > 2$	$\psi_j = \phi_1\psi_{j-1} + \phi_2\psi_{j-2}, j > 1$
ARMA(0, 1)	$\hat{z}_t(1) = \theta_0 - \theta_1(z_t - \hat{z}_{t-1}(1))$	$\sigma^2[e_t(1)] = \sigma_A^2$
	$\hat{z}_t(l) = \theta_0, l > 1$	$\sigma^2[e_t(l)] = (1+\theta_1^2)\sigma_A^2, l > 1$
ARMA(0, 2)	$\hat{z}_t(1) = \theta_0 - \theta_1(z_t - \hat{z}_{t-1}(1)) - \theta_2(z_{t-1} - \hat{z}_{t-2}(1))$	$\sigma^2[e_t(1)] = \sigma_A^2$
	$\hat{z}_t(2) = \theta_0 - \theta_2(z_t - \hat{z}_{t-1}(1))$	$\sigma^2[e_t(2)] = (1+\theta_1^2)\sigma_A^2$
	$z_t(l) = \theta_0, l > 2$	$\sigma^2[e_t(l)] = (1+\theta_1^2+\theta_2^2)\sigma_A^2, l > 2$
ARMA(1, 1)	$\hat{z}_t(1) = \mu + \phi_1(z_t - \mu) - \theta_1(z_t - \hat{z}_{t-1}(1))$	$\left[1 + (\phi_1 - \theta_1)^2\left(\dfrac{1-\phi_1^{2l-2}}{1-\phi_1^2}\right)\right]\sigma_A^2$
	$\hat{z}_t(l) = \mu + \phi_1\hat{z}_t(l-1), l > 1$	

3.9 EXERCISES

3.9.1   Using the general method that is described in Section 3.8, verify the forecast functions given in Table 3.5.

3.9.2   For the forecast functions given in Table 3.5, verify that the forecasts tend to the process mean and the variance of the forecast error tends to the process variance, as the lead time increases.

Chapter 4

Forecasting stationary time series

4.1 STAGES IN THE BOX–JENKINS APPROACH TO FORECASTING

It is advisable at this point to dwell on the concept of a *time series model*, as distinct from the *observed time series*, which is assumed to be a realization of some underlying *stochastic process*. We cannot observe this underlying stochastic process and so we can never be absolutely sure that we have correctly identified it. The most that we can say is that we have found a model, a realization of which would have similar characteristic properties to those of the observed time series. We cannot say that we have identified the underlying stochastic process as being identical to our selected model. All that we can say is that we have found a model which gives an adequate representation of the observed time series. It is conceivable that we may find more than one model, each of which gives an adequate representation according to our criteria. However, this will not cause problems, as such multiple models will usually be found to have fairly similar structure and to give similar short term forecasts.

The Box–Jenkins approach to time series analysis may be divided into three main stages, as shown in Figure 4.1:

(1) Selecting a suitable class of models for fitting to the observed time series.
(2) Fitting an appropriate model from this class to the observed time series.
(3) Using the fitted model to make forecasts of future values of the time series.

The first stage of the Box–Jenkins approach has been described as the selection of a suitable class of models from which to choose an appropriate model for the observed time series. If a study of the characteristics of the observed time series indicated that the observed time series is *stationary*, then a suitable class of models is the class of ARMA models described in the previous chapter. The reader will recall from Sections 2.4 and 2.6 that the observed time series is regarded as stationary if the means and standard deviations of subsets are approximately the same and the sample ACF either dies down quickly or cuts off after a particular lag. However, suppose that the sample ACF dies down extremely slowly or indicates a seasonal pattern: then the observed time series is non-stationary in the mean.

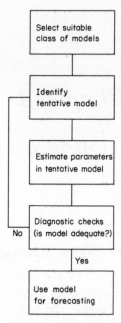

Figure 4.1   Stages
in the Box–Jenkins
approach

Similarly, a plot of the means and standard deviations of the subsets may indicate that the observed time series is non-stationary in the variance. In such cases, to find an appropriate model for the observed time series, we must select from a class of *non-stationary* models or a class of *seasonal* models. Such classes will be described in Chapters 5 and 6.

The second stage of the Box–Jenkins approach consists of selecting an appropriate model from the chosen class of models for fitting to the observed time series. This stage may be further subdivided into a cycle of three stages: (a) *identification*, (b) *estimation*, and (c) *diagnostic checking*. At the *identification* stage, by comparing the sample ACF and PACF of the observed time series with the theoretical ACF and PACF of models from the chosen class, a *tentative model* is selected such that the characteristics of a realization of the tentative model would resemble those of the observed time series. This identification stage is probably the most difficult stage in the Box–Jenkins approach and requires a skill that only comes with experience. If an incorrect model is selected at this stage, no great harm is done as this incorrect model will be discarded at a later stage in the analysis. It is quite possible that more than one tentative model is selected at this stage. In such a case, the subsequent stages of analysis may be applied to each of the tentative models.

At the *estimation* stage, the tentative model is fitted to the observed time series and the parameters in this model are estimated. Finally, *diagnostic checks* are applied to the fitted model to see if it adequately represents the observed time series. If no lack of fit is indicated, the model is ready for use in *forecasting* future values of the observed time series. If these tests detect inadequacies in the model, they will also indicate how the model should be altered to obtain a better fit. This leads to a new tentative model and a new cycle of identification, estimation, and diagnostic checking. This iterative cycle is repeated until an adequate model is found. If more than one tentative model has been selected at the identification stage, we may conceivably end up with more than one model, each of which gives an adequate representation of the observed time series according to our criteria. However, as has been said earlier, this will not cause problems as such multiple models will usually be found, on closer examination, to have very similar structure and similar short term forecasts. In the following three sections in this chapter, the techniques involved in identification, estimation, and diagnostic checking are described in detail. In the remaining sections in this chapter, these techniques are used to fit models to examples of stationary time series. In each of these examples, once an appropriate model has been fitted, the results of the last chapter are used to forecast future values of the time series.

4.2 IDENTIFICATION OF A TENTATIVE MODEL

The basic technique in the identification stage is the comparison of the sample ACF and PACF of the observed time series with the theoretical ACF and PACF patterns of models from the chosen class. To simplify the discussion, suppose that the observed time series is stationary and hence the class of ARMA models has been chosen as a suitable class of models. The characteristic properties of the six most widely used models from this class were given in Table 3.3 which is repeated here in Table 4.1. In general, an autoregressive model of order p (an AR(p) model) is characterized by the fact that its theoretical PACF cuts off after lag p, while a moving average model of order q (an MA(q) model) is characterized by the fact that its theoretical ACF cuts off after lag q. On the other hand for a mixed auto-regressive moving average ARMA(p, q) model with p and q both positive, the theoretical ACF and PACF both tail off towards zero. Consider a realization of N observations of one of these ARMA models and the sample ACF and PACF of this realization. This ACF and this PACF will not agree exactly with the theoretical

Table 4.1 Characteristic properties of six ARMA models

Model	Theoretical ACF	Theoretical PACF
White noise	All autocorrelations zero	All partial autocorrelations zero
AR(1)	Tails off towards zero	Cuts off after lag 1
AR(2)	Tails off towards zero	Cuts off after lag 2
MA(1)	Cuts off after lag 1	Tails off towards zero
MA(2)	Cuts off after lag 2	Tails off towards zero
ARMA(1, 1)	Tails off towards zero	Tails off towards zero

ACF and PACF described above, since the sample autocorrelations and partial autocorrelations are only estimates of their theoretical counterparts, but we would expect them to exhibit the same general patterns as the theoretical ACF and PACF, provided we have at least 50 observations. Thus, for example, the sample ACF of a realization of an AR(1) model should tend to tail off towards zero and all partial autocorrelations in the PACF after lag 1 should be near zero. However, it often happens that the sample ACF of a realization of an AR(1) model has 'ripples' at large lags, instead of tailing off towards zero. This is due to the fact that the sample autocorrelations can have rather large variances and can be highly autocorrelated with each other. Thus apparent trends and ripples can occur in the sample ACF which have no basis in the theoretical ACF. Similarly the sample PACF of a realization of an AR(1) model can have a few large partial autocorrelations at large lags, instead of all the partial autocorrelations being near zero after lag one. The same problems arise with realizations of any ARMA model.

The identification process essentially consists of studying the sample ACF and PACF of the observed time series and then asking the question: do the sample ACF and PACF of the observed time series resemble those of a realization of a model from the chosen class of models and, if so, which model do they resemble? From the remarks made above, it is clear that it will often be quite difficult to answer this question and this is why identification is the most difficult stage of the Box–Jenkins approach. Indeed it has been said that identification is a technique that should not be attempted for the first time. However, skill is acquired with experience. It is obvious that the observed time series must contain at least 50 observations, so that the sample autocorrelations and partial autocorrelations will be reasonable estimates of their theoretical counterparts in the underlying stochastic process. It is also clear that we must look for the broad characteristics in the sample ACF and PACF and not attach importance to every detail. This may lead to some ambiguity as to which model to choose. However, even if the wrong tentative model is selected at this stage, its inadequacies will be detected when we come to apply diagnostic checks to the model. Suppose we are undecided between two or more tentative models at the identification stage. Then the subsequent stages of analysis may be applied to each of the tentative models. However, according to what Box and Jenkins call the *principle of parsimonious parameterization*, when it comes to a choice between two models at the identification stage, it is better to select the model with fewer parameters. There are two reasons for this. First, it may be difficult to estimate the model parameters accurately if the model has too many parameters. Secondly, the diagnostic checks may not detect that a complicated model contains more parameters than are needed to adequately represent the observed time series. Thus it is better to choose an initial tentative model with as few parameters as possible. If the diagnostic checks indicate that this model is inadequate, more parameters may be added later.

Confronted with the problem of distinguishing what is important from what is not important in the sample ACF and PACF, we look for what are called *tests of significance* of the sample autocorrelations and partial autocorrelations. By a test of significance of a sample autocorrelation r_k is meant a procedure for deciding whether the corresponding theoretical autocorrelation ρ_k is equal to zero or not. Recall that for a moving average model of order q (an MA(q) model), the ACF cuts off after lag q, i.e. $\rho_k = 0$ for all $k > q$. Thus for a realization of an MA(q) model, the sample autocorrelations r_k should all be near zero for $k > q$. In fact, it may be shown that if the theoretical autocorrelations ρ_k are all zero for $k > q$, then the sample autocorrelations r_k with $k > q$ are approximately normally distributed with mean 0 and a standard deviation that may be estimated by

$$\frac{1}{N^{1/2}} \left(1 + 2 \sum_1^q r_i^2 \right)^{1/2}$$

where N is the number of observations in the realization. The reader will recall that if a variable X is normal with mean μ and standard deviation σ, then the probability that a random value of X lies between the limits $\mu \pm (1.96)\sigma$ is 0.95. Applying this result to the sample autocorrelation r_k, we see that if for $k > q$ the theoretical autocorrelations ρ_k are all zero, then the sample autocorrelation r_k with $k > q$ should lie between the limits

$$\pm \frac{1.96}{N^{1/2}} \left(1 + 2 \sum_1^q r_i^2 \right)^{1/2}$$

with probability 0.95.

This leads us to adopt the following rule of thumb:

If the sample autocorrelation r_k lies outside the limits

$$\pm \frac{1.96}{N^{1/2}} \left(1 + 2 \sum_{i=1}^k r_i^2 \right)^{1/2} , \tag{4.1}$$

it is significantly different from zero and we conclude that $\rho_k \neq 0$. Otherwise, r_k is not significantly different from zero and we conclude that $\rho_k = 0$.

In some computer packages, the limits (4.1) are shown on the graphical display of the sample ACF to facilitate this test of significance. An equivalent procedure is to calculate the 't-ratio'

$$t_{r_k} = \frac{r_k}{(1/N^{1/2}) \left(1 + 2 \sum_1^k r_i^2 \right)^{1/2}} \tag{4.2}$$

and to adopt the following rule of thumb:

If the t-ratio t_{r_k} lies outside the limits ± 1.96, then r_k is significantly different from zero and we conclude that $\rho_k \neq 0$. Otherwise, r_k is not significantly different from zero and we conclude that $\rho_k = 0$.

For the TSERIES computer package which was used for the examples in this book, the t-ratios (4.2) are given beside the corresponding sample autocorrelations in the graphical display of the sample ACF.

It should be remembered that even if the theoretical autocorrelation ρ_k is zero, there is a probability of 0.05 or 1 in 20 that the sample autocorrelation r_k will lie outside the limits (4.1) by chance and that the t-ratio (4.2) will lie outside the limits ±1.96 by chance. Consequently, if we study 24 sample autocorrelations and find that one of them is significant, then we should bear in mind that the corresponding theoretical autocorrelation may, in fact, be zero and the sample autocorrelation has turned out to be significant by chance. In any case, the rules of thumb given here are only rough guidelines, because of the problems we have mentioned in estimating the theoretical autocorrelations.

A similar test of significance is available for the sample partial autocorrelations. Recall that for an autoregressive model of order p (an AR(p) model), the PACF cuts off after lag p, i.e. $\rho_{kk} = 0$ for all $k > p$. For a realization of an AR(p) model, the sample partial autocorrelations r_{kk} should all be near zero for $k > p$. In fact it may be shown that if the sample partial autocorrelations ρ_{kk} are all zero for $k > p$, then the sample partial autocorrelation r_{kk} with $k > p$ is approximately normally distributed with mean 0 and standard deviation $1/N^{1/2}$. Hence if $\rho_{kk} = 0$ for all $k > p$, the sample partial autocorrelation r_{kk} with $k > p$ should lie between the limits

$$\pm 1.96/N^{1/2}$$

with probability 0.95. This leads us to adopt the following rule of thumb:

If the sample partial autocorrelation r_{kk} lies outside the limits

$$\pm 1.96/N^{1/2}, \tag{4.3}$$

it is significantly different from zero and we conclude that $\rho_{kk} \neq 0$. Otherwise, r_{kk} is not significantly different from zero and we conclude that $\rho_{kk} = 0$.

In some computer packages, the limits (4.3) are shown on the graphical display of the sample PACF to facilitate this test of significance. An equivalent procedure is to calculate the t-ratio

$$t_{r_{kk}} = \frac{r_{kk}}{1/N^{1/2}} \tag{4.4}$$

and to adopt the following rule of thumb:

If the t-ratio $t_{r_{kk}}$ lies outside the limits ±1.96, then r_{kk} is significantly different from zero and we conclude that $\rho_{kk} \neq 0$. Otherwise r_{kk} is not significantly different from zero and we conclude that $\rho_{kk} = 0$.

For the TSERIES package which was used for the examples in this book, the t-ratios (4.4) are given beside the corresponding sample partial autocorrelations in the graphical display of the sample PACF. As was the case for the sample auto-correlations, if we study 24 sample partial autocorrelations and find that one of them is significant, we should bear in mind that the corresponding theoretical partial autocorrelation may in fact be zero and the sample partial autocorrelation has turned out to be significant by chance. Again, these rules of thumb should be regarded as rough guidelines, rather than hard and fast rules, for the reasons already given.

In selecting a model from the class of ARMA models, another problem that arises is that of deciding if a constant term θ_0 should be included in the model. It may be shown that for an ARMA(p, q) model, the constant term θ_0 is related to process mean μ as follows:

$$\theta_0 = \mu(1 - \phi_1 - \phi_2 \ldots -\phi_p). \tag{4.5}$$

Thus the constant term θ_0 will be zero if and only if the process mean μ is zero. The mean μ of the stochastic process which generated the observed time series is estimated from the sample mean $\bar{z}$ and only if this sample mean differs significantly from zero should a constant term be included in the model. A simple rule of thumb is as follows:

> If the sample mean $\bar{z}$ is large compared with the sample standard deviation $\hat{\sigma}_z$, include a constant term in the model.

A more complicated rule of thumb is available which involves estimating the standard deviation of $\bar{z}$, but this will not be discussed here. In modelling non-stationary time series, including a constant term in the model has important implications for forecasting. This will be discussed in the next chapter.

4.3 ESTIMATION OF MODEL PARAMETERS

Once a tentative model has been selected as described in the previous section, the next problem is to estimate the unknown parameters in this tentative model. Recall that for an ARMA(p, q) model, the one step ahead forecasts error

$$e_{t-1}(1) = Z_t - \hat{z}_{t-1}(1)$$

is just the random shock A_t. Thus the observed value of the one step ahead forecast error,

$$z_t - \hat{z}_{t-1}(1)$$

is equal to a_t, the realization of the random shock A_t at time t. Now the forecast $\hat{z}_{t-1}(1)$ depends on the parameters of the model and hence so does $z_t - \hat{z}_{t-1}(1)$. For example, for the AR(1) model, we have from (3.11) that

$$\hat{z}_{t-1}(1) = \mu + \phi_1(z_{t-1} - \mu)$$

and so

$$z_t - \hat{z}_{t-1}(1) = z_t - \mu - \phi_1(z_{t-1} - \mu),$$

where

$$\mu = \theta_0/(1 - \phi_1).$$

Consider the sum of squares

$$\sum_{t=1}^{N} (z_t - \hat{z}_{t-1}(1))^2, \qquad (4.6)$$

whose value depends on the unknown parameters in the model, $\theta_0, \phi_1, \ldots, \phi_p,$ $\theta_1, \ldots, \theta_q$, as well as on the observations $z_1, z_2, \ldots, z_N$. For example, for the AR(1) model the sum of squares is

$$\sum_{t=1}^{N} (z_t - \mu - \phi_1(z_{t-1} - \mu))^2,$$

whose value depends on the unknown parameters θ_0 and ϕ_1 in the model. Now according to the *principle of least squares*, the *least squares estimates* of the unknown parameters $\theta_0, \phi_1, \ldots, \phi_p, \theta_1, \ldots, \theta_q$ are those values of $\theta_0, \phi_1, \ldots, \phi_p,$ $\theta_1, \ldots, \theta_q$ for which the sum of squares (4.6) is minimum. Since the sum of squares (4.6) depends on the observations $z_1, z_2, \ldots, z_N$ as well as on the values of the unknown parameters $\theta_0, \phi_1, \ldots, \phi_p, \theta_1, \ldots, \theta_q$, the values of these parameters for which the sum of squares (4.6) is minimum will also depend on the observations $z_1, z_2, \ldots, z_N$. Thus each of the least squares estimates of these parameters is a function of the observations $z_1, z_2, \ldots, z_N$. These least squares estimates are denoted by $\hat{\theta}_0, \hat{\phi}_1, \ldots, \hat{\phi}_p, \hat{\theta}_1, \ldots, \hat{\theta}_q$. For example, for the AR(1) model, the least squares estimates of θ_0 and ϕ_1 are those values of θ_0 and ϕ_1 for which the sum of squares

$$\sum_{t=1}^{N} (z_t - \mu - \phi_1(z_{t-1} - \mu))^2$$

is minimum. These least squares estimates are functions of the observations $z_1, z_2, \ldots, z_N$ and are denoted by $\hat{\theta}_0$ and $\hat{\phi}_1$. In general, it is not possible to find expressions for the least squares estimates of the parameters of ARMA(p, q) models in terms of the observations $z_1, z_2, \ldots, z_N$. A *non-linear least squares computer algorithm* must be used which searches the sum of squares function (4.6) to locate the minimum. However, for one or two unknown parameters, it is feasible to evaluate the sum of squares function (4.6) for a number of possible values of each parameter. For example, for an AR(1) model with $\theta_0 = 0$, we could evaluate the sum of squares (4.6) for a sequence of values of ϕ_1 between -1 and 1, say $\phi_1 = -1.0, -0.9, \ldots, 0.8, 0.9, 1.0$. By plotting these values, we can get an idea of the shape of the sum of squares function when plotted against ϕ_1 and a rough estimate of where the minimum occurs. This will be illustrated in the next section.

This procedure, which is known as *grid search,* is recommended for any new time series which has not been studied before.

In evaluating the sum of squares (4.6) for some ARMA models, *starting value problems* will arise in that the sum of squares will depend on some of the realizations a_0, a_{-1}, ... which cannot be calculated or on the realizations z_0, z_{-1}, ... which have not been observed. In the examples in this chapter, it will be seen how these starting value problems are overcome. Another problem is that some computer programs for finding the least squares estimates require us to provide *preliminary estimates* of these parameters. One approach to this problem is to use the relationships that have been established between the model parameters and the theoretical autocorrelations. For example, for the AR(1) model, we have

$$\rho_1 = \phi_1,$$

so that a preliminary estimate of ϕ_1 is provided by the sample autocorrelation r_1. In general, it is necessary to check that these preliminary estimates satisfy the stationarity and invertibility conditions required by the model. An alternative approach is to set the preliminary estimates of all parameters except the constant term θ_0 equal to some small number, say 0.1. There are two reasons for this. First, these preliminary estimates will usually satisfy the stationarity and invertibility conditions required by the model. A second reason for using preliminary estimates like 0.1 is that the final estimates obtained by computer programs are not very sensitive to the preliminary estimates used. Since for an ARMA(p, q) model we have from (4.5) that

$$\theta_0 = \mu(1 - \phi_1 - \phi_2 \ldots - \phi_p),$$

a preliminary estimate of the constant term θ_0 is given by

$$\bar{z}(1 - \hat{\phi}_1 - \hat{\phi}_2 \ldots - \hat{\phi}_p), \tag{4.7}$$

where $\hat{\phi}_1$, $\hat{\phi}_2$, ..., $\hat{\phi}_p$ are preliminary estimates of ϕ_1, ϕ_2, ..., ϕ_p, respectively. In some computer packages, including the TSERIES package, the user has the option of finding least squares estimates in one of two ways:

Method 1
If it has been decided to include a constant term θ_0 in the model, then a preliminary estimate of θ_0 is obtained using (4.7). Then assuming that the parameter θ_0 has the value given by this estimate, least squares estimates are found for the other parameters in the model. A final estimate of θ_0 is obtained by substituting the corresponding least squares estimates in (4.5).

Method 2
If it has been decided to include a constant term θ_0 in the model, least squares estimates are found for all the parameters in the model, including the constant term θ_0.

Now, while the estimates found using Method 2 are the true least squares estimates, it will usually be found that the estimates found using Method 1 are very good approximations and give very similar forecasts. The advantage of Method 1 is that it reduces by one the number of parameters to be estimated using the method of least squares. Unless otherwise stated, Method 1 will be used for all the examples in this book in order to simplify the discussion of these examples.

4.4 DIAGNOSTIC CHECKS OF THE TENTATIVE MODEL

Once the least squares estimates of the unknown parameters in the tentative model have been obtained as described in the last section, the fitted model should first be checked to see that the parameter estimates satisfy the stationarity and invertibility conditions required by the model. Otherwise the tentative model is unacceptable and usually means that the observed time series has not been properly differenced to achieve stationarity. Differencing will be described in the next chapter.

Next, the parameter estimates should be checked to see if they are significantly different from zero, i.e. if the parameters of which they are estimates are in fact zero. A rule of thumb is as follows:

A parameter estimate is significantly different from zero if it lies outside the limits ±1.96 times its 'estimated standard error'.

The expression for the estimated standard error will depend on the model being fitted, as shown in Table 4.2. Thus for an AR(1) model, the estimated standard

Table 4.2   Estimated standard errors of least squares estimates of ARMA models

Model	Parameter estimate	Estimated standard error
AR(1)	$\hat{\phi}_1$	$\left[\dfrac{1 - (\hat{\phi}_1)^2}{N}\right]^{1/2}$
AR(2)	$\hat{\phi}_1, \hat{\phi}_2$	$\left[\dfrac{1 - (\hat{\phi}_2)^2}{N}\right]^{1/2}$
MA(1)	$\hat{\theta}_1$	$\left[\dfrac{1 - (\hat{\theta}_1)^2}{N}\right]^{1/2}$
MA(2)	$\hat{\theta}_1, \hat{\theta}_2$	$\left[\dfrac{1 - (\hat{\theta}_2)^2}{N}\right]^{1/2}$
ARMA(1, 1)	$\hat{\phi}_1$	$\left[\dfrac{(1 - (\hat{\phi}_1)^2)(1 - \hat{\phi}_1\hat{\theta}_1)^2}{N(\hat{\phi}_1 - \hat{\theta}_1)^2}\right]^{1/2}$
ARMA(1, 1)	$\hat{\theta}_1$	$\left[\dfrac{(1 - (\hat{\theta}_1)^2)(1 - \hat{\phi}_1\hat{\theta}_1)^2}{N(\hat{\phi}_1 - \hat{\theta}_1)^2}\right]^{1/2}$

error of the least squares estimate $\hat{\phi}_1$ is

$$\left(\frac{1-(\hat{\phi}_1)^2}{N}\right)^{1/2}.$$

In some computer packages, including TSERIES, the estimated standard errors are shown next to the parameter estimates. An equivalent procedure is to calculate the t-ratio

$$\frac{\text{parameter estimate}}{\text{estimated standard error}} \qquad (4.8)$$

and to adopt the following rule of thumb:

> If the t-ratio (4.8) lies outside the limits ±1.96, the parameter estimate is significantly different from zero.

As before, these rules of thumb should be regarded as rough guidelines, rather than hard and fast rules, since a parameter estimate may be non-significant due to the small number of observations in the time series. For a larger number of observations, the estimate of this parameter may be significant.

In the TSERIES package, the t-ratios (4.8) are shown next to the parameter estimates. If a parameter estimate is significant, then this is an indication that the corresponding term should be included in the model. On the other hand, if the parameter estimate is not significant, then we may consider dropping the term corresponding to this parameter from the model. However, if we consider that this parameter estimate is non-significant due to the small number of observations in the time series, then we should retain the corresponding term in the model. It is also important to check whether certain parameter estimates are close to 1 in value. This may indicate that it would be preferable to use a non-stationary model for the time series. Such models are described in Sections 5.3 and 5.4 and this problem is discussed there.

After these preliminary checks, the main tests of model adequacy are based on a study of the *residuals* of the fitted model. Recall that if the model that we have fitted is the correct ARMA model, then the observed value of the one step ahead forecast error

$$e_{t-1}(1) = z_t - \hat{z}_{t-1}(1)$$

is equal to a_t, the realization of the random shock at time t. However, the forecast $\hat{z}_{t-1}(1)$ depends on the true values of the model parameters and we only have estimates of these true values. For example, for the AR(1) model, we have from (3.11) that the forecast $\hat{z}_{t-1}(1)$ is given by

$$\hat{z}_{t-1}(1) = \mu + \phi_1(z_{t-1} - \mu).$$

If the unknown parameters are replaced by their least squares estimates in calculating the one step ahead forecast $\hat{z}_{t-1}(1)$, the observed one step ahead forecast error

$$z_t - \hat{z}_{t-1}(1)$$

is called the *residual at time* t (since it is the difference between the observed value at time t and the forecast using our fitted model) and is denoted by $\hat{a}_t$. Thus for the AR(1) model, the residual at time t is

$$z_t - \hat{\mu} - \hat{\phi}_1(z_{t-1} - \hat{\mu}),$$

where $\hat{\mu} = \hat{\theta}_0/(1 - \hat{\phi}_1)$ and $\hat{\theta}_0$ and $\hat{\phi}_1$ are the least squares estimates of θ_0 and ϕ_1. Note that the minimum value of the sum of squares (4.6), which is attained when the least squares estimates are used for the unknown parameters, is just the *sum of the squared residuals*

$$\sum_{1}^{N} (\hat{a}_t)^2. \tag{4.9}$$

This is also known as the *residual sum of squares.*

Now *if* our fitted model is of the correct form and *if* the least squares estimates equal the true values of the model parameters, then the residual $\hat{a}_t$ is just the observed one step ahead forecast error, which in turn is a realization a_t of the random shock A_t. In other words, if our fitted model is correct, the residuals $\hat{a}_t$ should be a realization of a white noise process, since the random shocks A_t form a white noise process. The reader will recall that a sequence of random variables A_t is said to form a white noise process if they are independent and normally distributed with the same mean 0 and the same variance σ_A^2. The residuals are studied to see if they look like a realization of a process with these properties.

Firstly, it is recommended that the residuals be plotted against time. If the plot indicates that the variability of the residuals increases with time, this suggests that the residuals are not a realization of a process with constant variance and that the observed time series is not stationary in the variance. A *normal probability plot* of the residuals will test if the residuals are a realization of a sequence of normal variables. If this assumption is true, the plotted points should lie near a straight line. For the prediction intervals given here to be accurate, it is essential that this assumption is valid. Another graphical check on model adequacy is the *cumulative periodogram of the residuals*, which is usually provided by computer packages for time series analysis. If the plotted points cross the critical lines on this graph, the model is judged inadequate. Further details on the interpretation of the cumulative periodogram are given in the references in Appendix A.1. Examples of these graphical tests will be given later in this chapter.

The characteristic feature of a white noise process is that all the theoretical autocorrelations (and hence all the theoretical partial autocorrelations) are zero and so the theoretical ACF and PACF are as shown in Figures 3.1 and 3.2. Thus in the sample ACF of any realization of a white noise model, all the sample autocorrelations should be near zero. Now if our fitted model is correct, then the residuals are a realization of a white noise process and so the sample autocorrelations and sample partial autocorrelations of the residuals should all be near zero. Thus an obvious check on the adequacy of the fitted model is to calculate the sample autocorrelations of the residuals and the sample partial autocorrelations of the residuals. Then by studying the sample ACF and sample PACF of the residuals, we can use the techniques developed in Section 4.2 on model identification to decide if the sample ACF and PACF of the residuals resemble those of a realization of a white noise process or of some other ARMA model. In particular, if according to the rules of thumb used in that section none of the sample autocorrelations of the residuals or the sample partial autocorrelations of the residuals is significantly different from zero, we have no reason to doubt that the residuals are a realization of a white noise process. Suppose that we study the first 24 sample autocorrelations of the residuals and the first 24 sample partial autocorrelations of the residuals. Even if one of these sample autocorrelations is significant or one of the sample partial autocorrelations is significant, this could have occurred by chance and we should not immediately conclude that the model is inadequate. However, if the first sample autocorrelation of the residuals is significant, this suggests that a moving average term of order one should be included in the model. Similarly, if the first sample partial autocorrelation of the residuals is significant, this suggests that an autoregressive term of order one should be included in the model. If the sample ACF of the residuals exhibits 'peaks' at seasonal lags (e.g. lags 12 and 24 for monthly data) and the sample autocorrelations at these lags are significant, this indicates that a seasonal model should have been used. Such models are described in Chapter 6.

As well as studying the significance of individual sample autocorrelations of the residuals, we can also test whether, say, the first 20 sample autocorrelations of the residuals, taken as a whole, are small enough for the residuals to resemble a realization of a white noise process. Recall that for a realization of a white noise process, the sample autocorrelations should all be near zero. Let

$$r_l(\hat{a})$$

be the sample autocorrelation of lag l for the residuals and consider the expression

$$Q = N \sum_{l=1}^{k} (r_l(\hat{a}))^2$$

where N is the number of residuals for the observed time series. Thus Q is just the sum of the squares of the first k sample autocorrelations $r_l(\hat{a})$, multiplied by N. The larger these sample autocorrelations are, the larger Q will be, and vice versa, so that if Q is too large, this indicates that the autocorrelations $r_l(\hat{a})$ are too large for the residuals to resemble a realization of a white noise process. Thus if Q is too big, this indicates that the model is inadequate. To determine how big Q must be before the model is judged inadequate, we make use of the following result. If the fitted model is adequate, then the random variable Q has a probability distribution of known form. This probability distribution is called a 'chi-square distribution with $(k - r)$ degrees of freedom', where r is the total number of parameters in the fitted model. From tables of this probability distribution (e.g. Table A.2.2 in Appendix A.2), it is possible to find a *critical value* such that the probability is 0.05 that a random value of Q exceeds this critical value. Then our rule of thumb is as follows:

If the calculated value of Q exceeds the critical value determined from chi-squared tables, this value of Q is too big and the fitted model is judged inadequate. Otherwise, the fitted model is regarded as being adequate, at least according to this test.

This test is known as the *portmanteau lack of fit test* and Q is known as the *Box–Pierce chi-square statistic*. It will be illustrated in the examples later in this chapter. The number of sample autocorrelations k included in the expression Q is usually taken to be at least 20. In the TSERIES package, k is chosen so that $k - r = 20$ for each model. Thus k will depend on the number of parameters r in each model. In the TSERIES package, the value of Q is given below the graphical display of the sample ACF of the residuals. The critical value of Q for 20 degrees of freedom is 31.41, as can be seen from Table A.2.2 in Appendix A.2, so in this book the following rule of thumb will be used:

If the value of Q exceeds 31.41, the model is judged inadequate.

Note that if a constant term is included in the model, this must be taken into account in calculating r, the number of parameters in the model. This lack of fit test is a weak test in that several different models may pass this test and be judged as adequate models for the observed time series.

We have seen that a study of the sample autocorrelations of the residuals may indicate model inadequacies and suggest that a new parameter be included in the model. On other occasions, even though our diagnostic tests have not detected any inadequacies in the fitted model, we may consider including a further parameter in the model in the hope that the new model is a better fit than the old one. This is known as *overfitting*. When the new model is fitted, if the parameter estimate of the new parameter is not significantly different from zero, then the term corresponding to the new parameter may not be worth including in the model. In this case, the estimates of the other parameters in the new model will be similar to the corresponding estimates in the old model. To see if the new tentative model is a better fit than the old tentative model, we calculate the *residual variance* for each model. This residual variance is given by

$$\frac{1}{N-1} \sum_{t=1}^{N} (\hat{a}_t - \bar{\hat{a}}_t)^2, \tag{4.10}$$

where

$$\bar{\hat{a}}_t = \frac{1}{N} \sum_{1}^{N} \hat{a}_t$$

is the *residual mean*. If the residual mean is near zero and N is large, the residual variance is approximately equal to the following expression:

$$\frac{1}{N} \sum_{t=1}^{N} (\hat{a}_t)^2. \tag{4.11}$$

By comparing (4.11) and (4.9), we see that the residual variance is just the minimum value of the sum of squares function divided by N. It may be shown that, for ARMA models, this residual variance is an estimate of σ_A^2, the variance of the random shocks A_t for that model. Now since the random shocks are the unpredictable component of a model, the smaller the value of σ_A^2 the better the model for forecasting purposes. Thus in comparing two models, the model with the smaller residual variance is preferable.

To illustrate the concept of overfitting, suppose that the current tentative model is a white noise model. Then we should first consider adding an autoregressive parameter of order one to the model, resulting in an AR(1) model. If this gives no improvement in terms of lower residual variance, we consider adding a moving average term to the original tentative model, resulting in an MA(1) model. If this gives no improvement in terms of lower residual variance, the original white noise model is retained. It is inadvisable to add an autoregressive parameter of order one and simultaneously a moving average parameter of order one, resulting in an ARMA(1, 1) model, because, as has already been mentioned in Section 3.7, an ARMA(1, 1) model with $\phi_1 = \theta_1$ reduces to a white noise model. Consequently, overfitting an ARMA(1, 1) model to a white noise model could lead to estimation problems, since we see from Table 4.2 that if the parameter estimates $\hat{\theta}_1$ and $\hat{\phi}_1$ are similar, the estimated standard errors of these estimates will be very large and so the parameter estimates may be very inaccurate. As a general rule, it is inadvisable to add an autoregressive parameter and a moving average parameter simultaneously to a model, as these parameters may cancel one another out.

Suppose we have to choose between two or more adequate models with much the same residual variance. Then according to the *principle of parsimonious parameterization*, we should choose the model with the fewest parameters. If the models have the same number of parameters, then it often happens that these different models, on closer examination, are really very similar and give similar short term forecasts. In this case, it really doesn't matter which model we select for forecasting purposes. If the alternative models are similar but the forecasts produced by these models are different, the following approach may be used. Suppose the observed time series consists of 100 observations. Then the alternative models are fitted to the first 90 observations and forecasts are calculated for the next 10 observations using each method. These forecasts are compared with the actual values of the next 10 observations and the forecast errors are calculated. Then a measure of the forecasting accuracy of each model is obtained by calculating the *mean squared error* (MSE) of the forecasts. This mean squared error is just the sum of the squares of the forecast errors, divided by the number of forecasts. The model with minimum MSE is then chosen as the optimal type of model for forecasting and its parameters are estimated again by fitting it to all the 100 observations currently available. This updated model is used to forecast future values of the time series.

4.5 EXAMPLE 4.1

In this section we apply the techniques described in previous sections in this chapter to analysing the time series 4.1 given in Appendix A.3.

Choice of a class of models

The plot of this time series is given in Figure 4.2 and indicates that the time series oscillates rapidly. An observation above the mean tends to be followed by an observation below the mean. Means and standard deviations of subsets of this time series are given in Table 4.7 at the end of this chapter and are plotted in Figure 4.3 which indicates that the time series is stationary in the variance. The sample ACF and PACF are given in Figures 4.4 and 4.5. The sample ACF has ripples at large lags, but for low lags it dies down rapidly towards zero so we conclude that the time series is stationary in the mean. Hence the class of ARMA models is a suitable class from which to choose tentative models for the time series.

Identification

If we study the sample ACF in Figure 4.4, we see that only the first sample auto-correlation r_1 is significant since its t-ratio of -4.923 lies outside the limits ± 1.96. However, the second sample autocorrelation is nearly significant, as its t-ratio is 1.746. The sample autocorrelation r_{21} is also nearly significant, since its t-ratio is

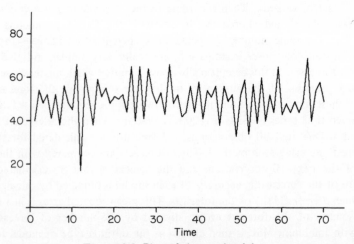

Figure 4.2 Plot of time series 4.1

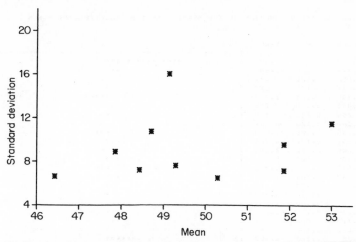

Figure 4.3 Plot of means and standard deviations of subsets of time series 4.1

70 OBSERVATIONS IN THE WORKING SERIES

MEAN AND STANDARD DEVIATION OF THE WORKING SERIES   IDENTIFICATION RUN
MEAN=   0.4969E 02
STANDARD DEVIATION=   0.9205E 01

AUTOCORRELATION FUNCTION OF THE WORKING SERIES   IDENTIFICATION RUN

	VALUE	S.E.	T VALUE	−1.0	0.0	1.0
1	−0.588	0.120	−4.923	I	****************	I
2	0.272	0.155	1.746	I	********	I
3	−0.078	0.162	−0.478	I	**	I
4	0.018	0.163	0.113	I	*	I
5	0.096	0.163	0.553	I	***	I
6	−0.149	0.163	−0.909	I	****	I
7	0.170	0.165	1.029	I	*****	I
8	−0.090	0.168	−0.537	I	***	I
9	0.100	0.169	0.595	I	***	I
10	−0.139	0.169	−0.822	I	****	I
11	0.190	0.171	1.111	I	*****	I
12	−0.206	0.174	−1.186	I	******	I
13	0.219	0.178	1.233	I	******	I
14	−0.255	0.181	−1.404	I	*******	I
15	0.220	0.186	1.179	I	******	I
16	−0.124	0.190	−0.650	I	****	I
17	−0.070	0.191	−0.368	I	**	I
18	0.119	0.192	0.622	I	****	I
19	−0.200	0.193	−1.039	I	******	I
20	0.207	0.196	1.060	I	******	I
21	−0.348	0.199	−1.751	I	*********	I
22	0.281	0.207	1.355	I	********	I
23	−0.235	0.213	−1.106	I	******	I
24	0.104	0.216	0.480	I	***	I

Figure 4.4 Sample ACF for time series 4.1

PARTIAL AUTCCORRELATION FUNCTICN UF THE WORKING SERIES   IDENTIFICATION RUN

	VALUE	S.E.	T VALUE	-1.0	0.0	1.0
1	-0.588	0.120	-4.923	I	****************	I
2	-0.114	C.120	-0.956	I	***	I
3	0.052	C.120	0.431	I	**	I
4	0.031	0.120	0.262	I	*	I
5	0.158	0.120	1.318	I	*****	I
6	-0.033	0.120	-0.279	I	*	I
7	0.054	0.120	0.450	I	**	I
8	0.062	0.120	0.517	I	**	I
9	0.105	0.120	0.879	I	***	I
10	-0.091	0.120	-0.764	I	***	I
11	0.096	0.120	0.804	I	***	I
12	-0.104	C.120	-0.868	I	***	I
13	0.087	0.120	0.732	I	***	I
14	-0.159	0.120	-1.327	I	****	I
15	0.031	0.120	0.263	I	*	I
16	-0.023	0.120	-0.195	I	*	I
17	-0.146	0.120	-1.224	I	****	I
18	-0.076	0.120	-0.637	I	**	I
19	-0.119	C.120	-0.997	I	***	I
20	-0.010	0.120	-0.082	I	*	I
21	-0.257	0.120	-2.152	I	*******	I
22	-0.073	0.120	-0.613	I	**	I
23	-0.112	0.120	-0.933	I	***	I
24	-0.075	0.120	-0.625	I	**	I

Figure 4.5 Sample PACF for time series 4.1

−1.751, but this is probably due to a ripple occurring at large lags. From the sample PACF in Figure 4.5, we see that the first sample partial autocorrelation r_{11} is significant, but none of the other partial autocorrelations approach significance, except for the sample partial autocorrelation at lag 21, which is probably significant by chance. Thus the sample PACF resembles that of a realization of a stochastic process for which the theoretical PACF cuts off after lag 1. This immediately suggests an AR(1) model. When we look again at the sample ACF, we could conclude that this sample ACF resembles a realization of a stochastic process for which the theoretical ACF cuts off after lag 1, since only the first sample autocorrelation is significant. However, since the second sample autocorrelation is nearly significant, we conclude instead that the sample ACF resembles a realization of a stochastic process for which the theoretical ACF tails off towards zero. The theoretical ACF and PACF of an AR(1) model with $\phi_1 < 0$ were given in Figures 3.5 and 3.6, which are repeated here in Figures 4.6 and 4.7. It is seen that the sample ACF and PACF resemble those of a realization of this model and so the AR(1) model is chosen as a tentative model for this time series. The sample mean and standard deviation of the time series are shown in Figure 4.4 under the heading 'Mean and standard deviation of the working series'. In the present case, the 'working series' is the same as the original time series, as the original time series has not been transformed or differenced. Thus the sample mean is

$$\bar{z} = 0.4969 \times 10^2 = 49.69$$

and the sample standard deviation is

$$\hat{\sigma}_z = 0.920 \times 10^1 = 9.2.$$

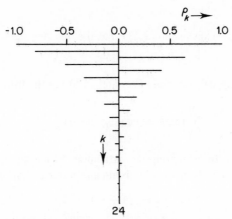

Figure 4.6 Theoretical ACF for AR(1) model with $\phi_1 < 0$

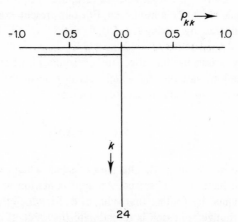

Figure 4.7 Theoretical PACF for AR(1) model with $\phi_1 < 0$

Since the sample mean is large compared with the sample standard deviation, we conclude that a constant term should be included in the model. Thus a tentative model is the AR(1) model

$$Z_t = \theta_0 + \phi_1 Z_{t-1} + A_t$$

where we expect ϕ_1 to be negative. Since $\rho_1 = \phi_1$ for this model, a preliminary estimate of ϕ_1 is given by the sample autocorrelation r_1 and we see from Figure 4.4 that

$$r_1 = -0.588.$$

Estimation

For the AR(1) model, we have from (3.11) that the one step ahead forecast is

$$\hat{z}_{t-1}(1) = \mu + \phi_1(z_{t-1} - \mu)$$

and so for the AR(1) model, the sum of squares (4.6) has the form

$$\sum_{t=1}^{N} (z_t - \mu - \phi_1(z_{t-1} - \mu))^2, \tag{4.12}$$

where $\mu = \theta_0/(1 - \phi_1)$. In estimating the parameters θ_0 and ϕ_1, we will use Method 1 described in Section 4.3. Thus we will obtain a preliminary estimate of θ_0 using

$$\hat{\theta}_0 = \hat{z}(1 - r_1),$$

and so our preliminary estimate of θ_0 is given by

$$\hat{\theta}_0 = (49.69)(1 - (-0.588)) = 78.9077.$$

Assuming that $\theta_0 = 78.9077$, the least squares estimate of ϕ_1 is that value of ϕ_1 for which the sum of squares (4.12) is minimum. For our present example, the sum of squares (4.12) is evaluated by setting $N = 70$, $\theta_0 = 78.9077$, and substituting the values of the observed time series $z_1 = 40$, $z_2 = 54$, ..., $z_{70} = 49$. A *starting value problem* immediately arises in that the sum of squares (4.12) involves z_0, the realization of the random variable Z_0, which has not been observed. The easiest way out of this problem is to study the sum of squares

$$\sum_{t=2}^{N} (z_t - \mu - \phi_1(z_{t-1} - \mu))^2 \tag{4.13}$$

where the summation begins at $t = 2$. This sum of squares involves only the values $z_1, z_2, \ldots, z_{70}$ which have been observed. An approximation to the least squares estimate of ϕ_1 is obtained by finding that value of ϕ_1 for which this sum of squares is minimum. An alternative approach is to estimate the value of z_0 using the technique known as *back forecasting*, which may be outlined as follows. It involves three steps.

Step 1
Find the least squares estimate of ϕ_1 using (4.13) and hence find the forecast $\hat{z}_N(1)$ of the observation at time $N + 1$. Assume for the moment that the value of the observation at time $N + 1$ is $\hat{z}_N(1)$, so that we have a time series of $(N + 1)$ known observations $z_1, z_2, \ldots, z_N, z_{N+1}$.

Step 2
Reverse the order of this time series of $(N + 1)$ observations to create the time series $z_{N+1}, z_N, \ldots, z_2, z_1$. Using a sum of squares similar to (4.13), find the least squares estimate of ϕ_1 and forecast one 'future' observation, which can be taken as an estimate of z_0.

Step 3

Using the sum of squares (4.12), find the least squares estimates of ϕ_1 using the estimate of z_0 obtained in Step 2.

In general, for an AR(p) model the sum of squares

$$\sum_{t=1}^{N} (z_t - \hat{z}_{t-1}(1))^2$$

will depend on $z_0, z_{-1}, \ldots, z_{-p+1}$ which have not been observed and to overcome this starting value problem we may study the sum of squares

$$\sum_{t=p+1}^{N} (z_t - \hat{z}_{t-1}(1))^2,$$

where the summation extends from $t = p + 1$ to $t = N$. If the time series contains at least 50 observations, this will make very little difference to the values of the least squares estimates. Alternatively, we can estimate the values of $z_0, z_{-1}, \ldots, z_{-p+1}$ using back forecasting as described above for the case of the AR(1) model.

Since the sum of squares (4.12) involves just one unknown parameter ϕ_1, we can use *grid search* to study the shape of the sum of squares function when plotted as a function of ϕ_1 and get a rough estimate of where the minimum occurs. Suppose we evaluate the sum of squares (4.12) for the following sequence of values of ϕ_1: $-0.8, -0.7, \ldots, 0.0, 0.1$. The results are shown in Figure 4.8. Thus for $\phi_1 = 0.1$, the value of the sum of squares (4.12) is

$$65927217 \times (0.1) \times 10^{-3} = 6592.7217.$$

If we plot these values of the sum of squares function and draw a smooth curve through these points, we see that the sum of squares function has the shape shown in Figure 4.9 and that the minimum occurs near $\phi_1 = -0.6$. Thus our preliminary estimate of ϕ_1, $\phi_1 = -0.538$, is fairly close to the least squares estimate.

Figure 4.10 shows the computer printout when the TSERIES package is used to find the least squares estimate of ϕ_1. It is seen that the sum of squares function is evaluated for a sequence of values of ϕ_1, beginning with the preliminary estimate $\phi_1 = 0.1$, and that this sequence of estimates converges on the least squares estimate

```
                    GRIC RUN LSING AR(1) MODEL


                    FACTOR =    0.10000-03


                    PARAMETER #  1
 -C.8000   -0.7000   -0.6000   -0.5000   -0.4000   -0.3000   -0.2000   -0.1000   -0.0000   C.1000
-----------------------------------------------------------------------------------------------

 40239691  38491601  37854270  38447306  40150888  43005035  47009749  52165013  58470837  65927217
```

Figure 4.8 Grid search for AR(1) model of time series 4.1

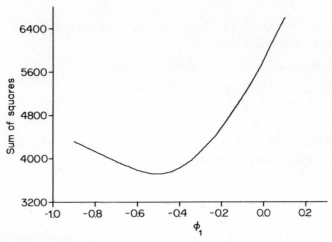

Figure 4.9 Sum of squares function for AR(1) model of time
series 4.1

ESTIMATICN RUN USING AR(1) MCDEL

TERMS IN THE ASSUMED STATICNARY (DIFFERENCED) MCDEL
  1 REGULAR AUTCREGRESSIVE TERM(S)

THE SAMPLE MEAN OF THE WORKING SERIES IS TO BE USED AS AN ESTIMATE OF THE TRUE MEAN

A CCNSTANT TERM IS TC BE INCLUDED IN THE MCCEL

BEGINING ESTIMATICN
ITERATICN   SUM OF SQUARES   PARAMETER VALUES
  0   0.6592722D 04   0.1CCCOC
  1   0.5778848D 04 -0.010000
  2   0.5104193D 04 -0.120000
  3   0.4568754D C4 -0.230000
  4   0.4172533D C4 -0.339999
  5   0.3915528D 04 -0.449999
  6   0.3797742D 04 -0.555999
  7   0.37894220 04 -0.596344
  8   0.3789405D 04 -0.597584
  9   0.3789405D C4 -0.597594

TERM#   TYPE   ORDER   ESTIMATE   STD. ERROR   T VALUE
----
  1   REG. AR   1   -0.5980   0.0964   -6.2054

    ESTIMATED EXPANDED MODEL LAG COEFFICIENTS

    AUTCREGRESSIVE TERMS
                1
            -0.5980

    MCVING AVERAGE TERMS

                    NCNE

    ESTIMATED MEAN CF THE WORKING SERIES=   49.6857
    THIS YIELDS A CCNSTANT TERM=   79.3974

Figure 4.10 The fitted AR(1) model for time series 4.1

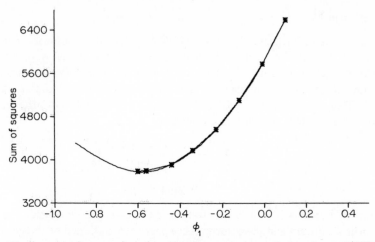

Figure 4.11 Convergence to the least squares estimate for AR(1) model of time series 4.1

$\hat{\phi}_1 = -0.597994$ and, for this least squares estimate, the sum of squares function attains the minimum value

$$0.3789405 \times 10^4 = 3789.405.$$

This is illustrated in Figure 4.11. Our final estimate of θ_0 is obtained from the relation

$$\theta_0 = \mu(1 - \phi_1).$$

Taking the sample mean $\bar{z} = 49.4857$ as an estimate of μ and using the least squares estimate $\hat{\phi}_1 = -0.597994$ for ϕ_1 gives the following estimate for θ_0:

$$\hat{\theta}_0 = 49.6857(1 - (-0.597994))$$

$$= 79.3974,$$

as shown at the bottom of Figure 4.10. Thus our tentative fitted model is

$$Z_t = 79.3974 - (0.597994)Z_{t-1} + A_t.$$

If Method 2 had been used and least squares estimates of θ_0 and ϕ_1 obtained, the fitted model would be

$$Z_t = 79.4928 - (0.598227)Z_{t-1} + A_t.$$

It is seen that these parameter estimates differ only slightly from those obtained using Method 1.

Diagnostic checks

The least squares estimate $\hat{\theta}_1 = -0.597994$ satisfies the stationary condition $-1 < \phi_1 < 1$. In Figure 4.10 the term $\phi_1 Z_{t-1}$ in the AR(1) model is referred to as a *regular* autoregressive term of order 1, to distinguish from a *seasonal* autoregressive term which will be introduced later. The least squares estimate of ϕ_1 is $\hat{\phi}_1 = -0.5980$, correct to four decimal places, and from Table 4.2 the standard error of this estimate is given by the expression

$$\left(\frac{1 - (\hat{\phi}_1)^2}{N}\right)^{1/2} = \left(\frac{1 - (-0.5980)^2}{70}\right)^{1/2}$$

$$= 0.0964,$$

as shown in Figure 4.10. Since the t-ratio for this estimate lies outside the limits ± 1.96, it is significant and the autoregressive parameter ϕ_1 should be retained in the model.

A plot of the residuals for this AR(1) model is shown in Figure 4.12 and indicates that the variability of the residuals is constant over time. A normal probability plot of the residuals is shown in Figure 4.13 and is consistent with the assumption that the residuals are a realization of a sequence of normal variables. The cumulative periodogram of the residuals is shown in Figure 4.14 and since the plotted points do not cross the critical lines on this graph, this graphical test does not detect any model inadequacy.

The sample ACF and PACF of the residuals are shown in Figure 4.15 and 4.16. None of the sample autocorrelations of the residuals are significant, except for that at lag 21 and this is probably significant by chance. Likewise, none of the sample partial autocorrelations of the residuals are significant, except for that at lag 21 and

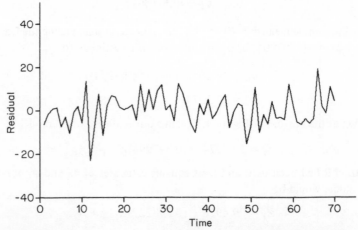

Figure 4.12 Plot of the residuals for the AR(1) model of time series 4.1

Figure 4.13 Normal probability plot of the residuals for the AR(1) model of time series 4.1

again this is probably significant by chance. Thus the sample ACF and PACF of the residuals do not detect any model inadequacies. The Box–Pierce chi-square statistic Q has the value $Q = 15.962$. Since this is less than 31.41 which is the critical value of Q for 20 degrees of freedom, this test does not detect any model inadequacy. From Figure 4.16 we see that the residual variance for the AR(1) model is 54.6065.

Finally, we overfit the AR(2) model and the ARMA(1, 1) model. The results are shown in Table 4.3. We see that for the AR(2) overfit, the estimate of the new parameter ϕ_2 is $\hat{\phi}_2 = -0.1210$ and that this is not significant, since its t-ratio is -0.9961, which lies between the limits ±1.96. The residual variance for the overfit is 54.6041, which is only very slightly below that for the AR(1) model. Consequently the AR(2) model does not give an appreciably better fit than the AR(1) model and so the AR(2) overfit is rejected. The ARMA(1, 1) overfit is rejected on similar grounds. Consequently, the AR(1) model is regarded as the best available model for the time series.

Forecasting

For the fitted AR(1) model, the forecasts at origin 70 for the next 10 time periods are shown in Figure 4.17 and plotted in Figure 4.18. From (3.11) we see that for

CUMULATIVE NORMALIZED PERIODOGRAM OF THE RESIDUALS   L AND U ARE 80% LOWER AND UPPER K-S LIMITS

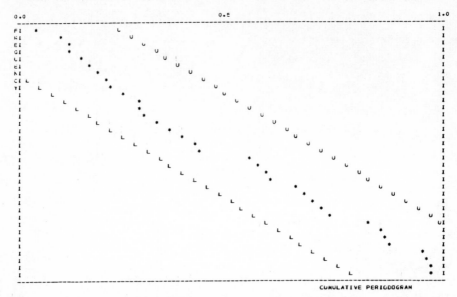

Figure 4.14 Cumulative periodogram of the residuals for the AR(1) model of time series 4.1

AUTCCORRELATION FUNCTION OF THE RESIDUALS   ESTIMATION RUN USING AR(1) MODEL

	VALUE	S.E.	T VALUE	-1.0	0.0	1.0
1	-0.061	0.120	-0.508	I	**	I
2	-0.044	0.120	-0.366	I	**	I
3	0.107	0.120	0.889	I	***	I
4	0.050	0.122	0.410	I	**	I
5	0.082	0.122	0.673	I	***	I
6	-0.076	0.123	-0.616	I	**	I
7	0.130	0.123	1.059	I	****	I
8	0.062	0.125	0.497	I	**	I
9	-0.008	0.126	-0.061	I	*	I
10	-0.012	0.126	-0.098	I	*	I
11	0.059	0.126	0.465	I	**	I
12	-0.061	0.126	-0.485	I	**	I
13	0.039	0.127	0.310	I	**	I
14	-0.141	0.127	-1.111	I	****	I
15	0.113	0.129	0.876	I	***	I
16	-0.115	0.130	-0.885	I	***	I
17	-0.148	0.132	-1.121	I	****	I
18	0.001	0.134	0.006	I	*	I
19	-0.120	0.134	-0.893	I	***	I
20	-0.070	0.136	-0.515	I	**	I
21	-0.279	0.136	-2.047	I	*******	I
22	0.044	0.144	0.305	I	**	I
23	-0.128	0.144	-0.888	I	****	I
24	-0.045	0.146	-0.309	I	**	I

BOX-PIERCE TEST   CHISQUARE STATISTIC WITH   20 DEGREES OF FREEDOM =   15.962

Figure 4.15 Sample ACF of the residuals for the AR(1) model of time series 4.1

	VALUE	S.E.	T VALLE	-1.0	0.0	1.0
1	-0.061	0.120	-0.508		**	
2	-0.048	0.120	-0.400		**	
3	0.102	0.120	0.851		***	
4	0.061	0.120	0.514		**	
5	0.100	0.120	0.834		***	
6	-0.072	0.120	-0.603		**	
7	0.126	0.120	1.082		****	
8	0.051	0.120	0.425		**	
9	0.019	0.120	0.158		*	
10	-0.037	0.120	-0.311		*	
11	0.046	0.120	0.386		**	
12	-0.098	0.120	-0.817		***	
13	0.052	0.120	0.438		**	
14	-0.177	0.120	-1.479		*****	
15	0.120	0.120	1.001		****	
16	-0.171	0.120	-1.427		*****	
17	-0.081	0.120	-0.681		***	
18	-0.094	0.120	-0.784		***	
19	-0.063	0.120	-0.530		**	
20	-0.126	0.120	-1.057		****	
21	-0.230	0.120	-1.928		******	
22	-0.008	0.120	-0.071		*	
23	-0.151	0.120	-1.267		****	
24	0.034	0.120	0.286		*	

STATISTICS COMPUTED FROM THE RESIDUALS

RESIDUAL MEAN= 0.0554
RESIDUAL VARIANCE= 54.6065

Figure 4.16 Sample PACF of the residuals for the AR(1) model of time series 4.1

the AR(1) model the forecast at origin t and lead time l is given by

$$\hat{z}_t(l) = \mu + \phi_1^l(z_t - \mu),$$

where μ is the process mean. Here $z_{70} = 49$ and, using $\bar{z} = 49.6857$ as our estimate of μ and $\hat{\phi}_1 = -0.597994$ as our estimate of ϕ_1, the forecast at origin 70 with lead time 2 is

$$\hat{z}_{70}(2) = 49.6857 + (-0.597994)^2(49 - 49.6857)$$

$$= 49.440,$$

as shown in Figure 4.17. From (3.16), the 95% prediction limits for a forecast at origin t and lead time l are

$$\hat{z}_t(l) \pm 1.96((1 + \phi_1^2)\sigma_A^2)^{1/2}.$$

Using the residual variance 54.6065 as our estimate of σ_A^2, this gives the 95% prediction limits for a forecast at origin 70 and lead time 2 as

$$49.440 \pm 1.96[(1 + (-0.597994)^2)(54.6065)]^{1/2},$$

resulting in a lower limit of 32.561 and an upper limit of 66.320, as shown in Figure 4.17. The reader will observe that the forecasts rapidly converge to the process mean 49.6857.

Table 4.3 Fitted models for time series 4.1

Model type	Fitted model	Residual variance	Q statistic
AR(1)	$Z_t = 79.3974 - (0.5980)Z_{t-1} + A_t$ $\quad\quad\quad\quad (t = -6.2054)$	54.6065	15.962
AR(2)	$Z_t = 88.9244 - (0.6692)Z_{t-1} - (0.1210)Z_{t-2} + A_t$ $\quad\quad\quad\quad (t = -5.5576) \quad (t = -0.9961)$	54.6041	17.772
ARMA(1, 1)	$Z_t = 74.4180 - (0.4978)Z_{t-1} + A_t - (0.1590)A_{t-1}$ $\quad\quad\quad\quad (t = -2.8632) \quad\quad\quad\quad (t = 0.7986)$	54.7568	17.614

FORECASTS FROM PERIOD 70

| | | 95 PERCENT LIMITS | |
PERIOD	FORECAST	LOWER	UPPER
71	50.096	35.609	64.582
72	49.440	32.561	66.320
73	49.832	32.176	67.489
74	49.598	31.672	67.524
75	49.738	31.717	67.760
76	49.654	31.599	67.710
77	49.704	31.637	67.772
78	49.674	31.603	67.746
79	49.692	31.619	67.766
80	49.682	31.608	67.756

Figure 4.17 Forecasts for time series 4.1 using the AR(1) model

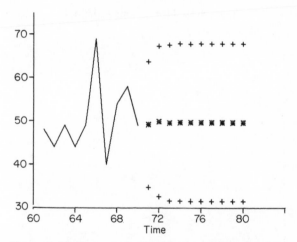

Figure 4.18 Plot of forecasts for time series 4.1 using the AR(1) model. —— Time series, *** forecasts, +++ 95% prediction limits

4.6 EXAMPLE 4.2

In this section we analyse time series 4.2 given in Appendix A.3.

Choice of a class of models

The plot of the time series is given in Figure 4.19 and indicates that the time series oscillates rapidly. Means and standard deviations of subsets of this time series are given in Table 4.7 at the end of this chapter and are plotted in Figure 4.20 which indicates that the time series is stationary in the variance. The sample ACF and PACF are given in Figures 4.21 and 4.22. It is seen that the sample ACF dies away

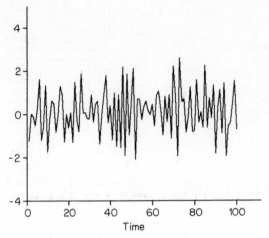

Figure 4.19 Plot of time series 4.2

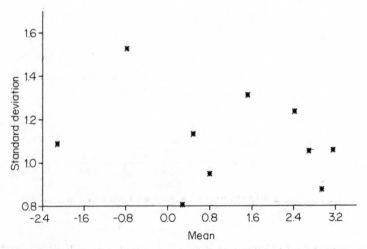

Figure 4.20 Plot of means and standard deviations of subsets of time
series 4.2

rapidly towards zero, apart from a few moderately large autocorrelations at a few
large lags, so we conclude that the time series is stationary in the mean. Hence the
class of ARMA models is a suitable class from which to choose a tentative model
for this time series.

Identification

From the sample ACF in Figure 4.21, only the first sample autocorrelation r_1 is
significant. Thus the sample ACF resembles that of a realization of a stochastic

100 CBSERVATIONS IN THE WORKING SERIES

MEAN AND STANDARD DEVIATION CF THE WORKING SERIES   IDENTIFICATION RUN
MEAN=   0.1141E 00
STANDARD DEVIATION=   0.1082E 01

AUTCCORRELATION FUNCTION OF THE WORKING SERIES   IDENTIFICATIUN RUN

```
         VALUE    S.E.   T VALUE  -1.0                      0.0                          1.0
                                   +--------------------------------------------------------+
  1     -0.470   C.100   -4.7C1   I                 ************                            I
  2      0.051   J.120    0.422   I                           **                            I
  3     -0.001   0.120   -0.012   I                           *                             I
  4      0.066   C.120    0.550   I                           **                            I
  5     -0.054   J.121   -0.448   I                          **                             I
  6     -0.104   0.121   -0.864   I                         ***                             I
  7      0.163   0.122    1.335   I                           *****                         I
  8      0.015   0.124    0.122   I                           *                             I
  9     -0.161   0.124   -1.297   I                      *****                              I
 10      0.052   0.126    0.415   I                           **                            I
 11      0.127   0.126    1.003   I                           ****                          I
 12     -0.016   C.128   -0.122   I                           *                             I
 13     -0.053   0.128   -0.414   I                          **                             I
 14      0.077   C.128    C.600   I                           **                            I
 15      0.013   C.128    0.105   I                           *                             I
 16     -0.119   0.128   -0.925   I                         ***                             I
 17      0.101   C.129    0.777   I                           ***                           I
 18     -0.011   0.130   -0.C84   I                           *                             I
 19     -0.045   0.130   -0.343   I                          **                             I
 20      0.052   C.13C    0.398   I                           **                            I
 21     -0.024   0.130   -0.184   I                           *                             I
 22      0.023   0.131    0.173   I                           *                             I
 23     -0.033   0.131   -0.249   I                           *                             I
 24     -0.008   C.131   -0.058   I                           *                             I
                                   +--------------------------------------------------------+
```

Figure 4.21 Sample ACF for time series 4.2

PARTIAL AUTCCORRELATIUN FUNCTION OF THE WORKING SERIES   IDENTIFICATIUN RUN

```
         VALUE    S.E.   T VALUE  -1.0                      0.0                          1.0
                                   +--------------------------------------------------------+
  1     -0.470   0.100   -4.701   I                 ************                            I
  2     -0.219   0.100   -2.186   I                      ******                             I
  3     -0.101   0.100   -1.013   I                         ***                             I
  4      0.043   0.100    0.431   I                           **                            I
  5      0.012   C.10C    0.120   I                           *                             I
  6     -0.158   0.100   -1.582   I                        ****                             I
  7      0.032   0.10C    0.316   I                           *                             I
  8      0.141   0.100    1.405   I                           ****                          I
  9     -0.081   C.100   -0.812   I                         ***                             I
 10     -0.089   0.100   -0.891   I                         ***                             I
 11      0.103   0.100    1.027   I                           ***                           I
 12      0.150   C.100    1.500   I                           ****                          I
 13      0.089   0.100    0.891   I                           ***                           I
 14      0.088   0.100    0.883   I                           ***                           I
 15      0.046   C.100    0.462   I                           **                            I
 16     -0.065   0.100   -0.654   I                          **                             I
 17      0.082   C.100    0.818   I                           ***                           I
 18      0.029   0.100    0.289   I                           *                             I
 19     -0.093   0.100   -0.933   I                         ***                             I
 20      0.058   C.100    0.575   I                           **                            I
 21      0.037   C.100    0.367   I                           *                             I
 22     -0.028   0.100   -0.281   I                           *                             I
 23     -0.014   0.100   -0.142   I                           *                             I
 24     -0.073   0.100   -0.734   I                          **                             I
                                   +--------------------------------------------------------+
```

Figure 4.22 Sample PACF for time series 4.2

process in which the theoretical ACF cuts off after lag 1, suggesting an MA(1) model. In the sample PACF in Figure 4.22, the first and second partial autocorrelations are significant and the sample PACF resembles that of a stochastic process in which the theoretical PACF tails off towards zero, again suggesting an MA(1) model. The theoretical ACF and PACF of an MA(1) model with $\theta_1 > 0$ were given in Figures 3.16 and 3.17 which are repeated here as Figures 4.23 and 4.24. It is seen that the sample ACF and PACF resemble those of a realization of this model and so the MA(1) model is chosen as a tentative model for this time series. The mean and standard deviation of the time series are $\bar{z} = 0.1141$ and $\hat{\sigma}_z = 1.082$. Since the mean

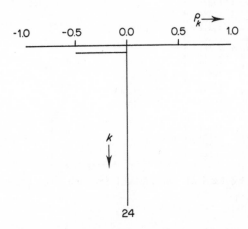

Figure 4.23 Theoretical ACF for MA(1)
model with $\theta_1 > 0$

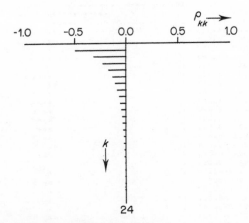

Figure 4.24 Theoretical PACF for MA(1)
model with $\theta_1 > 0$

is small compared with the standard deviation, no constant term is included in the model. Thus a tentative model is the MA(1) model

$$Z_t = A_t - \theta_1 A_{t-1}$$

where we expect θ_1 to be positive.

Estimation

For the MA(1) model, we have from (3.22) that the one step ahead forecasts are given by

$$\hat{z}_0(1) = \theta_0 - \theta_1(\hat{a}_0),$$

$$\hat{z}_1(1) = \theta_0 - \theta_1(z_1 - \hat{z}_0(1)),$$

$$\vdots$$

$$\hat{z}_{t-1}(1) = \theta_0 - \theta_1(z_{t-1} - \hat{z}_{t-2}(1)), \tag{4.14}$$

where $\hat{a}_0$ is an estimate of a_0, the realized value of A_0. Thus for the MA(1) model, the sum of squares (4.6) is given by

$$\sum_{t=1}^{N} (z_t - \hat{z}_{t-1}(1))^2 \tag{4.15}$$

where $\hat{z}_{t-1}(1)$ is calculated recursively from (4.14) for $t \geqslant 1$.

There is a starting value problem in that the sum of squares (4.15) depends on $\hat{a}_0$, an estimate of a_0, the realized value of A_0. One solution to this problem is to set a_0 equal to zero, the unconditional mean of the random variable A_0, and then calculate $\hat{z}_{t-1}(1)$ recursively from (4.14). In general, for an MA(q) model, we can set $\hat{a}_0 = 0$, $\hat{a}_{-1} = 0$, ..., $\hat{a}_{-q+1} = 0$. An alternative approach is to estimate $\hat{a}_0, \hat{a}_{-1}, \ldots, \hat{a}_{-q+1}$ using the technique known as *back forecasting*, which was outlined in the previous section. Since the sum of squares (4.15) depends on only one parameter θ_1, we can use grid search to study the shape of the sum of squares function when plotted as a function of θ_1 and get a rough estimate of where the minimum lies. The results are shown in Figure 4.25, indicating that the minimum lies near $\theta_1 = 0.5$. Figure 4.26 shows the computer printout when the TSERIES package is used to find the least squares estimate of θ_1 using Method 1. The least squares estimate of θ_1 is $\hat{\theta}_1 = 0.4743$, so that the tentative fitted model is

$$Z_t = A_t - (0.4743)A_{t-1}.$$

In Figure 4.26, the term $\theta_1 A_{t-1}$ is referred to as a *regular* moving average term of order 1 to distinguish it from a *seasonal* moving average term which will be described later.

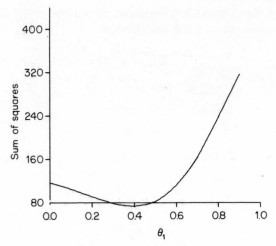

Figure 4.25 Sum of squares function for MA(1)
model of time series 4.2

ÉSTIMATICN RUN LSING MA(1) MCDEL

TERMS IN THE ASSUMED STATICNARY (DIFFERENCEC) MCDEL
  0 REGULAR AUTOREGRESSIVE TERM(S)
  0 SEASCNAL AUTCREGRESSIVE TERM(S)
  1 REGULAR MOVING AVERAGE TERM(S)
  0 SEASCNAL MCVING AVERAGE TERM(S)

THE WCRKING SERIES IS NCT TC EE CENTEKED--MEAN ASSUMED EQUAL TC 0.

NO CCNSTANT TERM IN THE MODEL

TERM#	TYPE	ORDER	ESTIMATE	STD. ERROR	T VALUE
1	REG. MA	1	0.4743	0.C884	5.3631

Figure 4.26 The fitted MA(1) model for time series 4.2

Diagnostic checks

The least squares estimate $\hat{\theta}_1 = 0.4743$ satisfies the invertibility condition
$-1 < \theta_1 < 1$. From Figure 4.26, we see that this parameter estimate is significant
and so the moving average term $\theta_1 A_{t-1}$ should be retained in the model. The plot
of the residuals, the normal probability plot of the residuals, and the cumulative
periodogram of the residuals do not detect any model inadequacies and are not
given here. The sample ACF and PACF of the residuals are shown in Figures 4.27
and 4.28 and do not detect any model inadequacies. The results of overfitting an

AUTCCORRELATICN FUNCTICN OF THE RESIDUALS   ESTIMATION RUN USING MA(1) MODEL

	VALUE	S.E.	T VALUE	-1.0	0.0	1.0
1	-0.123	0.100	-1.229	I	****	I
2	0.019	0.101	0.190	I	*	I
3	0.027	C.102	0.266	I	*	I
4	0.056	C.102	0.554	I	**	I
5	-0.069	0.102	-0.674	I	**	I
6	-0.086	C.102	-0.835	I	***	I
7	0.154	C.103	1.499	I	*****	I
8	0.023	0.105	0.220	I	*	I
9	-0.141	0.105	-1.335	I	****	I
10	0.076	0.107	C.708	I	**	I
11	0.190	0.108	1.758	I	*****	I
12	0.056	C.111	0.506	I	**	I
13	-0.004	0.111	-0.037	I	*	I
14	C.088	0.111	C.790	I	***	I
15	0.014	0.112	0.121	I	*	I
16	-0.094	0.112	-0.841	I	***	I
17	0.072	0.113	0.639	I	**	I
18	0.003	0.113	0.023	I	*	I
19	-0.033	0.113	-0.294	I	*	I
20	0.043	0.113	0.375	I	**	I
21	-0.006	0.114	-0.055	I	*	I
22	0.018	C.114	0.154	I	*	I
23	-0.016	C.114	-0.143	I	*	I
24	0.033	C.114	0.286	I	*	I

BOX-PIERCE TEST   CHISQUARE STATISTIC WITH   20 DEGREES CF FREEDOM =   14.552

Figure 4.27 Sample ACF of the residuals for the MA(1) model of time series 4.2

PARTIAL AUTCCORRELATICN FUNCTICN CF THE RESIDUALS   ESTIMATION RUN USING MA(1) MODEL

	VALUE	S.E.	T VALUE	-1.0	0.0	1.0
1	-0.123	0.100	-1.229	I	****	I
2	0.004	C.100	0.042	I	*	I
3	0.030	0.100	0.303	I	*	I
4	0.064	0.100	0.642	I	**	I
5	-0.056	0.100	-0.558	I	**	I
6	-0.106	C.100	-1.058	I	***	I
7	0.134	C.100	1.336	I	****	I
8	0.066	0.100	0.655	I	**	I
9	-0.131	0.100	-1.313	I	****	I
10	0.040	0.100	0.401	I	**	I
11	0.198	0.100	1.984	I	******	I
12	0.122	0.100	1.220	I	****	I
13	0.039	0.100	0.390	I	**	I
14	0.042	C.100	0.416	I	**	I
15	-0.014	0.100	-0.135	I	*	I
16	-0.039	0.100	-0.363	I	*	I
17	0.095	0.100	0.953	I	***	I
18	-0.041	0.100	-0.415	I	**	I
19	-0.067	C.100	-0.669	I	**	I
20	0.096	0.100	0.958	I	***	I
21	-0.015	0.100	-0.150	I	*	I
22	-0.052	0.100	-0.522	I	**	I
23	-0.011	0.100	-0.113	I	*	I
24	-0.022	0.100	-0.218	I	*	I

STATISTICS COMPUTED FROM THE RESIDUALS

RESIDUAL MEAN= 0.2220
RESIDUAL VARIANCE= 0.9186

Figure 4.28 Sample PACF of the residuals for the MA(1) model of time series 4.2

Table 4.4 Fitted models for time series 4.2

Model type	Fitted model	Residual variance	Q statistic
MA(1)	$Z_t = A_t - (0.4743)A_{t-1}$ $\quad\quad (t = 5.3631)$	0.9186	14.552
MA(2)	$Z_t = A_t - (0.5619)A_{t-1} + (0.1449)A_{t-2}$ $\quad\quad (t = 5.6227) \quad\quad (t = -1.4331)$	0.9096	15.232
ARMA(1, 1)	$Z_t = -(0.2164)Z_{t-1} + A_t - (0.3249)A_{t-1}$ $\quad\quad (t = -1.0985) \quad\quad (t = 1.6985)$	0.9142	15.727

MA(2) model and an ARMA(1, 1) model are shown in Table 4.4. Both these overfits are rejected and the MA(1) model is regarded as the best available model for the time series.

Forecasting

For the fitted MA(1) model, the forecasts at origin 100 for the next 10 time periods are shown in Figure 4.29 and plotted in Figure 4.30. The reader will recall that, for an MA(1) model, the forecast for two or more time periods ahead is just the process mean, which is zero in this example.

FORECASTS FROM PERIOD 100

| | | 95 PERCENT | LIMITS |
PERIOD	FORECAST	LOWER	UPPER
101	-0.023	-1.902	1.356
102	0.0	-2.080	2.080
103	0.0	-2.080	2.080
104	0.0	-2.080	2.080
105	0.0	-2.080	2.080
106	0.0	-2.080	2.080
107	0.0	-2.080	2.080
108	0.0	-2.080	2.080
109	0.0	-2.080	2.080
110	0.0	-2.080	2.080

Figure 4.29 Forecasts for time series 4.2 using the MA(1) model

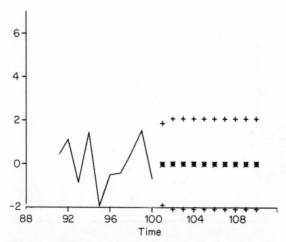

Figure 4.30 Plot of forecasts for time series 4.2 using the MA(1) model. —— Time series, *** forecasts, +++ 95% prediction limits

4.7 EXAMPLE 4.3

In this section we analyse time series 2.1, which was previously studied in Chapter 2.

Choice of a class of models

The plot of the time series is given in Figure 4.31 and indicates that the time series oscillates rapidly. Means and standard deviations of subsets of this time series are given in Table 4.7 at the end of this chapter and are plotted in Figure 4.32 which

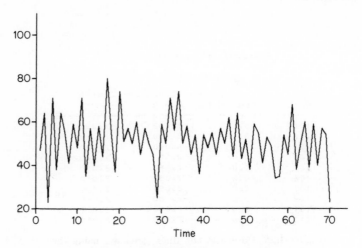

Figure 4.31 Plot of time series 2.1

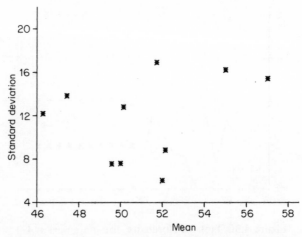

Figure 4.32 Plot of means and standard deviations of subsets of time series 2.1

indicates that the time series is stationary in the variance. The sample ACF and PACF are given in Figures 4.33 and 4.34. It is seen that the sample ACF dies away quickly towards zero, apart from a few moderately large autocorrelations for a few large lags, indicating that the time series is stationary in the mean. Hence the class of ARMA models is a suitable class from which to choose a tentative model for the time series.

Identification

The sample ACF in Figure 4.33 appears to tail off towards zero. While the first two sample autocorrelations r_1 and r_2 are significant, the third sample autocorrelation r_3 is nearly significant. In the sample PACF in Figure 4.3, the first sample partial auto-correlation is significant and the second sample partial autocorrelation is nearly significant, but none of the other sample partial autocorrelations are close to signifi-cance. Thus the sample PACF resembles that of a stochastic process for which the theoretical PACF cuts off after lag one or lag two, suggesting an AR(1) model or an AR(2) model. According to the principle of parsimonious parameterization, we should first fit an AR(1) model. From Figure 4.33, the sample mean is $\bar{z} = 51.13$ and the sample standard deviation is $\hat{\sigma}_z = 11.9$. Since the sample mean is large com-

70 CBSERVATIONS IN THE WORKING SERIES

MEAN AND STANDARD DEVIATION CF THE WORKING SERIES IDENTIFICATION RUN
MEAN= C.5113E 02
STANDARD DEVIATION= 0.1191E 02

AUTCCORRELATION FUNCTION OF THE WORKING SERIES IDENTIFICATION RUN

```
         VALUE   S.E.   T VALUE  -1.0                    0.0                          1.0
                                  +----------------------------------------------------------+
   1    -0.390  0.120  -3.262   I              **********  I
   2     0.304  0.136   2.230   I                   ********  I
   3    -0.166  0.146  -1.135   I                   *****  I
   4     0.071  0.145   0.476   I                   **  I
   5    -0.097  0.149  -0.651   I                   ***  I
   6    -0.047  0.150  -3.314   I                   **  I
   7     0.035  0.150   0.236   I                   *  I
   8    -0.043  0.150  -0.289   I                   **  I
   9    -0.005  0.150  -0.032   I                   *  I
  10     0.014  0.150   0.056   I                   *  I
  11     0.110  0.150   0.731   I                   ***  I
  12    -0.069  0.152  -0.454   I                   **  I
  13     0.148  0.152   0.974   I                   ****  I
  14     0.036  0.154   0.232   I                   *  I
  15    -0.007  0.154  -0.043   I                   *  I
  16     0.173  0.154   1.122   I                   *****  I
  17    -0.111  0.157  -0.709   I                   ***  I
  18     0.020  0.158   0.126   I                   *  I
  19    -0.047  0.158  -0.299   I                   **  I
  20     0.016  0.158   0.102   I                   *  I
  21     0.022  0.158   0.141   I                   *  I
  22    -0.079  0.158  -0.497   I                   **  I
  23    -0.010  0.159  -0.060   I                   *  I
  24    -0.073  0.159  -0.460   I                   **  I
                                  +----------------------------------------------------------+
```

Figure 4.33 Sample ACF for time series 2.1

PARTIAL AUTCCORRELATIUN FUNCTICN OF THE WORKING SERIES IDENTIFICATION RUN

	VALUE	S.E.	T VALUE	-1.0	0.0	1.0
1	-0.390	0.120	-3.262		**********	
2	0.180	0.120	1.504		*****	
3	0.002	0.120	0.019		*	
4	-0.044	0.120	-0.370		**	
5	-0.069	0.120	-0.581		**	
6	-0.121	0.120	-1.009		****	
7	0.020	0.120	0.165		*	
8	0.005	0.120	0.041		*	
9	-0.056	0.120	-0.473		**	
10	0.004	0.120	0.031		*	
11	0.143	0.120	1.195		****	
12	-0.009	0.120	-0.075		*	
13	0.092	0.120	0.769		***	
14	0.167	0.120	1.397		*****	
15	-0.001	0.120	-0.011		*	
16	0.221	0.120	1.846		*******	
17	0.053	0.120	0.442		**	
18	-0.105	0.120	-0.880		***	
19	0.042	0.120	0.353		**	
20	0.050	0.120	0.417		**	
21	0.056	0.120	0.466		**	
22	-0.042	0.120	-0.353		**	
23	-0.137	0.120	-1.145		****	
24	-0.163	0.120	-1.367		*****	

Figure 4.34 Sample PACF for time series 2.1

pared with the sample standard deviation, a constant term should be included in the model. Thus a tentative model is the AR(1) model

$$Z_t = \theta_0 + \phi_1 Z_{t-1} + A_t.$$

Estimation and diagnostic checking

The fitted AR(1) model is given in Table 4.5. The term $\phi_1 Z_{t-1}$ should be retained in this model, since the estimate of the parameter ϕ_1 is significant. The sample ACF and PACF of the residuals are given in Figures 4.35 and 4.36 and do not detect any model inadequacies, nor do any of the graphical tests. The results of overfitting an AR(2) model are also shown in Table 4.5. We see that while the second order autoregressive parameter estimate $\hat{\phi}_2 = 0.1939$ is not quite significant, the AR(2) model has a lower residual variance. Consequently, it may be preferred over the AR(1) model, in which case the new tentative model is the AR(2) model

$$Z_t = \theta_0 + \phi_1 Z_{t-1} + \phi_2 Z_{t-2} + A_t.$$

The result of a grid search for the estimates of ϕ_1 and ϕ_2 is shown in Figure 4.37. For this set of values of ϕ_1 and ϕ_2, the minimum value of the sum of squares is

$$79070567 \times 0.1 \times 10^{-3} = 7907.0567$$

and this occurs when $\phi_1 = -0.4$ and $\phi_2 = 0.2$. We can get an idea of the shape of the sum of squares surface as a function of ϕ_1 and ϕ_2 by plotting *contours* by hand on this grid. By a *contour* is meant a curve through all the points of this grid with approximately the same value. Thus one such contour is drawn through all the

Table 4.5 Fitted models for time series 2.1

Model type	Fitted model	Residual variance	Q statistic
AR(1)	$Z_t = 72.8571 - (0.4250)Z_{t-1} + A_t$ $(t = -3.7065)$	118.2873	12.084
AR(2)	$Z_t = 58.8788 - (0.3455)Z_{t-1} + (0.1939)Z_{t-2} + A_t$ $(t = -2.7687) \quad (t = 1.5535)$	115.8504	10.165
AR(3)	$Z_t = 58.2544 - (0.3480)Z_{t-1} + (0.1972)Z_{t-2} + (0.1114)Z_{t-3} + A_t$ $(t = -2.7005) \quad (t = 1.4857) \quad (t = 0.0885)$	117.5923	10.259
ARMA(2, 1)	$Z_t = 56.551 - (0.3134)Z_{t-1} + (0.2074)Z_{t-2} + A_t - (0.0335)A_{t-1}$ $(t = -0.4833) \quad (t = 0.7000) \qquad\qquad (t = 0.0503)$	117.5866	10.303

Table 4.6 Fitted models for time series 4.5

Model type	Fitted model	Residual variance	Q statistic
ARMA(1, 1)	$Z_t = (0.6316)Z_{t-1} + A_t - (0.1415)A_{t-1}$ $(t = 4.1955) \quad (t = 0.7477)$	1.0588	19.317
ARMA(2,1)	$Z_t = -(0.2151)Z_{t-1} + (0.4723)Z_{t-2} + A_t + (0.7018)A_{t-1}$ $(t = -0.6412) \quad (t = 2.9222) \quad (t = -1.9587)$	1.0532	17.692
ARMA(1, 2)	$Z_t = (0.9501)Z_{t-1} + A_t - (0.5817)A_{t-1} - (0.3850)A_{t-2}$ $(t = 8.0203) \quad (t = 4.1043) \quad (t = 3.7775)$	1.1877	36.765

Table 4.7 Means and standard deviations of subsets of the time series used in this chapter

Time series 4.1

Subset	Mean	Standard deviation
1–7	46.4	6.6
8–14	49.1	16.1
15–21	50.3	6.5
22–28	53.0	11.6
29–35	51.9	7.2
36–42	48.4	7.2
43–49	47.9	8.9
50–56	48.7	10.8
57–63	49.3	7.6
64–70	51.9	9.6
1–70	49.7	9.2

Time series 4.2

Subset	Mean	Standard deviation
1–10	−0.2	1.1
11–20	0.0	0.8
21–30	0.1	1.0
31–40	0.3	0.9
41–50	−0.1	1.5
51–60	0.3	1.1
61–70	0.3	1.1
71–80	0.2	1.3
81–90	0.2	1.2
91–100	0.1	1.1
1–100	0.1	1.1

Time series 2.1

Subset	Mean	Standard deviation
1–7	51.7	16.9
8–14	50.1	12.8
15–21	57.0	15.4
22–28	52.0	6.1
29–35	55.0	16.2
36–42	50.0	7.6
43–49	52.1	8.8
50–56	49.6	7.6
57–63	46.3	12.2
64–70	47.4	13.8
1–70	51.1	11.9

Time series 4.3

Subset	Mean	Standard deviation
1–10	0.1	0.9
11–20	0.0	0.9
21–30	−0.1	0.6
31–40	0.3	0.4
41–50	−0.2	0.8
51–60	−0.6	1.3
61–70	−0.3	0.7
71–80	0.4	1.3
81–90	−0.3	0.8
91–100	−0.3	1.0
1–100	−0.1	0.9

Time series 4.4

Subset	Mean	Standard deviation
1–20	−0.03	0.15
21–40	0.02	0.13
41–60	−0.01	0.28
61–80	−0.01	0.18
81–100	0.01	0.09
101–120	−0.01	0.08
121–140	0.02	0.11
141–160	0.01	0.13
161–180	−0.03	0.13
181–200	0.01	0.11
201–220	−0.02	0.10
1–224	0.00	0.14

Time series 4.5

Subset	Mean	Standard deviation
1–10	−0.2	1.3
11–20	−0.4	1.8
21–30	1.2	1.4
31–40	−0.5	0.7
41–50	−0.1	1.2
51–60	−0.1	1.3
61–70	0.2	0.7
71–80	0.2	0.7
81–90	−0.7	0.7
91–100	−0.4	1.0
1–100	−0.1	−1.2

AUTCCORRELATICN FUNCTICN OF THE RESIDUALS   ESTIMATICN RUN USING   AR(1) MCDEL

	VALUE	S.E.	T VALUE	-1.0	0.0	1.0
1	0.073	0.120	0.614	I	**	I
2	0.153	0.120	1.274	I	****	I
3	-0.042	0.123	-0.341	I	**	I
4	-0.047	0.123	-0.379	I	**	I
5	-0.122	0.123	-0.987	I	****	I
6	-0.111	0.125	-0.884	I	***	I
7	0.015	0.126	0.116	I	*	I
8	-0.057	0.126	-0.447	I	**	I
9	-0.031	0.127	-0.248	I	*	I
10	0.096	0.127	0.754	I	***	I
11	0.119	0.128	0.933	I	****	I
12	0.027	0.130	0.211	I	*	I
13	0.156	0.130	1.206	I	*****	I
14	0.095	0.132	0.714	I	***	I
15	0.093	0.133	0.699	I	***	I
16	0.182	0.134	1.352	I	*****	I
17	-0.072	0.138	-0.523	I	**	I
18	-0.044	0.138	-0.321	I	**	I
19	-0.045	0.138	-0.326	I	**	I
20	-0.009	0.139	-0.066	I	*	I
21	-0.005	0.139	-0.035	I	*	I
22	-0.110	0.139	-0.793	I	***	I
23	-0.077	0.140	-0.548	I	**	I
24	-0.123	0.140	-0.876	I	****	I

BCX-PIERCE TEST CHISQUARE STATISTIC WITH 20 DEGREES OF FREEDCM = 12.084

Figure 4.35 Sample ACF of the residuals for the AR(1) model of time series 2.1

PARTIAL AUTCCORRELATICN FUNCTICN OF THE RESIDUALS   ESTIMATION RUN USING   AR(1) MODEL

	VALUE	S.E.	T VALUE	-1.0	0.0	1.0
1	0.073	0.120	0.614	I	**	I
2	0.149	0.120	1.242	I	****	I
3	-0.064	0.120	-0.537	I	**	I
4	-0.064	0.120	-0.538	I	**	I
5	-0.102	0.120	-0.850	I	***	I
6	-0.085	0.120	-0.713	I	***	I
7	0.059	0.120	0.494	I	**	I
8	-0.045	0.120	-0.377	I	**	I
9	-0.059	0.120	-0.493	I	**	I
10	0.104	0.120	0.873	I	***	I
11	0.106	0.120	0.887	I	***	I
12	-0.027	0.120	-0.223	I	*	I
13	0.133	0.120	1.117	I	****	I
14	0.083	0.120	0.696	I	***	I
15	0.071	0.120	0.592	I	**	I
16	0.230	0.120	1.923	I	******	I
17	-0.099	0.120	-0.829	I	***	I
18	-0.063	0.120	-0.525	I	**	I
19	0.098	0.120	0.819	I	***	I
20	0.024	0.120	0.201	I	*	I
21	0.014	0.120	0.118	I	*	I
22	-0.109	0.120	-0.913	I	***	I
23	-0.167	0.120	-1.400	I	*****	I
24	-0.117	0.120	-0.983	I	***	I

STATISTICS CCMPUTED FRCM THE RESIDUALS

RESICUAL MEAN= 0.1814
RESICUAL VARIANCE=118.2873

Figure 4.36 Sample PACF of the residuals for the AR(1) model of time series 2.1

FACTOR =   0.10000-03

PARAM # 2		−0.8000	−0.7000	−0.6000	PARAMETER # 1 −0.5000	−0.4000	−0.3000	−0.2000	−0.1000	−0.0000
−0.5000	I	116615860	114461445	114102550	115539155	118771297	123753926	130622072	139240726	149654918
−0.4000	I	108625295	105734604	104639433	105339781	107835635	112127003	118213869	126096241	135774176
−0.3000	I	102395444	98768476	96937028	96901099	98660688	102215774	107566375	114712474	123654125
−0.2000	I	97926310	93563072	90955347	90223144	91246457	94065273	98679599	105089427	113294804
−0.1000	I	95217919	90118404	86814405	85305926	85592563	87675503	91553557	97227110	104696220
0.0	I	94270289	88434496	84394221	82149467	81700229	83046494	86188274	91125555	97858392
0.1000	I	95083295	88511233	83734688	80753662	79568148	80176143	82583647	86784650	92781205
0.2000	I	97657100	90348754	84835931	81118636	79196847	75070567	80739792	84204525	89464809
0.3000	I	*********	93947013	87657917	83244348	80586281	75723718	80656675	83385134	87909145
0.4000	I	*********	*********	92320620	87130770	83736437	82137601	82334284	84326468	88114202
0.5000	I	*********	*********	*********	92777934	88647338	86312231	85772639	87028536	90080000

Figure 4.37 Grid search for AR(2) model of time series 2.1

GRID RUN USING AR(2) MODEL

FACTOR =   0.10000-03

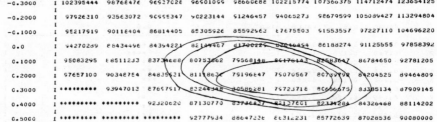

PARAM # 2		−0.8000	−0.7000	−0.6000	PARAMETER 1 −0.5000	−0.4000	−0.3000	−0.2000	−0.1000	−0.0000
−0.5000	I	116615860	114461445	114102550	115539155	118771297	123758926	130622072	139240726	149654918
−0.4000	I	108625295	105734604	104639433	105339781	107835635	112127003	118213869	126096241	135774176
−0.3000	I	102395444	98768476	96937028	96901099	98660688	102215774	107566375	114712474	123654125
−0.2000	I	97926310	93563072	90955347	90223144	91246457	94065273	98679599	105089427	113294804
−0.1000	I	95217919	90118404	86814405	85305926	85592563	87675503	91553557	97227110	104696220
0.0	I	94270289	88434496	84394221	82149467	81700229	83046494	86188274	91125555	97858392
0.1000	I	95083295	88511233	83734688	80753662	79568148	80176143	82583647	86784650	92781205
0.2000	I	97657100	90348754	84835931	81118636	79196847	75070567	80739792	84204525	89464809
0.3000	I	*********	93947013	87657917	83244348	80586281	75723718	80656675	83385134	87909145
0.4000	I	*********	*********	92320620	87130770	83736437	82137601	82334284	84326468	88114202
0.5000	I	*********	*********	*********	92777934	88647338	86312231	85772639	87028536	90080000

Figure 4.38 Sum of squares function for AR(2) model of time series 2.1

points for which the sum of squares is approximately 8000. These hand drawn
contours are shown in Figure 4.38 and indicate that the sum of squares surface has
a fairly pointed trough near $\phi_1 = -0.4$ and $\phi_2 = 0.2$. Thus the sum of squares
function will quickly increase in value as ϕ_1 and ϕ_2 move away from these values.
The results of overfitting an AR(3) model and an ARMA(2, 1) model are shown in
Table 4.5. Both these overfits are rejected for obvious reasons and it may be concluded that the AR(2) model is the best available model for this time series. It
should be noted that the AR(1) model gives almost as good a fit and some may
prefer to use this simpler model.

FORECASTS FROM PERIOD 70

PERIOD	FORECAST	95 PERCENT LIMITS LOWER	UPPER
71	61.403	40.302	82.503
72	42.125	19.801	64.449
73	56.231	32.949	79.513
74	47.620	24.046	71.194
75	53.330	29.618	77.042
76	49.688	25.922	73.454
77	52.053	28.264	75.842
78	50.530	26.731	74.329
79	51.515	27.712	75.317
80	50.879	27.075	74.684

Figure 4.39 Forecasts for time series 2.1 using the AR(2) model

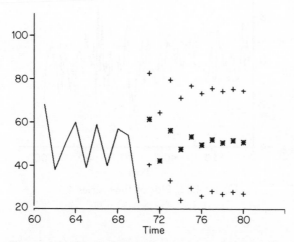

Figure 4.40 Plot of forecasts for time series 2.1 using the AR(2) model. —— Time series, *** forecasts. +++ 95% prediction limits

Forecasting

For the fitted AR(2) model, the forecasts at origin 70 for the next 10 time periods are shown in Figure 4.39 and plotted in Figure 4.40. The forecasts are seen to oscillate as they converge to the process mean. Note that while the last observed value of the time series is below average, the forecast for the next time period is above average and the forecast for the following time period is below average. This is what we would expect for the time series, since the first sample autocorrelation r_1 is negative and the second sample autocorrelation r_2 is positive. The complete TSERIES program for this example is given as program A.5.2 in Appendix A.5.

122

4.8 EXERCISES

4.8.1   The plot of time series 4.3 in Appendix A.3 is shown in Figure 4.41. The means and standard deviations of subsets are given in Table 4.7 and plotted in Figure 4.42. The sample ACF and PACF are given in Figures 4.43 and 4.44. Suggest a tentative model for this time series.

4.8.2   (a)   Figure 4.45 shows the results of a grid run when an MA(2) model is fitted to time series 4.4 in Appendix A.3. Parameter number 1 is θ_1 and parameter number 2 is θ_2. For this set of values of θ_1 and θ_2, what is the minimum value of the sum of squares and what are the corresponding values of θ_1 and θ_2? Draw contours on this grid and describe the shape of the sum of squares surface.

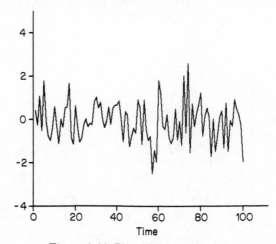

Figure 4.41   Plot of time series 4.3

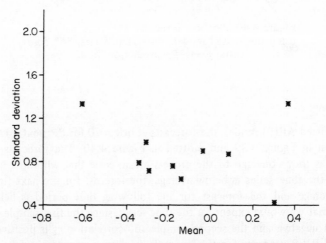

Figure 4.42   Plot of means and standard deviations of subsets of time series 4.3

100 OBSERVATIONS IN THE WORKING SERIES

MEAN AND STANDARD DEVIATION OF THE WORKING SERIES   IDENTIFICATION RUN
MEAN= -0.1165E 00
STANDARD DEVIATION=   0.9199E 00

AUTOCORRELATION FUNCTION OF THE WORKING SERIES   IDENTIFICATION RUN

```
      VALUE    S.E.   T VALUE  -1.0                    0.0                     1.0
                               +-----------------------------------------------+
 1   -0.024   0.100   -0.240   I                        *                      I
 2    0.166   0.100    1.658   I                    *****                      I
 3   -0.148   0.103   -1.440   I                    ****                       I
 4    0.055   0.105    0.527   I                      **                       I
 5   -0.181   0.105   -1.720   I                   *****                       I
 6    0.059   0.108    0.548   I                      **                       I
 7   -0.107   0.109   -0.988   I                    ***                        I
 8    0.008   0.110    0.074   I                       *                       I
 9   -0.051   0.110   -0.465   I                      **                       I
10    0.176   0.110    1.603   I                       *****                   I
11   -0.050   0.113   -0.444   I                      **                       I
12    0.230   0.113    2.039   I                       ******                  I
13   -0.135   0.117   -1.146   I                    ****                       I
14    0.045   0.119    0.382   I                      **                       I
15   -0.107   0.119   -0.895   I                    ***                        I
16    0.016   0.120    0.134   I                       *                       I
17   -0.295   0.120   -2.456   I              ********                         I
18   -0.009   0.127   -0.073   I                       *                       I
19   -0.050   0.127   -0.391   I                      **                       I
20    0.030   0.127    0.237   I                       *                       I
21   -0.088   0.127   -0.687   I                     ***                       I
22    0.028   0.128    0.216   I                       *                       I
23   -0.011   0.128   -0.088   I                       *                       I
24    0.078   0.128    0.607   I                       ***                     I
                               +-----------------------------------------------+
```

Figure 4.43 Sample ACF for time series 4.3

PARTIAL AUTOCORRELATION FUNCTION OF THE WORKING SERIES   IDENTIFICATION RUN

```
      VALUE    S.E.   T VALUE  -1.0                    0.0                     1.0
                               +-----------------------------------------------+
 1   -0.024   0.100   -0.240   I                        *                      I
 2    0.165   0.100    1.654   I                    *****                      I
 3   -0.145   0.100   -1.447   I                    ****                       I
 4    0.027   0.100    0.267   I                       *                       I
 5   -0.140   0.100   -1.401   I                    ****                       I
 6    0.030   0.100    0.297   I                       *                       I
 7   -0.053   0.100   -0.529   I                      **                       I
 8   -0.050   0.100   -0.496   I                      **                       I
 9   -0.006   0.100   -0.062   I                       *                       I
10    0.145   0.100    1.454   I                       ****                    I
11   -0.037   0.100   -0.372   I                       *                       I
12    0.176   0.100    1.755   I                       *****                   I
13   -0.108   0.100   -1.076   I                     ***                       I
14   -0.027   0.100   -0.275   I                       *                       I
15    0.011   0.100    0.112   I                       *                       I
16   -0.054   0.100   -0.539   I                      **                       I
17   -0.232   0.100   -2.315   I                 ******                        I
18   -0.044   0.100   -0.441   I                      **                       I
19    0.045   0.100    0.450   I                       **                      I
20   -0.051   0.100   -0.508   I                      **                       I
21   -0.097   0.100   -0.971   I                     ***                       I
22   -0.100   0.100   -1.001   I                     ***                       I
23    0.006   0.100    0.062   I                       **                      I
24    0.011   0.100    0.106   I                       *                       I
                               +-----------------------------------------------+
```

Figure 4.44 Sample PACF for time series 4.3

GRID RUN USING MA(2) MODEL

FACTOR =   0.1000D-06

PARAM # 2	PARAMETER # 1								
	−0.3000	−0.2000	−0.1000	0.0	0.1000	0.2000	0.3000	0.4000	0.5000
−0.4000	58694326	57022471	56017740	55677842	56004823	56979221	58561920	60706938	63369523
−0.3000	54827102	52971785	51848038	51374895	51509579	52222444	53488634	55293402	57651424
−0.2000	52722469	50503002	49127409	48451944	48394297	48909307	49979355	51619485	53898129
−0.1000	52007864	49264534	47526266	46586009	46323319	46677078	47635291	49240830	51614709
0.0	52548120	49090327	46871021	45599988	45111836	45327214	46239275	47920431	50551355
0.1000	54436332	49964365	47100597	45412392	44666442	44756777	45680560	47544921	50606980
0.2000	58113284	52053399	48266187	46022695	44962172	44929548	45921373	48090948	51825048
0.3000	64699255	55831531	50577149	47524758	46041380	45868480	46991749	49654259	54614572
0.4000	76848228	62382338	54521264	50157005	48035760	47672300	49037464	52662937	60569769
0.5000	101744309	74170926	61139534	54417828	51227819	50586728	52520806	58502506	96074822
0.6000	173659692	97866862	72735566	61327776	56202096	55215449	58703525	90037609	********

Figure 4.45 Grid search for MA(2) model of time series 4.4

AUTOCORRELATION FUNCTION OF THE RESIDUALS   ESTIMATION RUN USING MA(2) MODEL

	VALUE	S.E.	T VALUE	−1.0	0.0	1.0
1	0.019	0.067	0.289	I	*	I
2	0.033	0.067	0.486	I	*	I
3	−0.118	0.067	−1.768	I	***	I
4	−0.069	0.068	−1.021	I	**	I
5	−0.019	0.068	−0.285	I	*	I
6	−0.030	0.068	−0.447	I	*	I
7	0.018	0.068	0.260	I	*	I
8	−0.078	0.068	−1.137	I	**	I
9	−0.080	0.069	−1.159	I	**	I
10	0.042	0.069	0.612	I	**	I
11	−0.096	0.069	−1.384	I	***	I
12	0.031	0.070	0.444	I	*	I
13	−0.071	0.070	−1.016	I	**	I
14	0.019	0.070	0.265	I	*	I
15	0.003	0.070	0.042	I	*	I
16	−0.051	0.070	−0.722	I	**	I
17	0.144	0.070	2.050	I	****	I
18	−0.064	0.072	−1.178	I	***	I
19	0.030	0.072	0.419	I	*	I
20	−0.051	0.072	−0.708	I	**	I
21	0.026	0.072	0.356	I	*	I
22	0.048	0.072	0.667	I	**	I
23	0.100	0.072	1.374	I	***	I
24	−0.034	0.073	−0.460	I	*	I

BOX−PIERCE TEST   CHISQUARE STATISTIC WITH   20 DEGREES OF FREEDOM =   19.820

FIgure 4.46 Sample ACF of the residuals for MA(2) model of time series 4.4

(b) Figures 4.46 and 4.47 show the sample ACF and sample PACF of the residuals for the fitted MA(2) model and the value of the Q statistic. Do these tests detect any model inadequacies?

4.8.3 (a) The plot of time series 4.5 in Appendix A.3 is given in Figure 4.48. The means and standard deviations of subsets are given in Table 4.7 and plotted in Figure 4.49. The sample ACF and sample PACF are shown in Figures 4.50 and 4.51. Suggest a tentative model for this time series.

	VALUE	S.E.	T VALUE	-1.0	0.0	1.0
1	0.019	0.067	0.289	I	*	I
2	0.032	0.067	0.481	I	*	I
3	-0.120	0.067	-1.791	I	***	I
4	-0.066	0.067	-0.994	I	**	I
5	-0.009	0.067	-0.136	I	*	I
6	-0.040	0.067	-0.601	I	**	I
7	0.004	0.067	0.056	I	*	I
8	-0.085	0.067	-1.277	I	***	I
9	-0.091	0.067	-1.362	I	***	I
10	0.048	0.067	0.725	I	**	I
11	-0.115	0.067	-1.727	I	***	I
12	-0.002	0.067	-0.033	I	*	I
13	-0.072	0.067	-1.080	I	**	I
14	-0.012	0.067	-0.178	I	*	I
15	-0.007	0.067	-0.112	I	*	I
16	-0.080	0.067	-1.192	I	**	I
17	0.121	0.067	1.816	I	****	I
18	-0.095	0.067	-1.424	I	***	I
19	-0.003	0.067	-0.050	I	*	I
20	-0.042	0.067	-0.623	I	**	I
21	0.017	0.067	0.259	I	*	I
22	0.026	0.067	0.364	I	*	I
23	0.107	0.067	1.595	I	***	I
24	-0.081	0.067	-1.212	I	***	I

Figure 4.47 Sample PACF of the residuals for MA(2) model of time series 4.4

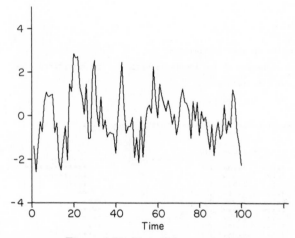

Figure 4.48 Plot of time series 4.5

(b) Figure 4.52 shows the computer printout when a particular ARMA model is fitted to this time series. Identify this model. Which parameter estimates are significant?

(c) Table 4.6 shows the results of fitting three models to this time series. Which of these three models would you select for this time series?

4.8.4 (This exercise is intended for readers with access to computer packages using the Box-Jenkins approach and the only information provided about each time series is the time series itself.) Suggest tentative models for time series 6.6, 6.9, and 6.12 in Appendix A.3.

126

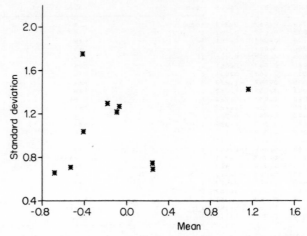

Figure 4.49 Plot of means and standard deviations of
subsets of time series 4.5

100 OBSERVATIONS IN THE WORKING SERIES

MEAN AND STANDARD DEVIATION OF THE WORKING SERIES   IDENTIFICATION RUN
MEAN= -0.7510E-01
STANDARD DEVIATION=   0.1197E 01

AUTOCORRELATION FUNCTION OF THE WORKING SERIES   IDENTIFICATION RUN

             VALUE   S.E.   T VALUE -1.0   0.0   1.0
                                       +---+
       1   0.499   0.100   4.986   I   *************   I
       2   0.308   0.122   2.519   I   *********   I
       3   0.131   0.130   1.010   I   ****   I
       4   0.048   0.131   0.364   I   **   I
       5   -0.176   0.131 -1.337   I   *****   I
       6   -0.200   0.134 -1.493   I   *****   I
       7   -0.256   0.137 -1.874   I   *******   I
       8   -0.184   0.141 -1.304   I   *****   I
       9   -0.052   0.144 -0.361   I   **   I
      10   0.018   0.144   0.123   I   *   I
      11   0.112   0.144   0.781   I   ***   I
      12   0.134   0.145   0.923   I   ****   I
      13   0.200   0.146   1.370   I   ******   I
      14   0.117   0.149   0.787   I   ****   I
      15   0.029   0.150   0.194   I   *   I
      16   -0.143   0.150 -0.956   I   ****   I
      17   -0.130   0.151 -0.863   I   ****   I
      18   -0.194   0.152 -1.275   I   *****   I
      19   -0.173   0.155 -1.118   I   *****   I
      20   -0.133   0.157 -0.850   I   ****   I
      21   -0.082   0.158 -0.523   I   ***   I
      22   -0.005   0.158 -0.029   I   *   I
      23   0.040   0.158   0.251   I   **   I
      24   -0.048   0.158 -0.304   I   **   I
                                       +---+

Figure 4.50 Sample ACF for time series 4.5

PARTIAL AUTOCORRELATION FUNCTION OF THE WORKING SERIES   IDENTIFICATION RUN

```
        VALUE    S.E.   T VALUE   -1.0                    0.0                              1.0
                                    +-----------------------------------------------------+
 1      0.499    0.100    4.986    I                      *************                    I
 2      0.079    0.100    0.794    I                      ***                              I
 3     -0.067    0.100   -0.667    I                    **                                 I
 4     -0.019    0.100   -0.186    I                      *                                I
 5     -0.249    0.100   -2.494    I              *******                                  I
 6     -0.036    0.100   -0.364    I                      *                                I
 7     -0.101    0.100   -1.012    I                   ***                                 I
 8      0.020    0.100    0.199    I                      *                                I
 9      0.142    0.100    1.415    I                      ****                             I
10     -0.006    0.100   -0.065    I                      *                                I
11      0.093    0.100    0.935    I                      ***                              I
12     -0.028    0.100   -0.277    I                      *                                I
13      0.074    0.100    0.735    I                      **                               I
14     -0.053    0.100   -0.533    I                    **                                 I
15     -0.094    0.100   -0.935    I                   ***                                 I
16     -0.142    0.100   -1.418    I                  ****                                 I
17      0.026    0.100    0.260    I                      *                                I
18     -0.034    0.100   -0.339    I                      *                                I
19      0.006    0.100    0.056    I                      *                                I
20      0.040    0.100    0.397    I                      **                               I
21     -0.060    0.100   -0.595    I                    **                                 I
22      0.027    0.100    0.274    I                      *                                I
23     -0.060    0.100   -0.595    I                    **                                 I
24     -0.206    0.100   -2.056    I              ******                                   I
                                    +-----------------------------------------------------+
```

Figure 4.51 Sample PACF for time series 4.5

ESTIMATION RUN USING ARMA(1,1) MODEL

TERMS IN THE ASSUMED STATICNARY (DIFFERENCED) MODEL
    1 REGULAR AUTOREGRESSIVE TERM(S)
    0 SEASONAL AUTOREGRESSIVE TERM(S)
    1 REGULAR MOVING AVERAGE TERM(S)
    0 SEASONAL MOVING AVERAGE TERM(S)

TERM#	TYPE	ORDER	ESTIMATE	STD. ERROR	T VALUE
1	REG. AR	1	0.6316	0.1506	4.1955
2	REG. MA	1	0.1415	0.1893	0.7477

ESTIMATED EXPANDED MODEL LAG COEFFICIENTS

AUTOREGRESSIVE TERMS
            1
         0.6316

MOVING AVERAGE TERMS
            1
         0.1415

Figure 4.52 The fitted ARMA(1, 1) model for time series 4.5

Chapter 5

Forecasting non-stationary time series

5.1 TRANSFORMING A TIME SERIES TO ACHIEVE STATIONARITY

A time series may be non-stationary in the mean or non-stationary in the variance or both. In this section, we see how to transform a time series which is non-stationary in the variance. A time series may be non-stationary in the mean due to a trend or a seasonal pattern. In Section 5.2, we will see how to difference a time series to achieve stationarity in the mean. In Sections 5.3 to 5.7, we consider a class of models for time series which are non-stationary in the mean and fit such models to a number of examples of time series. Seasonal time series will be discussed in Chapter 6.

A simple graphical method for detecting non-stationarity in the variance was described in Section 2.4. The time series is divided into subsets and the mean and standard deviation of each subset is calculated. These means and standard deviations are then plotted: if the standard deviation is independent of the mean, the relationship between the means and standard deviations of the subsets should be a random scatter about a horizontal straight line, as shown in Figure 5.1. This indicates that the time series is stationary in the variance. However, for a number of time series encountered in business and economics, the variability of the time series increases as the mean of the time series increases and at approximately the same rate. In other words, the standard deviation is proportional to the mean. In this case, a plot of the means and standard deviations of the subsets will show a random scatter about an upward-sloping straight line which goes through the origin, as shown in Figure 5.2. In such cases, although the original time series is non-stationary in the variance, it is very easily transformed into a time series which is stationary in the variance. An appropriate transformation is the *logarithmic transformation*. If we consider the transformed time series z_t^*

$$z_t^* = \log_e(z_t)$$

which consists of the natural logarithms of the terms of the original time series, then a plot of the means and standard deviations of subsets of the time series z_t^* should show a random scatter about a horizontal straight line, indicating that the

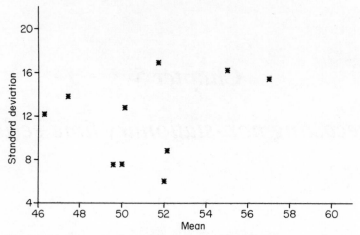

Figure 5.1 Plot of means and standard deviations of subsets of time series 2.1

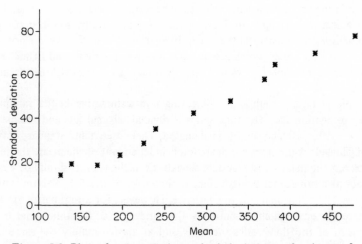

Figure 5.2 Plot of means and standard deviations of subsets of time series 2.4

transformed time series z_t^* is stationary in the variance. If this is not the case, other transformations may be tried. A useful one is the *square root transformation* in which we consider the transformed time series

$$z_t^* = (z_t)^{1/2}.$$

If a plot of the means and standard deviations of subsets of the transformed time series z_t^* shows a random scatter about a horizontal straight line, then this is the appropriate transformation. Many computer packages, including the TSERIES package, allow the user to apply such transformations to a time series. In some cases, it may not be clear from the plots which transformation is most appropriate. In such cases, it may be necessary to work with several transformed time series to discover which of the transformed time series produces the most accurate forecasts. More complicated techniques are available for choosing an appropriate transformation, but a choice based on a study of the plots described above is likely to be a reasonable one, provided the analyst is sufficiently experienced. Once a suitable transformation has been found so that the transformed time series is stationary in the variance, we can then look for an appropriate model for the transformed time series, using the methods described in subsequent sections. Forecasts for the transformed time series are then converted into forecasts for the original time series.

5.2 DIFFERENCING A TIME SERIES TO ACHIEVE STATIONARITY

Many of the time series encountered in business and economics are non-stationary in the mean. In fact, we would not expect such time series as stock prices, incomes, and sales to remain stationary in the mean. Instead we would expect these time series to exhibit upward or downward trends in the mean level or possibly random shifts to a new mean level. However, it is usually possible to transform such a time series into another time series which is stationary in the mean by a device known as *differencing*. The motivation for this is provided by a simple example. Consider the *deterministic* time series $3, 5, 7, 9, \ldots$ for which z_t is given by the expression

$$z_t = 2t + 1, \qquad t \geqslant 1.$$

The reader will recall that a *deterministic* time series is one with no random component in which future values are exactly determined by some mathematical function. This time series is plotted in Figure 5.3 and exhibits a *linear trend*. There

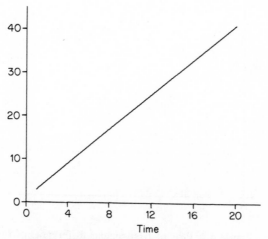

Figure 5.3 Plot of time series $z_t = 2t + 1$

are *systematic* changes in the *mean level* since the mean level is constantly increasing. However, the slope does not change, as the mean level is increasing at a constant rate. In fact, the trend line has slope 2 at all time points. Consider the time series obtained by subtracting consecutive values $5-3$, $7-5$, $9-7, \ldots$, giving the time series $2, 2, 2, 2, \ldots$. This second time series is said to consist of *first regular differences* of the original time series and is denoted by w_t where

$$w_t = z_t - z_{t-1}, \qquad t \geqslant 2.$$

Here

$$w_t = (2t+1) - (2(t-1)+1) = 2, \qquad t \geqslant 2.$$

Note that 2 was the slope of the linear trend line for the original time series. Note also that the number of observations in the time series of *first* regular differences is *one* less than the number of observations in the original time series. We say that one observation has been *lost in differencing*. The time series w_t is plotted in Figure 5.4 and is clearly stationary in the mean. In general, if a time series exhibits linear trend, i.e. systematic changes in mean level, but no change in slope, the time series of first regular differences will be stationary in the mean. If a time series exhibits random changes in level in that it oscillates around one mean level and then shifts to a new temporary level, the time series of first regular differences will again be stationary in the mean.

Another example is provided by the deterministic time series $1, 4, 9, 16, \ldots$ for which z_t is given by the expression

$$z_t = t^2, \qquad t \geqslant 1.$$

This time series is plotted in Figure 5.5 and exhibits *quadratic trend* or equivalently *systematic* changes in *slope* as well as in *mean level*, since both slope and mean level

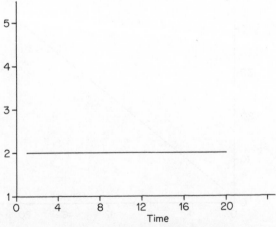

Figure 5.4 Plot of first regular differences of time series $z_t = 2t + 1$

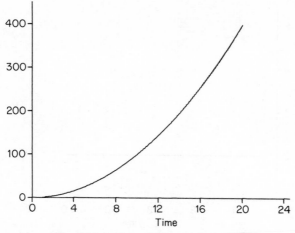

Figure 5.5 Plot of time series $z_t = t^2$

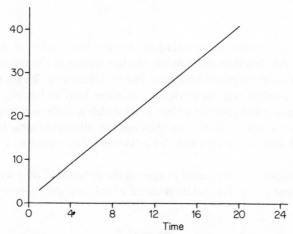

Figure 5.6 Plot of first regular differences of time
series $z_t = t^2$

are increasing over time. Subtracting consecutive values gives the time series of first regular differences $4-1=3$, $9-4=5$, $16-9=7,\ldots$. These first regular differences are plotted in Figure 5.6 and exhibit linear trend. By subtracting consecutive terms of this time series, we obtain the time series, 2, 2, 2, 2,... which is plotted in Figure 5.7 and is of course stationary in the mean. This latter time series is said to consist of *second regular differences* of the original time series $z_t = t^2$ and is related to the original time series z_t as follows:

$$w_t = [z_t - z_{t-1}] - [z_{t-1} - z_{t-2}]$$
$$= z_t - 2z_{t-1} + z_{t-2}, \qquad t \geq 3.$$

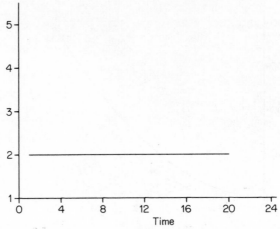

Figure 5.7 Plot of second regular differences of time series $z_t = t^2$

Note that the number of observations in the time series of *second* regular differences is *two* less than the number of observations in the original time series. We say that two observations have been lost in differencing. We see that for a time series which exhibits *systematic* changes in mean level and slope, taking second regular differences will produce a time series which is stationary in the mean. The same is true of a time series that exhibits *random* changes in mean level and slope, in that it will drift in one direction for a time and then temporarily shift direction for a time.

A special notation is often used to express the differenced time series in terms of the original time series. This notation uses the *backward shift operator B* defined as follows:

$$Bz_t = z_{t-1}.$$

Similarly

$$B^2z_t = BBz_t = Bz_{t-1} = z_{t-2}$$

and in general

$$B^kz_t = z_{t-k}.$$

Now the time series w_t of first regular differences of z_t is given by

$$w_t = z_t - z_{t-1}$$
$$= z_t - Bz_t$$
$$= (1 - B)z_t.$$

Similarly the time series w_t of second regular differences is given by

$$w_t = z_t - 2z_{t-1} + z_{t-2}$$
$$= z_t - 2Bz_t + B^2z_t$$
$$= (1 - 2B + B^2)\,z_t$$
$$= (1 - B)^2\,z_t.$$

In general, if d regular differences are taken, the difference time series w_t is related to the original time series z_t as follows:

$$w_t = (1 - B)^d z_t.$$

This notation is used to describe the differenced time series in many computer packages, including the TSERIES computer package.

If a time series is non-stationary in the mean due to random changes in mean level, then in any local segment of time the observations will look like those in any other segment, apart from the mean level. Similarly, if a time series is non-stationary in the mean due to random changes in mean level and slope, observations in different segments will look very much alike, apart from mean level and slope. The term *homogeneous* is used to describe such a time series which, although it is non-stationary in the mean, has basically the same appearance in different segments. We have seen that differencing such a time series produces a time series which is stationary in the mean. In general, a time series is said to be *homogeneously non-stationary in the mean* if taking one or more regular differences produces a time series which is stationary in the mean. We can readily find a model for such a time series by fitting an appropriate ARMA model to the stationary time series obtained by taking a suitable number of regular differences of the original time series. By 'undifferencing' this model, we arrive at a model for the original time series. This is illustrated in subsequent sections in this chapter.

An obvious question that now arises is: if a time series is non-stationary in the mean, how do we determine the number of regular differences that are necessary to produce a time series which is stationary in the mean? The number of regular differences required is denoted by d and is determined by studying the sample ACF of the original time series and of each of the differenced time series derived from it. The reader will recall that if the sample ACF of the original time series dies down extremely slowly, this is an indication that the original time series is non-stationary and that at least one regular difference is required. The sample ACF of the first regular differences should then be studied and if this cuts off or dies down quickly, then the time series of first regular differences is stationary and we may take $d = 1$. If, however, the sample ACF of the first regular differences dies down extremely slowly, the time series of first regular differences is non-stationary in the mean and at least two regular differences are required. The sample ACF of the second regular differences is then studied and if this cuts off or dies down quickly, the time series of second regular differences is stationary and we may take $d = 2$. A plot of the time series and of the differenced time series should also be inspected to see if the corresponding time series 'look' stationary, but the choice of d should be based on the appearance of the sample ACF's. For most of the non-seasonal time series encountered in practice, at least one regular difference is required to achieve stationarity. Very occasionally, two regular differences may be required, but rarely more than two. It is important to remember that d is defined to be the least number of regular differences needed to achieve stationarity. This is because further differences of a stationary time series are also stationary and nothing is gained by further differencing. Taking more regular differences than are needed to achieve stationarity is known as *overdifferencing* and should be avoided. The effect of over-differencing is to artificially introduce moving average terms into the model of the differenced time series and only serves to complicate this model unnecessarily. A very rough guide to the correct order of differencing may be obtained by study-ing the sample variance (or equivalently the sample standard deviation) of the original time series and of each of the differenced time series. It sometimes happens that the sample variance will decrease until a stationary time series is first obtained, but if further differences are taken the variance will increase again. However, it should be remembered that this is not always the case and so it is more important to study the sample ACF of the original time series and of each of the differenced time series to decide on the correct order of differencing to achieve stationarity.

5.3 THE RANDOM WALK MODEL

Many time series encountered in business and economics behave like realizations of a type of model known as a *random walk model*. In particular, it has been found that stock market prices can be modelled in this way. This model may be defined as follows:

$$Z_t = Z_{t-1} + \theta_0 + A_t \qquad (5.1)$$

where

$$A_t \sim \text{IN}(0, \sigma_A^2).$$

If the constant term θ_0 is zero, then Z_t, which represents the 'position' of the time series at time t, is given by Z_{t-1}, which represents the 'position' of the time series at time $(t-1)$, plus a random shock A_t. A stochastic process which develops in this way is known as a *random walk*, for obvious reasons. From (5.1), it follows that for any realization of this model with $\theta_0 = 0$, we have

$$z_t = z_0 + \sum_{i=1}^{t} a_i$$

and so z_t is just z_0 plus the sum of the realized random shocks up to time t. Because of this, the random walk model is called an *integrated* model because successive random shocks are accumulated or integrated over time. Depending on the sequence of realized random shocks that occur, it is possible for the realized time series to drift upwards or downwards from its starting value z_0. If a sequence of realized random shocks occur which are mainly positive in sign, then the realized time series will drift upwards. Similarly, if a sequence of realized random shocks occur which are mainly negative in sign, then the realized time series will drift downwards. If the positive and negative realized random shocks roughly cancel each other out, then of course the realized time series will not drift upwards or downwards.

If the constant term θ_0 in the model is non-zero, then it follows from (5.1) that

$$z_t = z_0 + \theta_0 t + \sum_{i=1}^{t} a_i$$

and so the realized time series will exhibit a linear trend with slope θ_0, upwards if θ_0 is positive and downwards if θ_0 is negative. Such a model is said to be a *random walk with trend*. Of course, the realized time series will also drift above and below the trend. The random walk model is characterized by the fact that the first regular differences of such a model form a white noise model. The random variables W_t corresponding to the first regular differences of the sequence of random variables Z_t in (5.1) are given by

$$W_t = Z_t - Z_{t-1}$$

$$= \theta_0 + A_t,$$

showing that the variables W_t do indeed form a white noise model. Consequently the characteristic properties of a random walk model are derived from those of a white noise model and are shown in Table 5.7 at the end of this chapter.

If an observed time series is a realization of a random walk model, then forecasting future values of the time series is trivial. From (5.1), we have

$$\hat{z}_t(1) = z_t + \theta_0$$

and in general

$$\hat{z}_t(l) = z_t + l\theta_0. \tag{5.2}$$

It may be shown that

$$\sigma^2[e_t(l)] = l\sigma_A^2 .$$

Since the 95% prediction limits for z_{t+l} are given by

$$\hat{z}_t(l) \pm 1.96(\sigma^2[e_t(l)])^{1/2} ,$$

we see that the forecasts increase or decrease linearly with l and the width of the prediction intervals increases with the square root of l. If $\theta_0 = 0$, we have from (5.2) that

$$\hat{z}_t(l) = z_t,$$

so that the forecast for all future time periods is just the last observed value of the time series. Stock market prices are often realizations of such a random walk and so the best forecast of tomorrow's price (and the price for all future days) is just today's price. Such a trivial forecast is unlikely to be very useful in practice.

The reader should observe that the random walk model

$$Z_t = Z_{t-1} + \theta_0 + A_t$$

is just the first order autoregressive AR(1) model

$$Z_t = \theta_0 + \phi_1 Z_{t-1} + A_t$$

with the parameter ϕ_1 set equal to 1. However, for this value of ϕ_1, the AR(1) model is non-stationary. If an observed time series appears to be a realization of an AR(1) model with ϕ_1 near 1, there are advantages in fitting a random walk model instead. We see from (3.15) that the forecasts $\hat{z}_t(l)$ for an AR(1) model are given by:

$$\hat{z}_t(l) = \mu + \phi_1^l (z_t - \mu).$$

Thus the forecasts are determined by the last observed value z_t of the time series, but ultimately converge to the process mean μ, which is estimated by the sample mean of the observed time series. However, for a random walk model, we see from (5.2) that the forecasts are determined only by the last observed value of the time series and not by the sample mean of the observed time series. As ϕ_1 approaches 1 in the AR(1) model, a realization of such a model can wander away from the process mean μ and not return for very long periods. In such circumstances, it is unreasonable to require forecasts for future time periods to depend on an estimate of this process mean and so it may be preferable to use a random walk model in which the forecasts depend only on the last observed value of the time series. However, if $\mu = \theta_0 = 0$, then there will be little difference between the short term forecasts produced by the two models.

5.4 AUTOREGRESSIVE INTEGRATED MOVING AVERAGE MODELS

The random walk model was described as an *integrated* model because it involved the accumulation or integration of successive random shocks. The first regular differences of a random walk model form a white noise model. Other integrated models are available whose first regular differences form other ARMA models. In this section, we first study models whose first regular differences form AR(1) and AR(2) models respectively. The first of these is known as the *autoregressive integrated model of order (1, 1)*, or, more briefly, the AR(1, 1) model. The second of these is known as the *autoregressive integrated model of order (2, 1)*, or, more briefly, the ARI(2, 1) model. In general, an ARI(p, d) model is one whose dth regular differences form an AR(p) model. The equation for an ARI(1, 1) model may be found as follows. If the first differences W_t form an AR(1) model, then

$$W_t = \theta_0 + \phi_1 W_{t-1} + A_t. \tag{5.3}$$

Setting $W_t = Z_t - Z_{t-1}$ in (5.3) gives

$$Z_t = \theta_0 + (1 + \phi_1) Z_{t-1} - \phi_1 Z_{t-2} + A_t.$$

The equation for an ARI(2, 1) model is found in a similar fashion. The characteristic properties of these models are derived from those of the AR(1) and AR(2)
models and are shown in Table 5.7. Forecasts for these models are easily found
using the general method of Section 3.8. Thus, for the ARI(1, 1) model, we have

$$Z_{t+l} = \theta_0 + (1 + \phi_1) Z_{t+l-1} - \phi_1 Z_{t+l-2} + A_{t+l}$$

and so

$$\hat{z}_t(1) = \theta_0 + (1 + \phi_1) z_t - \phi_1 z_{t-1},$$

$$\hat{z}_t(2) = \theta_0 + (1 + \phi_1) \hat{z}_t(1) - \phi_1 z_t,$$

$$\hat{z}_t(l) = \theta_0 + (1 + \phi_1) \hat{z}_t(l-1) - \phi_1 \hat{z}_t(l-2), \qquad l > 2.$$

Recall that for an AR(1) model, as the lead time increases, the forecasts tended
towards the process mean μ, where

$$\mu = \frac{\theta_0}{1 - \phi_1}.$$

From this it may be deduced that for the ARI(1, 1) model, as the lead time
increases, the forecasts tend towards a straight line with slope $\theta_0/(1 - \phi_1)$. As in the
case of the random walk model, if a non-zero constant term θ_0 is included in an
ARI(1, 1) model, a realization of this model will exhibit a linear trend with slope
$\theta_0/(1 - \phi_1)$, upwards or downwards depending on the sign of θ_0, and the forecasts
produced by such a model will eventually follow the same linear trend. It has been
found that ARI(1, 1) models and ARI(2, 1) models do not occur in practice as
frequently as the random walk model or the integrated moving average models to
be described next.

We now consider two models whose first regular differences form MA(1) and
MA(2) models respectively. The first of these is known as the *integrated moving
average model of order (1, 1)*, or, more briefly, the IMA(1, 1) model. The second of
these is known as the *integrated moving average model of order (1, 2)*, or, more
briefly, the IMA(1, 2) model. In general, an IMA(d, q) model is one whose dth
regular differences form an MA(q) model. The equation for an IMA(1, 1) model is
found as follows. If the first regular differences W_t form an MA(1) model, then

$$W_t = \theta_0 + A_t - \theta_1 A_{t-1}. \tag{5.4}$$

Setting $W_t = Z_t - Z_{t-1}$ in (5.4) gives

$$Z_t = \theta_0 + Z_{t-1} + A_t - \theta_1 A_{t-1}.$$

The reader should observe that this IMA(1, 1) model is a particular case of the
ARMA(1, 1) model

$$Z_t = \theta_0 + \phi_1 Z_{t-1} + A_t - \theta_1 A_{t-1}$$

with the parameter ϕ_1 set equal to 1. However, for this value of ϕ_1, the
ARMA(1, 1) model is non-stationary. If an observed time series appears to be a
realization of an ARMA(1, 1) model with ϕ_1 near 1, there are advantages in fitting

an IMA(1, 1) model instead. These advantages are similar to those which have already been discussed in the previous section for the case of the AR(1) and random walk models. The equation for an IMA(1, 2) model is found in a similar fashion. The characteristic properties of these models are derived from those of the MA(1) and MA(2) models and are shown in Table 5.7. Forecasts for these models are easily found using the general method of Section 3.8. Thus for the IMA(1, 1) model we have

$$\hat{z}_t(1) = \theta_0 + z_t - \theta_1(z_t - \hat{z}_{t-1}(1)),$$

$$\hat{z}_t(l) = \hat{z}_t(1) + (l-1)\,\theta_0, \qquad l > 1,$$

where the observed one step ahead forecast error $(z_t - \hat{z}_{t-1}(1))$ is used in place of a_t, the realized random shock at time t. The reader will recall that for the MA(1) model, the forecasts for lead time $l > 1$ consisted of the process mean μ which was equal to the constant term θ_0. Consequently, it is no surprise to find that for the IMA(1, 1) model the forecasts for lead time $l > 1$ lie on a straight line with slope θ_0 that originates at the value $\hat{z}_t(1)$ at time $(t + 1)$. In particular, for $\theta_0 = 0$, the forecasts are given by

$$\left.\begin{aligned}
\hat{z}_t(1) &= z_t - \theta_1(z_t - \hat{z}_{t-1}(1)), \\
\hat{z}_t(l) &= \hat{z}_t(1), \qquad l > 1.
\end{aligned}\right\} \tag{5.5}$$

In this case, the forecasts for all future time periods are the same and they all lie on a horizontal line that originates at the value $\hat{z}_t(1)$ at time $(t + 1)$. From (5.5), it follows that

$$\hat{z}_t(1) = (1 - \theta_1)\,z_t + \theta_1\hat{z}_{t-1}(1).$$

Setting $\alpha = 1 - \theta_1$, we get

$$\hat{z}_t(1) = \alpha z_t + (1 - \alpha)\,\hat{z}_{t-1}(1), \tag{5.6}$$

which is the formula for updating one step ahead forecasts using *simple exponential smoothing*. This equation may be interpreted as follows. Since the IMA(1, 1) model in non-stationary in the mean, there is no process mean. However, the forecast $\hat{z}_t(1)$ can be regarded as measuring the location or *level* of the process at time t. From (5.6), we now see that each new level is arrived at by averaging the new observation and the previous level. If α equals unity, then $\hat{z}_t(1) = z_t$, which ignores all evidence concerning level coming from previous observations. On the other hand, if α has some value close to zero, $\hat{z}_t(1)$ relies heavily on the previous value $\hat{z}_{t-1}(1)$, which has weight $1 - \alpha$. Only the small weight α is given to the new observation. From (5.6), it follows that

$$\hat{z}_t(1) = (1 - \theta_1)\,z_t + \theta_1(1 - \theta_1)\,z_{t-1} + \theta_1^2(1 - \theta_1)\,z_{t-2} + \dots,$$

from which it is clear that to get the forecast $\hat{z}_t(1)$ we 'smooth' (i.e. average) the current and previous observations. Since the condition $-1 < \theta_1 < 1$ is required for invertibility, it is clear that the weights used in calculating the above weighted average decay exponentially and hence this forecasting method is called *simple exponential smoothing.* It is intuitively appealing, since it gives the greatest weight to the most recent observation and yet does not completely ignore previous observations. This forecasting method is ideally suited to computers since we see from (5.6) that it is recursive in nature and requires at any time t only the current observation z_t and the forecast $\hat{z}_{t-1}(1)$. It was mentioned in Chapter 1 that simple exponential smoothing is very widely used in such areas as inventory control and has been found to give fairly accurate forecasts. We have now demonstrated that simple exponential smoothing will produce optimal forecasts for the IMA(1, 1) model in which $\theta_0 = 0$. In situations where this model is not appropriate, simple exponential smoothing may fail to give optimal forecasts. The optimal forecasts must be obtained by fitting an appropriate time series model. The IMA(1, 1) model is probably the most widely used of all the non-stationary models considered in this chapter.

The final model to be considered in this section is the *autoregressive integrated moving average model of order (1, 1, 1)*, or, more briefly, the ARIMA(1, 1, 1) model. The first regular differences of this model form an ARMA(1, 1) model. The equation for an ARIMA(1, 1, 1) model is found as follows. Since the first regular differences W_t form an ARMA(1, 1) model, we have

$$W_t = \theta_0 + \phi_1 W_{t-1} + A_t - \theta_1 A_{t-1}. \tag{5.7}$$

Setting $W_t = Z_t - Z_{t-1}$ in (5.7) gives

$$Z_t = \theta_0 + (1 + \phi_1) Z_{t-1} - \phi_1 Z_{t-2} + A_t - \theta_1 A_{t-1}.$$

The characteristic properties of this model are derived from those of an ARMA(1, 1) model and are shown on Table 5.7. Forecasts for this model are easily found using the general method of Section 3.8.

All the models considered so far in this section are particular cases of an ARIMA(p, 1, q) model whose first differences form an ARMA(p, q) model. The six models we have studied may be described in this notation as shown in Table 5.7. Thus a random walk model is an ARIMA(0, 1, 0) model, an ARI(1, 1) model is an ARIMA(1, 1, 0) model, etc. These six models that we have studied are the only ARIMA(p, 1, q) models that are usually needed in practice. More generally, an ARIMA(p, d, q) model is one whose dth regular differences form an ARMA(p, q) model. It has been found that ARIMA(p, d, q) models with $d \geqslant 2$ do not occur in practice as frequently as ARIMA(p, 1, q) models and so such models will not be discussed here.

The behaviour of forecasts for ARIMA(p, 1, q) models may be deduced from that of forecasts for ARMA(p, q) models and may be summarized as follows. For an ARMA(p, q) model, as the lead time increases, the forecasts tend towards the process mean μ, where

$$\mu = \frac{\theta_0}{1 - \phi_1 - \phi_2 \ldots - \phi_p}.$$

Consequently, for an ARIMA(p, 1, q) model, as the lead time increases, the forecasts tend towards a straight line with *slope μ*. Thus if the constant term θ_0 is zero, the forecasts tend towards a horizontal straight line, while if θ_0 is non-zero, the forecasts will tend towards a line which slopes upwards if θ_0 is positive and downwards if θ_0 is negative. In general for ARIMA(p, 1, q) models, the variance of the forecast errors increases without bound as the lead time increases and hence the width of prediction intervals increases without bound as the lead time increases.

It should be noted that the presence of a non-zero constant term in an ARIMA(p, 1, q) model has important implications both for the behaviour of a realization of this model and the behaviour of forecasts produced by this model. If θ_0 is non-zero, a realization of this model will exhibit a linear trend with slope μ where

$$\mu = \frac{\theta_0}{1 - \phi_1 - \phi_2 \ldots - \phi_p}.$$

Forecasts for this model will eventually follow the same linear trend. If the sample mean of the first regular differences of the observed time series is significantly different from zero, a non-zero constant term should be included in the model. However, if it is felt that it is unreasonable to assume that the future behaviour of the observed time series will follow the same upward or downward trend as in the past, then θ_0 should be set equal to zero in calculating forecasts of future values of the time series. This is equivalent to assuming that any future changes in mean level of the observed time series will be random changes rather than systematic changes, with equal long-run probability of either upward or downward movement. Many computer packages, including the TSERIES package, give the user this option in calculating forecasts.

5.5 EXAMPLE 5.1

In this section we analyse time series 5.1 given in Appendix A.3. The time series being studied consists of stock prices, so it is likely that the random walk model will be appropriate. The plot of the time series is shown in Figure 5.8 and seems to indicate that the time series is non-stationary in the mean due to random changes in mean level. The means and standard deviations of subsets of this time series are given in Table 5.8 at the end of this chapter and are plotted in Figure 5.9 which indicates that the time series is stationary in the variance. The sample ACF of the time series is given in Figure 5.10 and confirms that the time series is non-stationary in the mean, since the sample ACF dies down extremely slowly. In this figure, the 'working series' is defined to be

$$w_t = (1 - B^{12})^0 (1 - B)^0 z_t$$

where B is the backward shift operator described above. Since $(1 - B^{12})^0 = 1$ and $(1 - B)^0 = 1$, we have $w_t = z_t$, i.e. the working series w_t is just the original time series z_t.

The first regular differences of time series 5.1 are plotted in Figure 5.11 and appear to be stationary in the mean. This is confirmed by the sample ACF of the

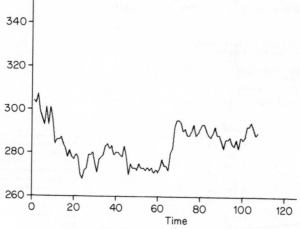

Figure 5.8 Plot of time series 5.1

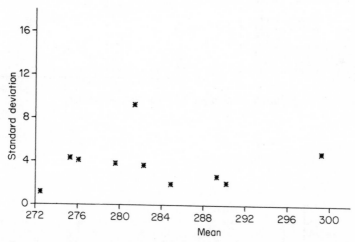

Figure 5.9 Plot of means and standard deviations of subsets of
time series 5.1

first regular differences, which is given in Figure 5.12. In this figure, the working
series is defined to be

$$w_t = (1 - B^{12})^0 (1 - B)^1 z_t$$
$$= (1 - B)^1 z_t$$

i.e. the working series w_t consists of the first regular differences of the original
time series z_t. The second regular differences of time series 5.1 are plotted in Figure
5.14 and appear to be stationary in the mean. This is confirmed by the sample

DIFFERENCED (WORKING) SERIES W(T)=(1−B^{12})^{0} (1−B)^{0} Z(T)

0 OBSERVATIONS LOST IN DIFFERENCING
107 OBSERVATIONS IN THE WORKING SERIES

MEAN AND STANDARD DEVIATION OF THE WORKING SERIES   IDENTIFICATION RUN
MEAN=   0.2836E 03
STANDARD DEVIATION=   0.8683E 01

AUTOCORRELATION FUNCTION OF THE WORKING SERIES   IDENTIFICATION RUN

```
          VALUE   S.E.   T VALUE  -1.0                    0.0                         1.0
                                  +------------------------------------------------------+
  1       0.885   0.097   9.157   I                       **********************         I
  2       0.800   0.155   5.166   I                       *******************            I
  3       0.699   0.190   3.688   I                       *****************              I
  4       0.629   0.212   2.961   I                       ****************               I
  5       0.583   0.229   2.543   I                       ***************                I
  6       0.549   0.243   2.265   I                       **************                 I
  7       0.481   0.254   1.894   I                       *************                  I
  8       0.401   0.262   1.528   I                       ***********                    I
  9       0.309   0.268   1.152   I                       *********                      I
 10       0.227   0.271   0.837   I                       ******                         I
 11       0.193   0.273   0.709   I                       ******                         I
 12       0.146   0.274   0.532   I                       ****                           I
 13       0.096   0.275   0.348   I                       ***                            I
 14       0.034   0.275   0.123   I                       *                              I
 15       0.004   0.275   0.016   I                       *                              I
 16      -0.046   0.275  -0.168   I                      **                              I
 17      -0.059   0.275  -0.215   I                      **                              I
 18      -0.075   0.276  -0.271   I                      **                              I
 19      -0.096   0.276  -0.347   I                     ***                              I
 20      -0.120   0.276  -0.436   I                    ****                              I
 21      -0.160   0.277  -0.579   I                   *****                              I
 22      -0.161   0.277  -0.579   I                   *****                              I
 23      -0.138   0.278  -0.495   I                    ****                              I
 24      -0.101   0.279  -0.362   I                     ***                              I
                                  +------------------------------------------------------+
```

Figure 5.10 Sample ACF for time series 5.1

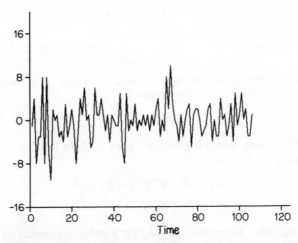

Figure 5.11 Plot of first regular differences of time
series 5.1

```
                                 12  0      1
DIFFERENCED (WORKING) SERIES W(T)=(1-B   ) (1-B) Z(T)


         1 OBSERVATIONS LOST IN DIFFERENCING
        106 OBSERVATIONS IN THE WORKING SERIES

     MEAN AND STANDARD DEVIATION OF THE WORKING SERIES        IDENTIFICATION RUN
     MEAN=  -0.1415E 00
     STANDARD DEVIATION=   0.3632E 01

     AUTOCORRELATION FUNCTION OF THE WORKING SERIES    IDENTIFICATION RUN
```

	VALUE	S.E.	T VALUE	-1.0	0.0	1.0
1	-0.155	0.097	-1.592	I	****	I
2	0.019	0.069	0.194	I	*	I
3	-0.069	0.099	-0.695	I	**	I
4	-0.089	0.100	-0.894	I	***	I
5	-0.031	0.101	-0.310	I	*	I
6	0.105	0.101	1.038	I	***	I
7	0.188	0.102	1.851	I	*****	I
8	-0.056	0.105	-0.530	I	**	I
9	0.048	0.105	0.453	I	**	I
10	-0.131	0.105	-1.245	I	****	I
11	0.063	0.107	0.589	I	**	I
12	0.010	0.107	0.057	I	*	I
13	0.041	0.107	0.382	I	**	I
14	-0.140	0.108	-1.303	I	****	I
15	0.153	0.109	1.403	I	****	I
16	-0.143	0.111	-1.284	I	****	I
17	-0.041	0.113	-0.363	I	**	I
18	0.005	0.113	0.575	I	*	I
19	0.036	0.113	0.319	I	*	I
20	0.043	0.114	0.378	I	**	I
21	-0.199	0.114	-1.752	I	*****	I
22	-0.008	0.117	-0.068	I	*	I
23	-0.051	0.117	-0.436	I	**	I
24	-0.041	0.117	-0.351	I	**	I

Figure 5.12 Sample ACF for first regular differences of time series 5.1

```
PARTIAL AUTOCORRELATION FUNCTION OF THE WORKING SERIES   IDENTIFICATION RUN
```

	VALUE	S.E.	T VALUE	-1.0	0.0	1.0
1	-0.155	0.097	-1.592	I	****	I
2	-0.005	0.097	-0.049	I	*	I
3	-0.069	0.097	-0.706	I	**	I
4	-0.114	0.097	-1.169	I	***	I
5	-0.066	0.097	-0.675	I	**	I
6	0.087	0.097	0.900	I	***	I
7	0.216	0.097	2.219	I	******	I
8	-0.005	0.097	-0.050	I	*	I
9	0.043	0.097	0.446	I	**	I
10	-0.078	0.097	-0.799	I	**	I
11	0.078	0.097	0.807	I	***	I
12	0.041	0.097	0.420	I	**	I
13	-0.002	0.097	-0.024	I	*	I
14	-0.199	0.097	-2.052	I	*****	I
15	0.125	0.097	1.283	I	****	I
16	-0.091	0.097	-0.932	I	***	I
17	-0.069	0.097	-0.706	I	**	I
18	-0.014	0.097	-0.146	I	*	I
19	0.065	0.097	0.674	I	**	I
20	0.065	0.097	0.674	I	**	I
21	-0.184	0.097	-1.896	I	*****	I
22	-0.121	0.097	-1.245	I	****	I
23	0.043	0.097	0.447	I	**	I
24	-0.085	0.097	-0.874	I	***	I

Figure 5.13 Sample PACF for first regular differences of time series 5.1

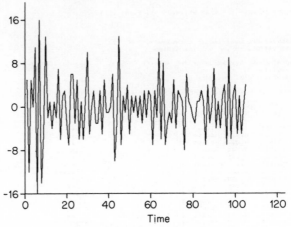

Figure 5.14 Plot of second regular differences of time
series 5.1

ACF of the second regular differences, which is given in Figure 5.15. However, from the plot of the second regular differences in Figure 5.14, it appears that the second regular differences have greater variability than the first regular differences, indicating that to take two regular differences will result in overdifferencing. This is confirmed by studying the sample standard deviations of time series 5.1 and its first and second regular differences. From Figures 5.10, 5.12, and 5.15, the sample standard deviations are 8.683 for $d = 0$, 3.632 for $d = 1$, and 5.543 for $d = 2$. Thus for the time series 5.1, it is appropriate to take only one regular difference to reduce the time series to stationarity and so the class of ARIMA$(p, 1, q)$ models is an appropriate class of models for this time series.

The sample PACF of the first regular differences of time series 5.1 is given in Figure 5.13. From Figures 5.12 and 5.13, we see that none of the sample auto-correlations or partial autocorrelations of the first regular differences are signifi-cantly different from zero. From the characteristic properties of ARIMA$(p, 1, q)$ models given in Table 5.7, we see that the random walk model is an appropriate model for time series 5.1. From Figure 5.12, the sample mean of the first regular differences is -0.1415, which is not large compared with the sample standard deviation of the first regular differences, which is 3.632, and so no constant term is included in the model. The fitted random walk model is shown in Figure 5.16, under the heading 'Estimated expanded model lag coefficients'. This shows that the fitted random walk model is

$$Z_t = Z_{t-1} + A_t.$$

The usual diagnostic checks do not detect any model inadequacies and are not given here. The results of overfitting an ARI(1, 1) model and IMA(1, 1) model are shown in Table 5.1. Both overfits are rejected and the random walk model is regarded as the best available model for time series 5.1. The forecasts at origin

Table 5.1 Fitted models for time series 5.1

Model type	Fitted model $(W_t = Z_t - Z_{t-1})$	Residual variance	Q statistic
Random walk	$W_t = A_t$	13.2095	23.859
ARI(1, 1)	$W_t = -(0.1531)\,W_{t-1} + A_t$ $(t = -1.5867)$	12.9002	20.786
IMA(1, 1)	$W_t = A_t - (0.1563)\,A_{t-1}$ $(t = 1.6219)$	12.8983	20.571

107 for the next 10 time periods are given in Figure 5.17 and plotted in Figure 5.18. The reader will recall that for a random walk model with $\theta_0 = 0$, the forecasts for all future time periods equal the last observed value of the time series, which is 289 in the present example. Notice that the width of the prediction intervals increases without bound as the lead time increases.

```
                                   12  0      2
DIFFERENCED (WORKING) SERIES W(T)=(1-B  ) (1-B) Z(T)


     2 OBSERVATIONS LOST IN DIFFERENCING
   105 OBSERVATIONS IN THE WORKING SERIES

MEAN AND STANDARD DEVIATION OF THE WORKING SERIES
MEAN=    0.1905E-01
STANDARD DEVIATION=    0.5543E 01

AUTOCORRELATION FUNCTION OF THE WORKING SERIES


         VALUE    S.E.   T VALUE  -1.0                    0.0                      1.0
                                   +-------------------------------------------------+
    1   -0.573   0.098   -5.870   I          ****************I                        I
    2    0.110   0.126    0.879   I                         ***                       I
    3   -0.030   0.127   -0.238   I                         *                         I
    4   -0.033   0.127   -0.262   I                         *                         I
    5   -0.033   0.127   -0.257   I                         *                         I
    6    0.020   0.127    0.155   I                         *                         I
    7    0.147   0.127    1.160   I                         ****                      I
    8   -0.157   0.128   -1.219   I                      ****                         I
    9    0.124   0.130    0.954   I                         ****                      I
   10   -0.161   0.131   -1.225   I                      *****                        I
   11    0.108   0.133    0.811   I                         ***                       I
   12   -0.035   0.134   -0.261   I                         *                         I
   13    0.089   0.134    0.665   I                         ***                       I
   14   -0.205   0.135   -1.522   I                     ******                        I
   15    0.253   0.138    1.841   I                         *******                   I
   16   -0.168   0.142   -1.183   I                      *****                        I
   17   -0.003   0.144   -0.024   I                         *                         I
   18    0.058   0.144    0.402   I                         **                        I
   19   -0.013   0.144   -0.091   I                         *                         I
   20    0.104   0.144    0.725   I                         ***                       I
   21   -0.189   0.145   -1.308   I                      *****                        I
   22    0.104   0.147    0.708   I                         ***                       I
   23   -0.021   0.148   -0.142   I                         *                         I
   24   -0.004   0.148   -0.029   I                         *                         I
                                   +-------------------------------------------------+
```

Figure 5.15 Sample ACF for second regular differences of time series 5.1

ESTIMATION RUN USING RANDOM WALK MODEL

ESTIMATED EXPANDED MODEL LAG COEFFICIENTS

AUTOREGRESSIVE TERMS
1
1.0000

MOVING AVERAGE TERMS

NONE

Figure 5.16 The fitted random walk model for
time series 5.1

ESTIMATION RUN USING RANDOM WALK MODEL

FORECASTS FROM PERIOD 107

PERIOD	FORECAST	95 PERCENT LIMITS LOWER	UPPER
108	289.000	281.875	296.125
109	289.000	278.924	299.076
110	289.000	276.659	301.341
111	289.000	274.750	303.250
112	289.000	273.068	304.932
113	289.000	271.547	306.453
114	289.000	270.149	307.851
115	289.000	268.847	309.153
116	289.000	267.625	310.375
117	289.000	266.469	311.531

Figure 5.17 Forecasts for time series 5.1 using the
random walk model

5.6 EXAMPLE 5.2

In this section we analyse time series 5.2 in Appendix A.3. The plot of the time
series is shown in Figure 5.19 and seems to indicate that the time series is non-
stationary in the mean due to random changes in mean level. The means and
standard deviations of subsets of this time series are given in Table 5.8 and plotted
in Figure 5.20, which indicates that the time series in stationary in the variance.
Plots of the first and second regular differences are given in Figures 5.22 and 5.25,
which indicate that these time series appear to be stationary in the mean. This is
confirmed by the sample ACF's of time series 5.2 and its first and second regular
differences, given in Figures 5.21, 5.23, and 5.26. The sample ACF of the time
series dies down extremely slowly, while that of its first and second regular

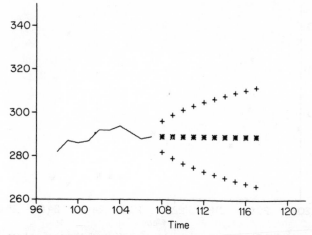

Figure 5.18 Plot of forecasts for time series 5.1 using the random walk model. ——— Time series, *** forecasts, +++ 95% prediction limits

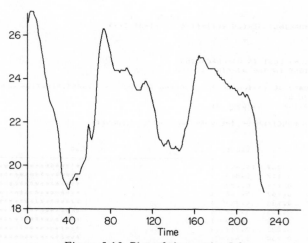

Figure 5.19 Plot of time series 5.2

differences die down quickly towards zero. Consequently the class of **ARIMA**-$(p, 1, q)$ models is an appropriate class of models of time series 5.2. The sample PACF of the first regular differences is shown in Figure 5.24 and cuts off after lag one, while the sample ACF of the first regular differences tails off towards zero, as shown in Figure 5.23. From Table 5.7 we see that the ARI(1, 1) model is an appropriate model for time series 5.2. Since the sample mean of the first regular differences is not large compared with the sample standard deviation of the first

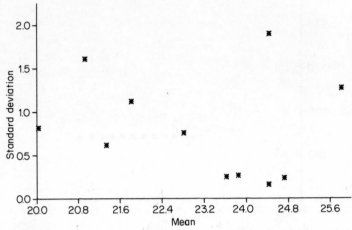

Figure 5.20 Plot of means and standard deviations of subsets of
time series 5.2

```
                                    12  0      0
DIFFERENCED (WORKING) SERIES W(T)=(1-B   ) (1-B) Z(T)


      0 OBSERVATICNS LOST IN DIFFERENCING
    226 OBSERVATIONS IN THE WORKING SERIES

MEAN AND STANDARD DEVIATICN OF THE WORKING SERIES      IDENTIFICATION RUN
MEAN=   0.2297E 02
STANDARD DEVIATICN=    0.2059E 01

AUTOCORRELATION FUNCTICN OF THE WORKING SERIES     IDENTIFICATION RUN
```

```
              VALUE    S.E.   T VALUE   -1.0                      0.0                            1.0
                                        +--------------------------+------------------------------+
    1         0.978    3.067   14.656   I                          ************************** I
    2         0.944    0.113    8.318   I                          ************************ I
    3         0.902    0.144    6.260   I                          *********************** I
    4         0.854    0.167    5.108   I                          ********************** I
    5         0.802    0.186    4.324   I                          ********************* I
    6         0.748    0.200    3.732   I                          ******************** I
    7         0.692    0.212    3.259   I                          ****************** I
    8         0.635    0.222    2.861   I                          ***************** I
    9         0.579    0.230    2.517   I                          **************** I
   10         0.523    0.236    2.214   I                          ************** I
   11         0.468    0.241    1.940   I                          ************* I
   12         0.413    0.245    1.685   I                          *********** I
   13         0.359    0.248    1.445   I                          ********** I
   14         0.305    0.251    1.218   I                          ******** I
   15         0.253    0.252    1.001   I                          ******* I
   16         0.201    0.253    0.791   I                          ****** I
   17         0.150    0.254    0.589   I                          **** I
   18         0.098    0.255    0.387   I                          *** I
   19         0.047    0.255    0.185   I                          * I
   20        -0.003    0.255   -0.012   I                         * I
   21        -0.052    0.255   -0.205   I                        ** I
   22        -0.101    0.255   -0.397   I                       *** I
   23        -0.151    0.255   -0.591   I                      **** I
   24        -0.200    0.255   -0.783   I                     ***** I
                                        +--------------------------+------------------------------+
```

Figure 5.21 Sample ACF for time series 5.2

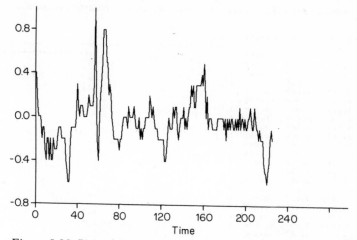

Figure 5.22 Plot of first regular differences of time series 5.2

DIFFERENCED (WORKING) SERIES W(T)=(1-B^{12})^0 (1-B)^1 Z(T)

    1 OBSERVATIONS LOST IN DIFFERENCING
    225 OBSERVATIONS IN THE WORKING SERIES

MEAN AND STANDARD DEVIATION OF THE WORKING SERIES   IDENTIFICATION RUN
MEAN=   -0.3467E-01
STANDARD DEVIATION=   0.2312E 00

AUTOCORRELATION FUNCTION OF THE WORKING SERIES   IDENTIFICATION RUN

```
         VALUE    S.E.   T VALUE   -1.0                    0.0                    1.0
                                   +--------------------------------------------------+
    1    0.805    0.067   12.082   I                       *********************** I
    2    0.653    0.101    6.457   I                       ****************** I
    3    0.526    0.118    4.446   I                       ************** I
    4    0.442    0.128    3.444   I                       *************I
    5    0.380    0.135    2.815   I                       **********I
    6    0.318    0.140    2.282   I                       *********I
    7    0.262    0.143    1.833   I                       *******I
    8    0.186    0.145    1.286   I                       *****I
    9    0.139    0.146    0.952   I                       ****I
   10    0.144    0.146    0.983   I                       ****I
   11    0.097    0.147    0.656   I                       ***I
   12    0.094    0.147    0.640   I                       ***I
   13    0.074    0.148    0.500   I                       **I
   14    0.073    0.148    0.496   I                       **I
   15    0.070    0.148    0.476   I                       **I
   16    0.072    0.148    0.485   I                       **I
   17    0.089    0.148    0.600   I                       ***I
   18    0.048    0.149    0.321   I                       **I
   19    0.041    0.149    0.278   I                       **I
   20    0.040    0.149    0.268   I                       **I
   21    0.044    0.149    0.293   I                       **I
   22    0.048    0.149    0.321   I                       **I
   23    0.000    0.149    0.002   I                       *I
   24   -0.052    0.149   -0.351   I                       **I
                                   +--------------------------------------------------+
```

Figure 5.23 Sample ACF for first regular differences of time series 5.2

PARTIAL AUTOCORRELATION FUNCTION OF THE WORKING SERIES   IDENTIFICATION RUN

	VALUE	S.E.	T VALUE	-1.0	0.0	1.0
1	0.805	0.067	12.082	I	**********************	I
2	0.010	0.067	0.157	I	*	I
3	-0.007	0.067	-0.108	I	*	I
4	0.051	0.067	0.759	I	**	I
5	0.027	0.067	0.406	I	*	I
6	-0.019	0.067	-0.290	I	*	I
7	-0.013	0.067	-0.198	I	*	I
8	-0.080	0.067	-1.200	I	**	I
9	0.020	0.067	0.307	I	*	I
10	0.117	0.067	1.755	I	****	I
11	-0.137	0.067	-2.049	I	****	I
12	0.094	0.067	1.404	I	***	I
13	-0.027	0.067	-0.401	I	*	I
14	0.034	0.067	0.516	I	*	I
15	0.006	0.067	0.094	I	*	I
16	0.012	0.067	0.173	I	*	I
17	0.043	0.067	0.646	I	**	I
18	-0.121	0.067	-1.818	I	****	I
19	0.060	0.067	0.901	I	**	I
20	-0.005	0.067	-0.076	I	*	I
21	0.038	0.067	0.568	I	*	I
22	-0.022	0.067	-0.328	I	*	I
23	-0.116	0.067	-1.742	I	***	I
24	-0.076	0.067	-1.133	I	**	I

Figure 5.24 Sample PACF for first regular differences of time series 5.2

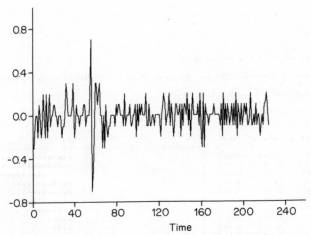

Figure 5.25 Plot of second regular differences of time
series 5.2

regular differences, no constant term is included in the model. From Figure 5.27, we see that the fitted ARI(1, 1) model is

$$Z_t = (1.8239)\,Z_{t-1} - (0.8239)\,Z_{t-2} + A_t.$$

The usual diagnostic checks do not detect any model inadequacies and are not given here. The results of overfitting an ARI(2, 1) model and an ARIMA (1, 1, 1)

DIFFERENCED (WORKING) SERIES w(T)=(1-B^{12})^0 (1-B)^2 Z(T)

2 OBSERVATIONS LOST IN DIFFERENCING
224 OBSERVATIONS IN THE WORKING SERIES

MEAN AND STANDARD DEVIATION OF THE WORKING SERIES
MEAN= -0.2679E-02
STANDARD DEVIATION= 0.1411E 00

AUTOCORRELATION FUNCTION OF THE WORKING SERIES

```
        VALUE    S.E.   T VALUE  -1.0                         0.0                        1.0
                                  +----------------------------------------------------------------+
 1     -0.079   0.067  -1.182    I                            **                                  I
 2     -0.065   0.067  -0.974    I                            **                                  I
 3     -0.122   0.068  -1.806    I                          ****                                  I
 4     -0.063   0.068  -0.926    I                            **                                  I
 5      0.013   0.069   0.193    I                             *                                  I
 6     -0.018   0.069  -0.266    I                             *                                  I
 7      0.049   0.069   0.717    I                            **                                  I
 8     -0.052   0.069  -0.753    I                            **                                  I
 9     -0.124   0.069  -1.791    I                          ****                                  I
10      0.122   0.070   1.735    I                            ****                                I
11     -0.122   0.071  -1.713    I                          ****                                  I
12      0.072   0.072   1.004    I                            **                                  I
13     -0.077   0.072  -1.060    I                            **                                  I
14      0.029   0.073   0.405    I                             *                                  I
15     -0.011   0.073  -0.153    I                             *                                  I
16     -0.058   0.073  -0.804    I                            **                                  I
17      0.171   0.073   2.361    I                            *****                               I
18     -0.101   0.075  -1.356    I                           ***                                  I
19     -0.013   0.075  -0.178    I                             *                                  I
20     -0.020   0.075  -0.268    I                             *                                  I
21     -0.007   0.075  -0.089    I                             *                                  I
22      0.135   0.075   1.795    I                            ****                                I
23      0.014   0.076   0.177    I                             *                                  I
24     -0.013   0.076  -0.177    I                             *                                  I
                                  +----------------------------------------------------------------+
```

Figure 5.26 Sample ACF for second regular differences of time series 5.2

ESTIMATION RUN USING ARI(1,1) MODEL

ESTIMATED EXPANDED MODEL LAG COEFFICIENTS

AUTOREGRESSIVE TERMS
            1   2
          1.8239   -0.8239

MOVING AVERAGE TERMS

            NONE

Figure 5.27 The fitted ARI(1, 1) model for
time series 5.2

model are shown in Table 5.2. Both overfits are rejected and the ARI(1, 1) model is regarded as the best available model for time series 5.2. The forecasts at origin 226 for the next 10 time periods are given in Figure 5.28 and plotted in Figure 5.29. The reader will recall that, for an ARI(1, 1) model with no constant term, the forecasts tend to a horizontal straight line as the lead time increases.

154

FORECASTS FROM PERIOD 226

PERIOD	FORECAST	95 PERCENT LIMITS LOWER	UPPER
227	18.635	18.372	18.898
228	18.499	17.952	19.046
229	18.387	17.531	19.243
230	18.295	17.120	19.470
231	18.219	16.723	19.716
232	18.156	16.342	19.971
233	18.105	15.978	20.231
234	18.062	15.632	20.493
235	18.027	15.302	20.752
236	17.998	14.988	21.008

Figure 5.28 Forecasts for time series 5.2 using the ARI(1, 1) model

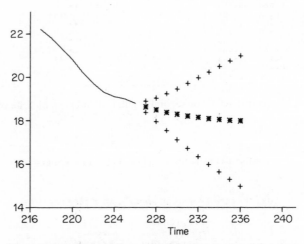

Figure 5.29 Plot of forecasts for time series 5.2 using the ARI(1, 1) model. —— Time series, *** forecasts, +++ 95% prediction limits

5.7 EXAMPLE 5.3

In this section we analyse time series 5.3 in Appendix A.3. The plot of the time series is shown in Figure 5.30 and seems to indicate that the time series is non-stationary in the mean due to random changes in mean level. The means and standard deviations of subsets of the time series are given in Table 5.8 and plotted in Figure 5.31, which indicates that the time series is stationary in the variance. Plots of the first and second regular differences are given in Figures 5.33 and 5.36,

Table 5.2 Fitted models for time series 5.2

Model type	Fitted model $(W_t = Z_t - Z_{t-1})$	Residual variance	Q statistic
ARI(1, 1)	$W_t = (0.8239)\, W_{t-1} + A_t$ $(t = 21.5462)$	0.0180	21.306
ARI(2, 1)	$W_t = (0.8310)\, W_{t-1} - (0.0086)\, W_{t-2} + A_t$ $(t = 12.4052) \quad (t = -0.1282)$	0.0181	25.434
ARIMA- (1, 1, 1)	$W_t = (0.8207)\, W_{t-1} + A_t + (0.0101)\, A_{t-1}$ $(t = 17.5438) \qquad (t = -0.1248)$	0.0181	25.424

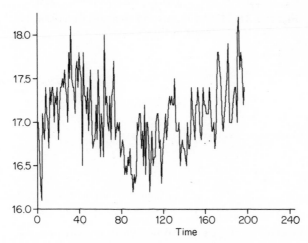

Figure 5.30 Plot of time series 5.3

which indicate that these time series appear to be stationary in the mean. However, taking more than one regular difference appears to result in overdifferencing, as the second regular differences have greater variability than the first regular differences. This is confirmed by the sample ACF's of time series 5.3 and of its first and second regular differences, given in Figures 5.32, 5.34, and 5.37. The sample ACF of time series 5.3 dies down extremely slowly, while that of its first regular differences appears to cut off after lag one and that of its second regular differences appears to cut off after lag 2. A study of the sample standard deviations of time series 5.3 and of its first and second regular differences indicates that taking two regular differences will result in overdiffercncing. Consequently the class of ARIMA- $(p, 1, q)$ models is an appropriate class for time series 5.3. The sample PACF of the first regular differences is shown in Figure 5.35 and tails off towards zero, while the sample ACF of the first regular differences cuts off after lag one, as shown in Figure 5.34. From Table 5.7, we see that the IMA(1, 1) model is an

156

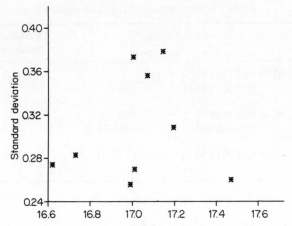

Figure 5.31 Plot of means and standard deviations of
subsets of time series 5.3

                                            12 0   0
DIFFERENCED (WORKING) SERIES W(T)=(1-B   ) (1-B) Z(T)

    0 OBSERVATIONS LOST IN DIFFERENCING
    197 OBSERVATIONS IN THE WORKING SERIES

MEAN AND STANDARD DEVIATION OF THE WORKING SERIES   IDENTIFICATION RUN
MEAN=   0.1706E 02
STANDARD DEVIATION=   0.3592E 00

AUTOCORRELATION FUNCTION OF THE WORKING SERIES   IDENTIFICATION RUN

            VALUE   S.E.   T VALUE -1.0   0.0   1.0
                                    +---+
     1   0.570   0.071   8.003   I   *************** **   I
     2   0.495   0.092   5.409   I   **************   I
     3   0.398   0.104   3.818   I   ***********   I
     4   0.356   0.112   3.185   I   *********   I
     5   0.327   0.117   2.787   I   *********   I
     6   0.350   0.122   2.871   I   **********   I
     7   0.392   0.127   3.090   I   ***********   I
     8   0.322   0.133   2.420   I   *********   I
     9   0.304   0.137   2.224   I   ********   I
    10   0.255   0.140   1.819   I   *******   I
    11   0.188   0.142   1.321   I   *****   I
    12   0.163   0.144   1.136   I   *****   I
    13   0.195   0.145   1.346   I   ******   I
    14   0.236   0.146   1.617   I   *******   I
    15   0.140   0.148   0.949   I   ****   I
    16   0.180   0.149   1.212   I   *****   I
    17   0.197   0.150   1.313   I   ******   I
    18   0.202   0.151   1.339   I   ******   I
    19   0.140   0.152   0.920   I   ****   I
    20   0.183   0.153   1.198   I   *****   I
    21   0.100   0.154   0.649   I   ***   I
    22   0.125   0.154   0.811   I   ****   I
    23   0.105   0.155   0.679   I   ***   I
    24   0.141   0.155   0.909   I   ****   I
                                    +---+

Figure 5.32 Sample ACF for time series 5.3

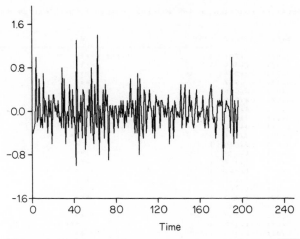

Figure 5.33 Plot of first regular differences of time series 5.3

DIFFERENCED (WORKING) SERIES W(T)=(1-B) (1-B) Z(T)

    1 OBSERVATIONS LOST IN DIFFERENCING
  196 OBSERVATIONS IN THE WORKING SERIES

MEAN AND STANDARD DEVIATION OF THE WORKING SERIES   IDENTIFICATION RUN
MEAN=   0.2041E-02
STANDARD DEVIATION=   0.3703E 00

AUTOCORRELATION FUNCTION OF THE WORKING SERIES   IDENTIFICATION RUN

	VALUE	S.E.	T VALUE	-1.0	0.0	1.0
1	-0.413	0.071	-5.781	I	***********	I
2	0.019	0.083	0.225	I	*	I
3	-0.066	0.083	-0.797	I	**	I
4	-0.011	0.083	-0.131	I	*	I
5	-0.069	0.083	-0.826	I	**	I
6	-0.020	0.083	-0.244	I	*	I
7	0.146	0.083	1.746	I	****	I
8	-0.068	0.085	-0.800	I	**	I
9	0.037	0.085	0.436	I	*	I
10	0.021	0.085	0.246	I	*	I
11	-0.046	0.085	-0.541	I	**	I
12	-0.064	0.085	-0.747	I	**	I
13	-0.011	0.085	-0.131	I	*	I
14	0.160	0.085	1.875	I	*****	I
15	-0.171	0.087	-1.964	I	*****	I
16	0.033	0.089	0.371	I	*	I
17	0.014	0.089	0.156	I	*	I
18	0.082	0.089	0.924	I	***	I
19	-0.123	0.089	-1.382	I	****	I
20	0.151	0.090	1.681	I	****	I
21	-0.128	0.091	-1.398	I	****	I
22	0.047	0.092	0.507	I	**	I
23	-0.067	0.092	-0.722	I	**	I
24	0.047	0.092	0.513	I	**	I

Figure 5.34 Sample ACF for first regular differences of time series 5.3

158

	VALUE	S.E.	T VALUE	-1.0	0.0	1.0
1	-0.413	0.071	-5.781	I	**********	I
2	-0.183	0.071	-2.564	I	*****	I
3	-0.165	0.071	-2.314	I	*****	I
4	-0.139	0.071	-1.947	I	****	I
5	-0.193	0.071	-2.696	I	*****	I
6	-0.214	0.071	-2.995	I	******	I
7	-0.002	0.071	-0.030	I	*	I
8	-0.047	0.071	-0.653	I	**	I
9	-0.018	0.071	-0.258	I	*	I
10	0.041	0.071	0.581	I	**	I
11	-0.005	0.071	-0.076	I	*	I
12	-0.077	0.071	-1.072	I	**	I
13	-0.102	0.071	-1.427	I	***	I
14	0.103	0.071	1.443	I	***	I
15	-0.085	0.071	-1.191	I	***	I
16	-0.127	0.071	-1.779	I	****	I
17	-0.096	0.071	-1.343	I	***	I
18	0.045	0.071	0.636	I	**	I
19	-0.074	0.071	-1.032	I	**	I
20	0.091	0.071	1.275	I	***	I
21	-0.074	0.071	-1.040	I	**	I
22	0.016	0.071	0.228	I	*	I
23	-0.066	0.071	-0.921	I	**	I
24	-0.043	0.071	-0.601	I	**	I

Figure 5.35 Sample PACF for first regular differences of time series 5.3

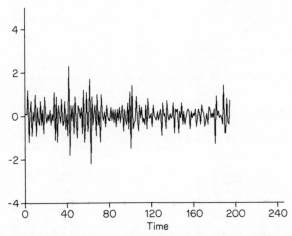

Figure 5.36 Plot of second regular differences of
time series 5.3

appropriate model for time series 5.3. Since the sample mean of the first regular differences is not large compared with the sample standard deviation, no constant term is included in the model. From Figure 5.38, we see that the fitted IMA(1, 1) model is

$$Z_t = Z_{t-1} + A_t - (0.7051) A_{t-1}.$$

```
                                12  0      2
DIFFERENCED (WORKING) SERIES W(T)=(1-B   ) (1-B) Z(T)


    2 OBSERVATIONS LOST IN DIFFERENCING
  195 OBSERVATIONS IN THE WORKING SERIES

MEAN AND STANDARD DEVIATION OF THE WORKING SERIES
MEAN=    0.3077E-02
STANDARD DEVIATION=    0.6232E 00

AUTOCORRELATION FUNCTION OF THE WORKING SERIES


            VALUE    S.E.   T VALUE  -1.0                      0.0                         1.0
                                      +----------------------------------------------------------+
   1       -0.652    0.072   -9.106   I          *****************                               I
   2        0.183    0.097    1.874   I                       *****                              I
   3       -0.044    0.099   -0.443   I                      **                                  I
   4        0.036    0.099    0.360   I                       *                                  I
   5       -0.039    0.099   -0.394   I                       *                                  I
   6       -0.040    0.099   -0.403   I                      **                                  I
   7        0.133    0.099    1.341   I                       ****                               I
   8       -0.113    0.100   -1.124   I                     ***                                  I
   9        0.042    0.101    0.411   I                       **                                 I
  10        0.023    0.101    0.231   I                       *                                  I
  11       -0.023    0.101   -0.223   I                       *                                  I
  12       -0.022    0.101   -0.219   I                       *                                  I
  13       -0.043    0.101   -0.427   I                      **                                  I
  14        0.178    0.101    1.761   I                       *****                              I
  15       -0.139    0.103   -1.839   I                     *****                                I
  16        0.078    0.105    0.742   I                       ***                                I
  17       -0.030    0.105   -0.282   I                       *                                  I
  18        0.093    0.105    0.884   I                       ***                                I
  19       -0.165    0.105   -1.570   I                     *****                                I
  20        0.197    0.107    1.845   I                       ******                             I
  21       -0.161    0.109   -1.485   I                     *****                                I
  22        0.102    0.110    0.924   I                       ***                                I
  23       -0.081    0.110   -0.739   I                     ***                                  I
  24        0.058    0.111    0.522   I                      **                                  I
                                      +----------------------------------------------------------+
```

Figure 5.37 Sample ACF for second regular differences of time series 5.3


```
          ESTIMATION RUN USING IMA(1,1) MODEL


          ESTIMATED EXPANDED MODEL LAG COEFFICIENTS

          AUTOREGRESSIVE TERMS
                     1
                  1.0000

          MOVING AVERAGE TERMS
                     1
                  0.7051
```

Figure 5.38 The fitted IMA(1, 1) model for
time series 5.3

The usual diagnostic checks do not detect any model inadequacies and are not given here. The results of overfitting an ARIMA(1, 1, 1) model and an IMA(1, 2) model are shown in Table 5.3. Both overfits are rejected and the IMA(1, 1) model is regarded as the best available model for time series 5.3. The forecasts at origin 197 for the next 10 time periods are given in Figure 5.39 and plotted in Figure 5.40. The reader will recall that, for an IMA(1, 1) model with no constant term,

Table 5.3 Fitted models for time series 5.3

Model type	Fitted model $(W_t = Z_t - Z_{t-1})$	Residual variance	Q statistic
IMA(1, 1)	$W_t = A_t - (0.7051) A_{t-1}$ $(t = 13.9032)$	0.1009	28.379
ARIMA- (1, 1, 1)	$W_t = (0.2187) W_{t-1} + A_t - (0.8252) A_{t-1}$ $(t = 2.3251)$ $(t = 15.3052)$	0.0994	22.183
IMA(1, 2)	$W_t = A_t - (0.6316) A_{t-1} - (0.1232) A_{t-2}$ $(t = 8.8747)$ $(t = 1.7270)$	0.0998	23.425

ESTIMATION RUN USING IMA(1.1) MODEL

FORECASTS FROM PERIOD 197

```
                       95 PERCENT LIMITS
PERIOD    FORECAST    LOWER       UPPER
------------------------------------------
 198      17.505      16.883      18.128
 199      17.505      16.856      18.154
 200      17.505      16.831      18.180
 201      17.505      16.806      18.205
 202      17.505      16.782      18.228
 203      17.505      16.759      18.251
 204      17.505      16.737      18.273
 205      17.505      16.716      18.295
 206      17.505      16.695      18.316
 207      17.505      16.674      18.337
```

Figure 5.39 Forecasts for time series 5.3 using the IMA(1, 1) model

the forecasts for all future time periods coincide with the forecast for the next time period, which is 17.705 in the present example. The complete TSERIES program for this example is given as program A.5.3 in Appendix A.5.

5.8 EXERCISES

5.8.1 Time series 5.4, 5.5, and 5.6 are given in Appendix A.3. Figures 5.41 to 5.64 provide relevant information for these time series. Identify tentative models for these time series.

5.8.2 Fitted models for these time series are shown in Tables 5.4 to 5.6. Which fitted model do you consider most appropriate for each time series?

5.8.3   (This exercise is intended for readers with access to computer packages using the Box–Jenkins approach and the only information provided about each time series is the time series itself.) Indentify tentative models for time series 6.7, 6.11, and 6.13 in Appendix A.3.

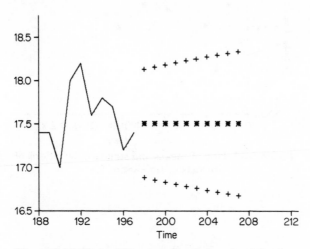

Figure 5.40 Plot of forecasts for time series 5.3 using
the IMA(1, 1) model. —— Time series, *** forecasts,
+++ 95% prediction limits

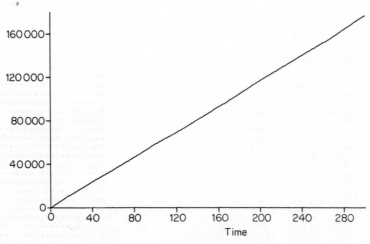

Figure 5.41 Plot of time series 5.4

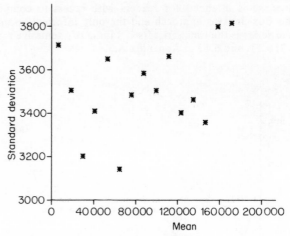

Figure 5.42 Plot of means and standard deviations of
subsets of time series 5.4

$$\text{DIFFERENCED (WORKING) SERIES } W(T)=(1-B^{12}) \; (1-B)^0 \; Z(T)$$

```
        0 OBSERVATICNS LOST IN CIFFERENCING
      300 OBSERVATIONS IN THE WORKING SERIES

MEAN AND STANDARD DEVIATION OF THE WORKING SERIES        IDENTIFICATION RUN
MEAN=    0.8798E 05
STANDARD DEVIATION=    0.5080E C5

AUTOCORRELATICN FUNCTICN OF THE WORKING SERIES    IDENTIFICATION RUN


            VALUE   S.E.   T VALUE  -1.0                    0.0                    1.0
                                     +-------------------------------------------------+
      1     0.990   0.058   17.144   I                      ***************************** I
      2     0.980   0.099    9.863   I                      ***************************** I
      3     0.970   0.128    7.602   I                      ****************************  I
      4     0.959   0.150    6.392   I                      ***************************   I
      5     0.949   0.169    5.606   I                      **************************    I
      6     0.939   0.186    5.043   I                      **************************    I
      7     0.929   0.201    4.613   I                      *************************     I
      8     0.919   0.215    4.270   I                      *************************     I
      9     0.909   0.228    3.989   I                      ************************      I
     10     0.899   0.240    3.750   I                      ************************      I
     11     0.889   0.251    3.545   I                      ***********************       I
     12     0.879   0.261    3.367   I                      ***********************       I
     13     0.869   0.271    3.210   I                      **********************        I
     14     0.859   0.280    3.069   I                      **********************        I
     15     0.849   0.288    2.943   I                      *********************         I
     16     0.839   0.297    2.828   I                      *********************         I
     17     0.829   0.304    2.723   I                      *********************         I
     18     0.819   0.312    2.626   I                      ********************          I
     19     0.809   0.319    2.536   I                      ********************          I
     20     0.799   0.326    2.453   I                      ********************          I
     21     0.789   0.332    2.375   I                      *******************           I
     22     0.779   0.338    2.303   I                      *******************           I
     23     0.769   0.344    2.235   I                      *******************           I
     24     0.759   0.350    2.170   I                      ******************            I
                                     +-------------------------------------------------+
```

Figure 5.43 Sample ACF for time series 5.4

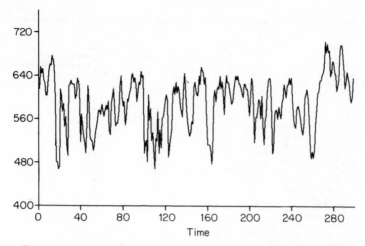

Figure 5.44 Plot of first regular differences of time series 5.4

DIFFERENCED (WORKING) SERIES W(T)=(1-B^{12})^0(1-B)^1 Z(T)

1 OBSERVATIONS LOST IN DIFFERENCING
299 OBSERVATIONS IN THE WORKING SERIES

MEAN AND STANDARD DEVIATION OF THE WORKING SERIES   IDENTIFICATION RUN
MEAN=   0.5907E 03
STANDARD DEVIATION=   0.4977E 02

AUTOCORRELATION FUNCTION OF THE WORKING SERIES   IDENTIFICATION RUN

```
        VALUE   S.E.   T VALUE  -1.0                   0.0                      1.0
                                 +--------------------------------------------------+
 1      0.781   0.058  13.509   I                      ****************************  I
 2      0.568   0.086   6.590   I                      ******************           I
 3      0.373   0.098   3.857   I                      ***********                  I
 4      0.237   0.103   2.307   I                      *******                      I
 5      0.195   0.104   1.871   I                      ******                       I
 6      0.177   0.106   1.675   I                      *****                        I
 7      0.221   0.107   2.069   I                      ******                       I
 8      0.230   0.108   2.124   I                      ******                       I
 9      0.197   0.110   1.791   I                      ******                       I
10      0.107   0.111   0.963   I                      ***                          I
11      0.036   0.111   0.326   I                      *                            I
12     -0.028   0.111  -0.251   I                      *                            I
13     -0.052   0.111  -0.464   I                     **                            I
14     -0.048   0.111  -0.429   I                     **                            I
15     -0.027   0.112  -0.240   I                      *                            I
16      0.015   0.112   0.133   I                      *                            I
17      0.045   0.112   0.401   I                      **                           I
18      0.051   0.112   0.453   I                      **                           I
19      0.029   0.112   0.260   I                      *                            I
20      0.035   0.112   0.313   I                      *                            I
21      0.015   0.112   0.136   I                      *                            I
22     -0.005   0.112  -0.045   I                      *                            I
23     -0.016   0.112  -0.140   I                      *                            I
24     -0.061   0.112  -0.542   I                     **                            I
                                 +--------------------------------------------------+
```

Figure 5.45 Sample ACF for first regular differences of time series 5.4

164

	VALUE	S.E.	T VALUE	-1.0	0.0	1.0
1	0.781	0.058	13.509	I	*********************	
2	-0.109	0.058	-1.880	I	***	
3	-0.076	0.058	-1.320	I	**	
4	-0.009	0.058	-0.147	I	*	
5	0.143	0.058	2.465	I	****	
6	0.010	0.058	0.169	I	*	
7	0.148	0.058	2.554	I	****	
8	-0.039	0.058	-0.671	I	*	
9	-0.048	0.058	-0.831	I	**	
10	-0.134	0.058	-2.315	I	****	
11	0.046	0.058	0.789	I	**	
12	-0.066	0.058	-1.147	I	**	
13	0.036	0.058	0.623	I	*	
14	-0.028	0.058	-0.488	I	*	
15	0.030	0.058	0.527	I	*	
16	0.024	0.058	0.419	I	*	
17	0.056	0.058	0.968	I	**	
18	-0.024	0.058	-0.412	I	*	
19	-0.009	0.058	-0.134	I	*	
20	0.073	0.058	1.269	I	**	
21	-0.053	0.058	-0.913	I	**	
22	-0.036	0.058	-0.629	I	*	
23	-0.007	0.058	-0.118	I	*	
24	-0.122	0.058	-2.105	I	****	

Figure 5.46 Sample PACF for first regular differences of time series 5.4

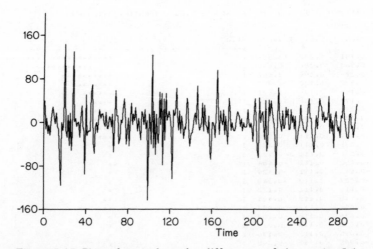

Figure 5.47 Plot of second regular differences of time series 5.4

DIFFERENCED (WORKING) SERIES w(T)=(1-B^{12})^0 (1-B)^2 Z(T)

2 OBSERVATIONS LOST IN DIFFERENCING
298 OBSERVATIONS IN THE WORKING SERIES

MEAN AND STANDARD DEVIATION OF THE WORKING SERIES
MEAN=   0.7047E-01
STANDARD DEVIATION=   0.3253E 02

AUTOCORRELATION FUNCTION OF THE WORKING SERIES

```
        VALUE    S.E.   T VALUE   -1.0                    0.0                        1.0
                                  +----------------------------------------------------+
 1     -0.011    0.058   -0.190   I                        *                           I
 2     -0.050    0.058   -0.866   I                       **                           I
 3     -0.116    0.058   -1.999   I                      ***                           I
 4     -0.232    0.059   -3.937   I                   ******                           I
 5     -0.053    0.062   -0.865   I                       **                           I
 6     -0.143    0.062   -2.311   I                     ****                           I
 7      0.082    0.063    1.301   I                        ***                         I
 8      0.098    0.063    1.539   I                        ***                         I
 9      0.124    0.064    1.944   I                        ****                        I
10     -0.050    0.065   -0.765   I                       **                           I
11     -0.017    0.065   -0.262   I                        *                           I
12     -0.095    0.065   -1.460   I                      ***                           I
13     -0.062    0.065   -0.943   I                       **                           I
14     -0.031    0.066   -0.472   I                        *                           I
15     -0.041    0.066   -0.625   I                       **                           I
16      0.038    0.066    0.575   I                        *                           I
17      0.051    0.066    0.780   I                        **                          I
18      0.063    0.066    0.958   I                        **                          I
19     -0.066    0.066   -1.001   I                       **                           I
20      0.048    0.066    0.717   I                        **                          I
21      0.005    0.066    0.074   I                        *                           I
22     -0.019    0.066   -0.282   I                        *                           I
23      0.071    0.066    1.068   I                        **                          I
24     -0.064    0.067   -0.962   I                       **                           I
                                  +----------------------------------------------------+
```

Figure 5.48 Sample ACF for second regular differences of time series 5.4

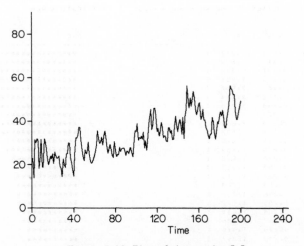

Figure 5.49 Plot of time series 5.5

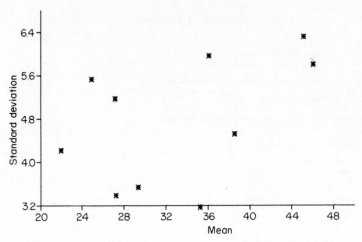

Figure 5.50 Plot of means and standard deviations of subsets of
time series 5.5

```
                                          12  0      0
DIFFERENCED (WORKING) SERIES W(T)=(1-B  ) (1-B) Z(T)


     0 OBSERVATIONS LOST IN DIFFERENCING
     200 OBSERVATIONS IN THE WORKING SERIES

MEAN AND STANDARD DEVIATION OF THE WORKING SERIES       IDENTIFICATION RUN
MEAN=   0.3316E 02
STANDARD DEVIATION=   0.5274E 01

AUTOCORRELATION FUNCTION OF THE WORKING SERIES    IDENTIFICATION RUN


         VALUE    S.E.    T VALUE   -1.0                    0.0                              1.0
                                    +-----------------------+--------------------------------+
  1      0.875    0.071   12.377    I                       ********************             I
  2      0.774    0.113    6.880    I                       ***********************          I
  3      0.724    0.137    5.302    I                       *********************            I
  4      0.680    0.155    4.451    I                       ********************             I
  5      0.671    0.169    3.967    I                       ********************             I
  6      0.656    0.182    3.604    I                       *******************              I
  7      0.634    0.193    3.278    I                       *******************              I
  8      0.619    0.204    3.041    I                       ******************               I
  9      0.608    0.213    2.856    I                       *****************                I
 10      0.576    0.221    2.603    I                       *****************                I
 11      0.536    0.229    2.346    I                       ***************                  I
 12      0.507    0.235    2.159    I                       **************                   I
 13      0.475    0.240    1.978    I                       *************                    I
 14      0.446    0.245    1.819    I                       ************                     I
 15      0.426    0.249    1.710    I                       ************                     I
 16      0.432    0.253    1.708    I                       ************                     I
 17      0.441    0.256    1.722    I                       ************                     I
 18      0.437    0.260    1.682    I                       ************                     I
 19      0.425    0.264    1.611    I                       ***********                      I
 20      0.397    0.267    1.486    I                       ***********                      I
 21      0.382    0.270    1.416    I                       **********                       I
 22      0.367    0.273    1.347    I                       **********                       I
 23      0.365    0.275    1.328    I                       **********                       I
 24      0.387    0.278    1.394    I                       **********                       I
                                    +-----------------------+--------------------------------+
```

Figure 5.51 Sample ACF for time series 5.5

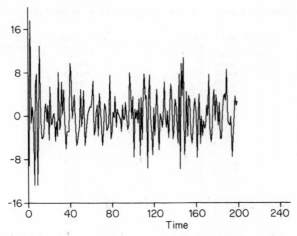

Figure 5.52 Plot of first regular differences of time series 5.5

```
                                      12  0     1
DIFFERENCED (WORKING) SERIES W(T)=(1-B   ) (1-B) Z(T)


        1 OBSERVATIONS LOST IN DIFFERENCING
       199 OBSERVATIONS IN THE WORKING SERIES

MEAN AND STANDARD DEVIATION OF THE WORKING SERIES        IDENTIFICATION RUN
MEAN=   0.1332E 00
STANDARD DEVIATION=   0.4438E 01

AUTCCORRELATION FUNCTION OF THE WORKING SERIES    IDENTIFICATION RUN


         VALUE    S.E.   T VALUE  -1.0                 0.0                 1.0
                                  +------------------------------------------+
  1     -0.118   0.071   -1.662   I                   ***                    I
  2     -0.171   0.072   -2.374   I                 *****                    I
  3     -0.050   0.074   -0.672   I                   **                     I
  4     -0.079   0.074   -1.073   I                   **                     I
  5     -0.026   0.074   -0.347   I                    *                     I
  6     -0.037   0.075   -0.503   I                    *                     I
  7     -0.016   0.075   -0.216   I                    *                     I
  8     -0.004   0.075   -0.050   I                    *                     I
  9      0.048   0.075    0.640   I                    **                    I
 10      0.031   0.075    0.413   I                    *                     I
 11      0.023   0.075    0.306   I .                  *                     I
 12      0.022   0.075    0.292   I                    *                     I
 13     -0.005   0.075   -0.065   I                    *                     I
 14     -0.039   0.075   -0.523   I                    *                     I
 15     -0.120   0.075   -1.594   I                  ***                     I
 16     -0.030   0.076   -0.396   I                    *                     I
 17      0.047   0.076    0.622   I                    **                    I
 18      0.044   0.076    0.584   I                    **                    I
 19      0.066   0.076    0.861   I                    **                    I
 20     -0.066   0.077   -0.862   I                   **                     I
 21      0.033   0.077    0.430   I                    *                     I
 22     -0.065   0.077   -0.844   I                   **                     I
 23     -0.088   0.077   -1.142   I                  ***                     I
 24      0.093   0.078    1.191   I                    ***                   I
                                  +------------------------------------------+
```

Figure 5.53 Sample ACF for first regular differences of time series 5.5

PARTIAL AUTOCORRELATION FUNCTION OF THE WORKING SERIES   IDENTIFICATION RUN

```
        VALUE   S.E.   T VALUE   -1.0                     0.0                          1.0
                                 +-------------------------------------------------------+
 1     -0.118   0.071   -1.662   I                        ***                            I
 2     -0.187   0.071   -2.640   I                        *****                          I
 3     -0.100   0.071   -1.417   I                        ***                            I
 4     -0.142   0.071   -1.999   I                        ****                           I
 5     -0.096   0.071   -1.355   I                        ***                            I
 6     -0.117   0.071   -1.651   I                        ***                            I
 7     -0.096   0.071   -1.349   I                        ***                            I
 8     -0.089   0.071   -1.255   I                        ***                            I
 9     -0.024   0.071   -0.335   I                        *                              I
10     -0.015   0.071   -0.211   I                        *                              I
11      0.008   0.071    0.118   I                        *                              I
12      0.025   0.071    0.353   I                        *                              I
13      0.019   0.071    0.266   I                        *                              I
14     -0.015   0.071   -0.209   I                        *                              I
15     -0.121   0.071   -1.702   I                        ****                           I
16     -0.084   0.071   -1.187   I                        ***                            I
17     -0.032   0.071   -0.456   I                        *                              I
18     -0.010   0.071   -0.141   I                        *                              I
19      0.037   0.071    0.517   I                        *                              I
20     -0.076   0.071   -1.076   I                        **                             I
21      0.011   0.071    0.155   I                        *                              I
22     -0.100   0.071   -1.417   I                        ***                            I
23     -0.134   0.071   -1.889   I                        ****                           I
24      0.017   0.071    0.242   I                        *                              I
                                 +-------------------------------------------------------+
```

Figure 5.54 Sample PACF for first regular differences of time series 5.5

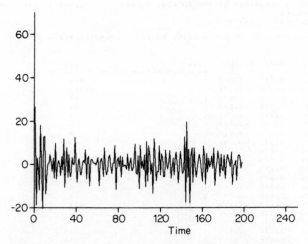

Figure 5.55 Plot of second regular differences of time
series 5.5

DIFFERENCED (WORKING) SERIES W(T)=(1-B^{12})^0 (1-B)^2 Z(T)

2 OBSERVATIONS LOST IN DIFFERENCING
198 OBSERVATIONS IN THE WORKING SERIES

MEAN AND STANDARD DEVIATION OF THE WORKING SERIES
MEAN=   0.5960E-01
STANDARD DEVIATION=   0.6617E 01

AUTOCORRELATION FUNCTION OF THE WORKING SERIES

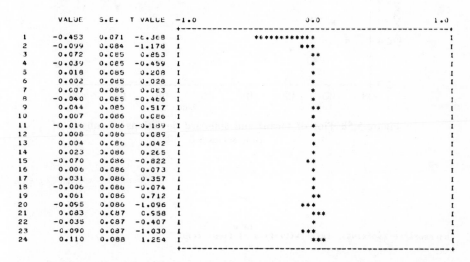

```
       VALUE   S.E.   T VALUE  -1.0                    0.0                    1.0
                              +------------------------------------------------+
 1    -0.453   0.071  -6.368   I          ************* I                       I
 2    -0.099   0.084  -1.178   I                  *** I                         I
 3     0.072   0.085   0.853   I                      ** I                      I
 4    -0.039   0.085  -0.459   I                     * I                        I
 5     0.018   0.085   0.208   I                      * I                       I
 6     0.002   0.085   0.028   I                      * I                       I
 7     0.007   0.085   0.083   I                      * I                       I
 8    -0.040   0.085  -0.466   I                     * I                        I
 9     0.044   0.085   0.517   I                      ** I                      I
10     0.007   0.086   0.086   I                      * I                       I
11    -0.016   0.086  -0.189   I                     * I                        I
12     0.008   0.086   0.089   I                      * I                       I
13     0.004   0.086   0.042   I                      * I                       I
14     0.023   0.086   0.265   I                      * I                       I
15    -0.070   0.086  -0.822   I                     ** I                       I
16     0.006   0.086   0.073   I                      * I                       I
17     0.031   0.086   0.357   I                      * I                       I
18    -0.006   0.086  -0.074   I                      * I                       I
19     0.061   0.086   0.712   I                      ** I                      I
20    -0.095   0.086  -1.096   I                  *** I                         I
21     0.083   0.087   0.958   I                      *** I                     I
22    -0.035   0.087  -0.407   I                     * I                        I
23    -0.090   0.087  -1.030   I                  *** I                         I
24     0.110   0.088   1.254   I                      *** I                     I
                              +------------------------------------------------+
```

Figure 5.56 Sample ACF for second regular differences of time sereis 5.5

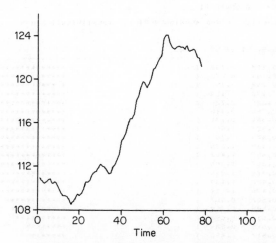

Figure 5.57 Plot of time series 5.6

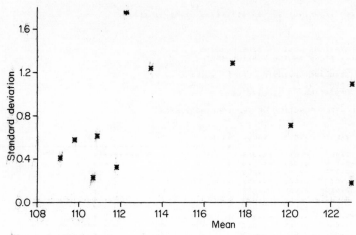

Figure 5.58 Plot of means and standard deviations of subsets of time series 5.6

DIFFERENCED (WORKING) SERIES W(T)=(1-B^{12})^0 (1-B)^0 Z(T)

    0 CBSERVATIONS LOST IN DIFFERENCING
    78 OBSERVATICNS IN THE WORKING SERIES

MEAN AND STANDARD DEVIATION UF THE WORKING SERIES   IDENTIFICATION RUN
MEAN=   0.1157E 03
STANDARD DEVIATION=   0.5506E 01

AUTCCORRELATION FUNCTION UF THE WORKING SERIES   IDENTIFICATION RUN

```
          VALUE   S.E.   T VALUE  -1.0                    0.0                    1.0
                                   +---------------------------------------------------+
   1     0.985   0.113   8.702   I                     ***********************  I
   2     0.965   0.194   4.970   I                     **********************   I
   3     0.942   0.248   3.795   I                     *********************    I
   4     0.916   0.290   3.154   I                     *********************    I
   5     0.888   0.325   2.729   I                     *********************    I
   6     0.859   0.355   2.418   I                     ********************     I
   7     0.827   0.381   2.171   I                     *******************      I
   8     0.792   0.403   1.965   I                     ******************       I
   9     0.757   0.423   1.792   I                     ******************       I
  10     0.720   0.440   1.638   I                     *****************        I
  11     0.681   0.455   1.497   I                     ****************         I
  12     0.638   0.467   1.366   I                     ****************         I
  13     0.596   0.478   1.245   I                     ***************          I
  14     0.551   0.488   1.130   I                     **************           I
  15     0.504   0.496   1.017   I                     *************            I
  16     0.455   0.502   0.907   I                     ************             I
  17     0.405   0.508   0.798   I                     ***********              I
  18     0.354   0.512   0.692   I                     **********               I
  19     0.303   0.515   0.589   I                     ********                 I
  20     0.255   0.517   0.494   I                     *******                  I
  21     0.207   0.519   0.400   I                     ******                   I
  22     0.160   0.520   0.308   I                     *****                    I
  23     0.115   0.520   0.221   I                     ***                      I
  24     0.070   0.521   0.135   I                     **                       I
                                   +---------------------------------------------------+
```

Figure 5.59 Sample ACF for time series 5.6

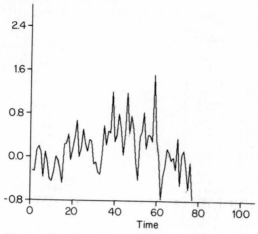

Figure 5.60 Plot of first regular differences of
time series 5.6

DIFFERENCED (WORKING) SERIES W(T)=(1-B^{12})^0 (1-B)^1 Z(T)

    1 CBSERVATICNS LOST IN DIFFERENCING
   77 OBSERVATIONS IN THE WORKING SERIES

MEAN AND STANDARD DEVIATION OF THE WORKING SERIES   IDENTIFICATION RUN
MEAN=   0.1336E 00
STANDARD DEVIATION=   0.4269E 00

AUTCCORRELATICN FUNCTION OF THE WORKING SERIES   IDENTIFICATION RUN

	VALUE	S.E.	T VALUE	-1.0	0.0	1.0
1	0.422	0.114	3.702	I	**********	I
2	0.272	0.133	2.046	I	********	I
3	0.162	0.140	1.157	I	*****	I
4	0.227	0.142	1.597	I	******	I
5	0.149	0.147	1.013	I	****	I
6	0.201	0.149	1.349	I	******	I
7	0.172	0.152	1.131	I	*****	I
8	0.026	0.155	0.170	I	*	I
9	0.040	0.155	0.253	I	**	I
10	0.054	0.155	0.352	I	**	I
11	0.177	0.155	1.139	I	*****	I
12	0.014	0.158	0.090	I	*	I
13	0.195	0.158	1.234	I	******	I
14	0.058	0.161	0.359	I	**	I
15	-0.076	0.161	-0.471	I	**	I
16	-0.180	0.162	-1.112	I	*****	I
17	0.076	0.164	0.463	I	**	I
18	0.016	0.165	0.096	I	*	I
19	-0.001	0.165	-0.008	I	*	I
20	0.041	0.165	0.245	I	**	I
21	0.001	0.165	0.003	I	*	I
22	-0.056	0.165	-0.338	I	**	I
23	-0.183	0.165	-1.109	I	*****	I
24	-0.036	0.168	-0.217	I	*	I

Figure 5.61 Sample ACF for first regular differences of time series 5.6

172

```
              VALUE    S.E.   T VALUE  -1.0                    0.0                           1.0
                                       +-------------------------------------------------------+
   1          0.422    0.114   3.702   I                        ***********                    I
   2          0.114    0.114   0.998   I                        ***                            I
   3          0.013    0.114   0.132   I                        *                              I
   4          0.162    0.114   1.419   I                        *****                          I
   5         -0.007    0.114  -0.061   I                        *                              I
   6          0.114    0.114   1.003   I                        ***                            I
   7          0.046    0.114   0.407   I                        **                             I
   8         -0.151    0.114  -1.325   I                    ****                               I
   9          0.041    0.114   0.361   I                        **                             I
  10          0.010    0.114   0.089   I                        *                              I
  11          0.146    0.114   1.277   I                        ****                           I
  12         -0.131    0.114  -1.152   I                    ****                               I
  13          0.222    0.114   1.949   I                        ******                         I
  14         -0.096    0.114  -0.843   I                     ***                               I
  15         -0.208    0.114  -1.821   I                  ******                               I
  16         -0.107    0.114  -0.941   I                     ***                               I
  17          0.204    0.114   1.788   I                        ******                         I
  18         -0.067    0.114  -0.591   I                      **                               I
  19          0.014    0.114   0.120   I                        *                              I
  20          0.083    0.114   0.732   I                        ***                            I
  21         -0.008    0.114  -0.073   I                        *                              I
  22         -0.079    0.114  -0.694   I                      **                               I
  23         -0.211    0.114  -1.852   I                  ******                               I
  24         -0.007    0.114  -0.057   I                        *                              I
                                       +-------------------------------------------------------+
```

Figure 5.62 Sample PACF for first regular differences of time series 5.6

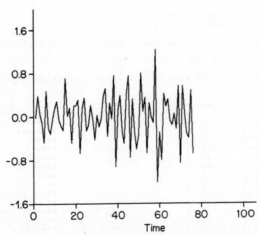

Figure 5.63 Plot of second regular differences
of time series 5.6

DIFFERENCED (WORKING) SERIES w(T)=(1-d^{12})^0 (1-B)^2 Z(T)

    2 OBSERVATIONS LOST IN DIFFERENCING
    76 OBSERVATIONS IN THE WORKING SERIES

MEAN AND STANDARD DEVIATION OF THE WORKING SERIES
MEAN= -0.6842E-02
STANDARD DEVIATION=   0.4430E 00

AUTOCORRELATION FUNCTION OF THE WORKING SERIES

```
        VALUE   S.E.   T VALUE  -1.0                        0.0                            1.0
                                +----------------------------------------------------------+
1      -0.353   0.115   -3.078   I                    *********                              I
2      -0.057   0.128   -0.445   I                          **                               I
3      -0.136   0.129   -1.062   I                        ****                               I
4       0.149   0.130    1.139   I                            ****                           I
5      -0.135   0.133   -1.020   I                        ****                               I
6       0.051   0.134    0.332   I                          **                               I
7       0.155   0.135    1.149   I                            *****                          I
8      -0.189   0.137   -1.379   I                       *****                               I
9       0.012   0.140    0.083   I                          *                                I
10     -0.099   0.140   -0.702   I                        ***                                I
11      0.279   0.141    1.971   I                          ********                         I
12     -0.313   0.148   -2.110   I                   ********                                I
13      0.269   0.157    1.713   I                          *******                          I
14     -0.021   0.163   -0.128   I                          *                                I
15     -0.035   0.163   -0.215   I                          *                                I
16     -0.282   0.163   -1.734   I                   ********                                I
17      0.312   0.169    1.845   I                          *********                        I
18      0.022   0.177    0.122   I                          *                                I
19     -0.123   0.177   -0.695   I                       ****                                I
20      0.087   0.178    0.487   I                          ***                              I
21      0.025   0.178    0.138   I                          *                                I
22      0.032   0.178    0.179   I                          *                                I
23     -0.207   0.178   -1.162   I                      ******                               I
24      0.220   0.182    1.211   I                          ******                           I
                                +----------------------------------------------------------+
```

Figure 5.64 Sample ACF for second regular differences of time series 5.6

Table 5.4 Fitted models for time series 5.4

Model type	Fitted model $(W_t = Z_t - Z_{t-1})$	Residual variance	Q statistic
ARI(1, 1)	$W_t = 127.4583 + (0.7842)\,W_{t-1} + A_t$ $\quad\quad\quad\quad\quad\quad (t = 21.7316)$	958.9731	36.373
ARI(2, 1)	$W_t = 141.7525 + (0.8706)\,W_{t-1} - (0.1106)\,W_{t-2} + A_t$ $\quad\quad\quad\quad\quad\quad (t = 15.0628) \quad\quad (t = -1.9129)$	950.8062	28.830
ARI(3, 1)	$W_t = 152.9852 + (0.8620)\,W_{t-1} - (0.0425)\,W_{t-2} - (0.0785)\,W_{t-3} + A_t$ $\quad\quad\quad\quad\quad\quad (t = 14.8471) \quad\quad (t = -0.5546) \quad (t = -1.3522)$	948.1292	25.435
ARIMA(2, 1, 1)	$W_t = 252.0225 - (0.0828)\,W_{t-1} + (0.6561)\,W_{t-2} + A_t + (0.9391)\,A_{t-1}$ $\quad\quad\quad\quad\quad\quad (t = -1.4917) \quad\quad (t = 12.2087) \quad\quad\quad\quad\quad (t = -37.5702)$	940.2690	30.687

Table 5.5 Fitted models for time series 5.5

Model type	Fitted model $(W_t = Z_t - Z_{t-1})$	Residual variance	Q statistic
IMA(1, 1)	$W_t = A_t - (0.1982)\,A_{t-1}$ $\quad\quad\quad\quad (t = 2.8400)$	19.2630	22.223
IMA(1, 2)	$W_t = A_t - (0.2290)\,A_{t-1} - (0.3220)\,A_{t-2}$ $\quad\quad\quad\quad (t = 3.3966) \quad\quad (t = 4.7766)$	18.0008	17.229
ARIMA(1, 1, 2)	$W_t = (0.5761)\,W_{t-1} + A_t - (0.7920)\,A_{t-1} - (0.1079)\,A_{t-2}$ $\quad\quad\quad (t = 5.1598) \quad\quad\quad\quad (t = 6.6128) \quad\quad (t = 1.1236)$	17.6917	14.065
IMA(1, 3)	$W_t = A_t - (0.2197)\,A_{t-1} - (0.2855)\,A_{t-2} - (0.1191)\,A_{t-3}$ $\quad\quad\quad\quad (t = 3.0977) \quad\quad (t = 4.0955) \quad\quad (t = 1.6795)$	17.9041	15.871

Table 5.6 Fitted models for time series 5.6

Model type	Fitted model $(W_t = Z_t - Z_{t-1})$	Residual variance	Q statistic
ARI(1, 1)	$W_t = (0.5060)\,W_{t-1} + A_t$ $(t = 4.9821)$	0.1511	29.853
ARIMA(1, 1, 1)	$W_t = (0.8676)\,W_{t-1} + A_t - (0.5437)\,A_{t-1}$ $(t = 8.7306)\qquad\qquad (t = 3.3254)$	0.1470	23.927
ARIMA(2, 1, 1)	$W_t = (1.1856)\,W_{t-1} - (0.2269)\,W_{t-2} + A_t - (0.8049)\,A_{t-1}$ $(t = 5.1982)\quad (t = -1.2487)\qquad\qquad (t = 4.4121)$	0.1458	26.281
ARIMA(1, 1, 2)	$W_t = (0.9388)\,W_{t-1} + A_t + (0.5728)\,A_{t-1} - (0.1462)\,A_{t-2}$ $(t = 12.8462)\qquad\qquad (t = 4.0259)\qquad (t = 1.1205)$	0.1462	26.089

Table 5.7 Characteristic properties of six ARIMA(p, 1, q) models

Model	ARIMA notation	Theoretical ACF	Theoretical ACF of first regular differences	Theoretical PACF of first regular differences
Random walk	ARIMA(0, 1, 0)	Dies away extremely slowly	All autocorrelations zero	All partial autocorrelations zero
ARI(1, 1)	ARIMA(1, 1, 0)	Dies away extremely slowly	Tails off towards zero	Cuts off after lag 1
ARI(2, 1)	ARIMA(2, 1, 0)	Dies away extremely slowly	Tails off towards zero	Cuts off after lag 2
IMA(1, 1)	ARIMA(0, 1, 1)	Dies away extremely slowly	Cuts off after lag 1	Tails off towards zero
IMA(1, 2)	ARIMA(0, 1, 2)	Dies away extremely slowly	Cuts off after lag 2	Tails off towards zero
ARIMA(1, 1, 1)	ARIMA(1, 1, 1)	Dies away extremely slowly	Tails off towards zero	Tails off towards zero

Table 5.8 Means and standard deviations of subsets of the time series used in this chapter

	Times series 5.1			Times series 5.2			Time series 5.3	
Subset	Mean	Standard deviation	Subset	Mean	Standard deviation	Subset	Mean	Standard deviation
1–10	299.2	4.8	1–20	25.8	1.3	1–20	17.0	0.4
11–20	282.3	3.7	21–40	20.9	1.6	21–40	17.5	0.3
21–30	275.3	4.3	41–60	20.0	0.8	41–60	17.1	0.4
31–40	279.6	3.8	61–80	24.4	1.9	61–80	17.1	0.4
41–50	276.1	4.1	81–100	24.4	0.2	81–100	16.6	0.3
51–60	272.5	1.2	101–120	23.6	0.3	101–120	16.7	0.3
61–70	281.4	9.3	121–140	21.3	0.6	121–140	17.0	0.3
71–80	290.2	2.1	141–160	21.8	1.1	141–160	17.0	0.3
81–90	289.3	2.7	161–180	24.7	0.2	161–180	17.2	0.3
91–100	284.9	2.0	181–200	23.9	0.3			
			201–220	22.8	0.8			
1–107	283.6	8.7	1–226	23.0	2.1	1–197	17.1	0.4

Time series 5.4

Subset	Mean	Standard deviation
1–20	6599.6	3714.0
21–40	18292.5	3506.8
41–60	29713.0	3201.5
61–80	40963.3	3410.6
81–100	52834.4	3650.7
101–120	64307.6	3141.4
121–140	75491.4	3483.5
141–160	87295.4	3584.5
161–180	99021.6	3504.2
181–200	11255.6	3661.1
201–220	23224.0	3401.3
221–240	34814.0	3462.6
241–260	46570.3	3357.9
261–280	58127.7	3797.1
281–300	71178.0	3814.3
1–300	87977.8	50805.9

Time series 5.5

Subset	Mean	Standard deviation
1–20	24.9	5.5
21–40	22.0	4.2
41–60	27.2	5.2
61–80	29.4	3.5
81–100	27.2	3.4
101–120	36.0	6.0
121–140	35.2	3.2
141–160	45.1	6.3
161–180	38.5	4.5
181–200	46.0	5.8
1–200	33.2	9.3

Time series 5.6

Subset	Mean	Standard deviation
1–7	110.7	0.2
8–14	109.8	0.6
15–21	109.1	0.4
22–28	110.9	0.6
29–35	111.8	0.3
36–42	113.5	1.3
43–49	117.3	1.3
50–56	120.1	0.7
57–63	123.0	1.1
64–70	123.0	0.2
1–78	115.7	5.5

Chapter 6

Forecasting seasonal time series

6.1 DIFFERENCING A SEASONAL TIME SERIES TO ACHIEVE STATIONARITY

Seasonal time series are studied in this chapter. In the present section, we see how to difference a seasonal time series to achieve stationarity in the mean. Simple models for seasonal time series are described in Section 6.2 and more complex models in Section 6.3. In Sections 6.4 to 6.6, these models are fitted to examples of seasonal time series. Finally, the Box–Jenkins approach to forecasting time series is reviewed in Section 6.7.

In Section 1.4, a time series was said to have a seasonal pattern if it exhibits a regular pattern which repeats itself after a certain number of basic time intervals. The number of time intervals after which the pattern recurs is known as the *period* of the seasonal pattern and is denoted by s. For monthly data, the pattern usually repeats itself after a year and so $s = 12$ months. For quarterly data, we usually have $s = 4$. In Section 2.6, it was mentioned that seasonal peaks and troughs are often easy to spot by visual examination of a plot of the time series. On many occasions, however, if the time series fluctuates considerably or if trend is present, seasonal peaks and troughs may not be easy to identify from a plot of the time series. Instead, the seasonal pattern may be detected from the sample ACF of the time series. If there is a seasonal pattern with a period of 12 time periods, we would expect to find a high positive correlation between observations that are 12 time periods apart and so the sample ACF should exhibit peaks at the seasonal lags 12, 24, 36, etc. By this is meant that these sample autocorrelations are larger in value than the sample autocorrelations at other lags. The stronger the trend in the time series, the less obvious this seasonal pattern will be as it will be swamped by the fact that the sample ACF will tend to die down extremely slowly. Thus if the sample ACF suggests that trend is present, one or more regular differences should first be taken before looking for a seasonal pattern in the sample ACF. Non-stationarity due to a seasonal pattern may be removed by taking one or more seasonal differences of the observed time series, as described below.

The general approach to determining the degree of differencing required to reduce a time series to stationarity may be outlined as follows:

Case 1

The sample ACF of the original time series z_t cuts off or dies down quickly towards zero. This indicates that the original time series is stationary in the mean and no differencing is required.

Case 2

The sample ACF of the original time series z_t cuts off or dies down quickly towards zero, except for spikes at the seasonal lags 12, 24, and 36, say. Attention is then focused on the sample autocorrelations r_{12}, r_{24}, r_{36}. If these sample autocorrelations cut off after r_{12} or r_{24}, or appear to die down quickly towards zero, then the original time series z_t is stationary in the seasonal pattern and no differencing is required. On the other hand, if these sample autocorrelations appear to die down extremely slowly towards zero, i.e. r_{12}, r_{24}, and r_{36} are all approximately the same size, then the time series z_t is said to be *non-stationary in the seasonal pattern*. This can be caused by a trend in the seasonal pattern or by random changes in mean level in the seasonal pattern. Just as non-stationarity in the mean can be removed by taking one regular difference, non-stationarity in the seasonal pattern can be removed by taking *one seasonal difference* of the original time series z_t. The differenced time series is denoted by

$$w_t = z_t - z_{t-12}, \qquad t \geqslant 13.$$

Note that when the seasonal pattern has period 12, the time series obtained by taking one seasonal difference contains 12 fewer observations than the original time series. We say that 12 observations have been lost in differencing. The number of seasonal differences taken is denoted by D. Here $D = 1$. The time series w_t obtained by taking one seasonal difference may be expressed as follows:

$$w_t = (1 - B^{12}) z_t, \qquad t \geqslant 13,$$

where B is the backward shift operator. The sample ACF of the first seasonal differences w_t is then studied. If this cuts off or dies down quickly towards zero, the time series w_t is stationary in the mean. If, on the other hand, this sample ACF dies down extremely slowly or if the sample autocorrelations are first persistently positive and then persistently negative, then the time series w_t should be regarded as non-stationary in the mean, and we should consider the time series obtained by taking first regular differences of w_t. The resulting time series is given by

$$w_t = (z_t - z_{t-12}) - (z_{t-1} - z_{t-13}), \qquad t \geqslant 14,$$

$$= z_t - z_{t-1} - z_{t-12} + z_{t-13}, \qquad t \geqslant 14.$$

Note that a total of 13 observations have been lost in differencing. This time series has been obtained by taking one seasonal difference ($D = 1$) and then one regular difference ($d = 1$) of the original time series. An alternative expression for w_t is

$$w_t = (1 - B)^1 (1 - B^{12}) z_t, \qquad t \geqslant 14,$$

as may be easily verified by multiplying out. For most time series encountered in practice, at most one regular difference and one seasonal difference are required to reduce a time series to stationarity and so it will usually be found that the sample ACF of w_t with $D = 1$ and $d = 1$ either cuts off or dies down quickly towards zero.

Case 3

The sample ACF of the original time series dies down extremely slowly, with or without peaks at the seasonal lags. This indicates that the original time series is non-stationary in the mean and one regular difference $(d = 1)$ should be taken. The sample ACF of the differenced time series

$$w_t = z_t - z_{t-1}, \qquad t \geqslant 1,$$

should then be studied. If this cuts off or dies down quickly towards zero, the time series of first regular differences is stationary in the mean. If the sample ACF of w_t dies down quickly towards zero except for spikes at the seasonal lags 12, 24, 36, then as in Case 2, attention is focused on the sample autocorrelations r_{12}, r_{24}, r_{36} of the time series w_t. As in Case 2, if these sample autocorrelations cut off after r_{12} or r_{24} or appear to die down quickly towards zero, the time series w_t is stationary in the mean and no further differencing is required. If, on the other hand, these sample autocorrelations appear to die down extremely slowly towards zero, the time series w_t is non-stationary in the seasonal pattern. As before, this can be removed by taking one seasonal difference of w_t. The resulting time series is given

$$w_t = (z_t - z_{t-1}) - (z_{t-12} - z_{t-13})$$
$$= z_t - z_{t-1} - z_{t-12} + z_{t-13}, \qquad t \geqslant 13,$$

which we have already encountered. This time series has been obtained by taking one regular difference $(d = 1)$ and then one seasonal difference $(D = 1)$ of the original time series. Thus the·order in which the differences are taken is irrelevant. As mentioned above in Case 2, at most one regular difference and one seasonal difference are normally required to reduce a time series to stationarity in the mean and so it will usually be found that the sample ACF of w_t with $d = 1$ and $D = 1$ either cuts off or dies down quickly towards zero.

From the above, it is evident that in the case of a seasonal time series with period 12, we need to consider at least the first 36 sample autocorrelations of the time series and its differences to decide on the degree of differencing required to achieve stationarity. Even with this, the precise meanings of such expressions as 'die down quickly' and 'die down extremely slowly' are rather arbitrary and may lead to some doubt as to the degree of differencing required. When the sample ACF of a time series or one of its differences leaves some doubt as to the stationarity of that time series, it is recommended that another difference (regular or seasonal) be taken. One advantage of doing this is that forecasts for non-stationary time series are not tied to a fixed mean, as is the case with forecasts for stationary time series. Another advantage is that in situations where the degree of differencing is in doubt,

182

it is generally the case that superior forecasts are obtained when the greater degree of differencing has been used. Plots of the original time series and of its differences should also be studied, but a decision on the degree of differencing required to achieve stationarity will usually be based on the sample ACF of the original time series and its differences. The sample standard deviations of the original time series and its regular and seasonal differences should also be studied to avoid over-differencing. If the sample standard deviation increases when a further difference is taken, this indicates that taking the extra difference will result in overdifferencing. If the original time series is stationary in the variance, it is easily shown that any regular or seasonal difference of the time series is also stationary in the variance.

6.2 SEASONAL AUTOREGRESSIVE AND MOVING AVERAGE MODELS

In Sections 6.2 and 6.3 we consider models for seasonal time series. We begin in the present section with simple models which, while they do not occur frequently in practice, are important building blocks for more general models of seasonal time series. The first model we study is the *seasonal autoregressive model of order 1*, or, more briefly, the SAR(1) model. We have previously studied a first order auto-regressive AR(1) model, which can be described as a *regular* autoregressive model to distinguish it from the model to be discussed here. In that model, we assumed that the variable Z_t, corresponding to the observation at time t, depends on the variable Z_{t-1}, but not on any of the variables $Z_{t-2}, Z_{t-3}, \ldots, Z_1$. Thus we are assuming that the observation at time t depends on the observation immediately preceding it, but not on any other observation preceding it. If a time series of monthly data has a seasonal pattern with period 12 (say), then it is reasonable to assume that the observation for January this year depends on the observations for January in previous years, but not on the observations for other months of previous years. Thus the observations at each January constitute a time series that is completely independent of the time series of observations for February or for any other month of the year. In such a case, the following model may be appropriate:

$$Z_t = \theta_0 + \phi_{12} Z_{t-12} + A_t$$

where

$$A_t = \text{IN}(0, \sigma_A^2).$$

In this model, the random variable Z_t is assumed to be a linear function of the random variable Z_{t-12}, plus a random shock A_t. This model is called a *seasonal autoregressive model of order 1 and period 12*, or, more briefly, an SAR(1)$_{12}$ model. Since this model is a simple generalization of an AR(1) model, its characteristic properties are easily found. It may be shown that the theoretical autocorrelations are given by

$$\rho_s = \phi_{12}^k, \qquad s = 12k,$$
$$\rho_s = 0, \qquad s \neq 12k.$$

We see that the theoretical autocorrelations are zero except for lags 12, 24, 36, ... and since the condition $-1 < \phi_{12} < 1$ is required for stationarity, the theoretical autocorrelations at these lags decline geometrically towards zero. The theoretical partial autocorrelations are given by

$$\rho_{12, 12} = \phi_{12}, \qquad \rho_{ss} = 0 \text{ otherwise.}$$

Thus the only non-zero theoretical partial autocorrelation occurs at lag 12. Thus the characteristic properties of an $SAR(1)_{12}$ model are that the theoretical ACF has spikes at lags 12, 24, 36, etc. and tails off towards zero and the theoretical PACF cuts off after a single spike at lag 12, as shown in Figures 6.1 and 6.2. These

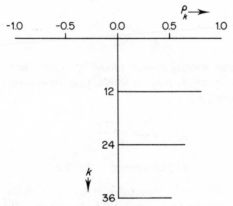

Figure 6.1 Theoretical ACF for $SAR(1)_{12}$ model with $\phi_{12} > 0$

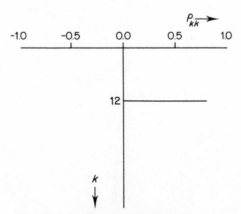

Figure 6.2 Theoretical PACF for $SAR(1)_{12}$ model with $\phi_{12} > 0$

184

characteristic properties are included in Table 6.7 at the end of the chapter. Seasonal autoregressive models of higher order are defined in a similar fashion and their characteristic properties may be deduced from those of regular autoregressive models.

The reader will recall that for a regular moving average model of order 1, or, more briefly, an MA(1) model, it emerged that the random variable Z_t was correlated with its predecessor Z_{t-1} and its successor Z_{t+1} but not with any other members of the sequence of variables $Z_1, Z_2, \ldots$. For a time series of monthly data which has a seasonal pattern with period 12 (say), it would be reasonable to consider a model for which the observation for this January is correlated with the observation for last January and the observation for next January, but not with any other observations. This will be the case for the following model:

$$Z_t = \theta_0 + A_t - \theta_{12} A_{t-12},$$

where

$$A_t \sim \text{IN}(0, \sigma_A^2).$$

This is called a *seasonal moving average model of order 1 and period 12*, or, more briefly, an SMA(1)$_{12}$ model. It may be shown that the theoretical autocorrelations for this model are given by

$$\rho_{12} = \frac{-\theta_{12}}{1 + \theta_{12}^2},$$

$$\rho_k = 0 \text{ otherwise}, \quad \text{for } k > 1.$$

Thus the theoretical ACF has a single spike at lag 12 as shown in Figure 6.3. This implies that a given observation is correlated only with the observations following and preceding it by 12 time periods. It may be shown that the theoretical PACF

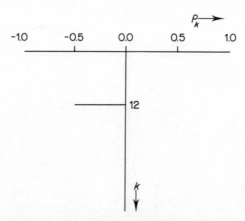

Figure 6.3 Theoretical ACF for SMA(1)$_{12}$
model with $\theta_{12} > 0$

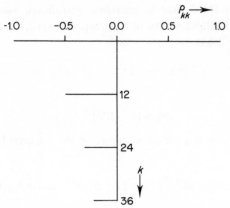

Figure 6.4 Theoretical PACF for SMA(1)$_{12}$
model with $\theta_{12} > 0$

has spikes at lags 12, 24, 36, etc. and tails off towards zero, as shown in Figure 6.4. These characteristic properties are included in Table 6.7 at the end of the chapter. Seasonal moving average models of higher order are defined in a similar fashion and their characteristic properties may be deduced from those of regular moving average models.

6.3 MULTIPLICATIVE SEASONAL MODELS

An obvious generalization of the seasonal autoregressive and seasonal moving average models is the mixed seasonal autoregressive moving average model of the form:

$$Z_t = \phi_{12} Z_{t-12} + \ldots + \phi_{12P} Z_{t-12P} + A_t - \theta_{12} A_{t-12} - \ldots - \theta_{12Q} A_{t-12Q}.$$

Generalizing further, consider a seasonal stochastic process for which D seasonal differences are required to produce a stationary seasonal model, resulting in the model

$$W_t = \phi_{12} W_{t-12} + \ldots + \phi_{12P} W_{t-12P} + A_t - \theta_{12} A_{t-12} - \ldots - \theta_{12Q} A_{t-12Q}$$

where

$$W_t = (1 - B^{12})^D Z_t.$$

The model is called a *seasonal autoregressive integrated moving average model of order (P, D, Q)* and period 12, or, more briefly, an SARIMA$(P, D, Q)_{12}$ model. Such a model would explain one of the features of a seasonal time series with period 12, i.e. that an observation for a particular month, say April, is related to the observations for previous Aprils. However, such a model assumes that observations within a particular year are independent of each other, whereas in practice the observation for April in a particular year will be related to observations for the other months of that year. This problem may be overcome as follows. For the time series of observations for a particular month of the year, say April, the following SARIMA-$(P, D, Q)_{12}$ model is fitted:

$$W_t = \phi_{12} W_{t-12} + \ldots + \phi_{12P} W_{t-12P} + A'_t - \theta_{12} A'_{t-12} - \ldots - \theta_{12Q} A'_{t-12Q}$$

where

$$W_t = (1 - B^{12})^D Z_t.$$

An alternative form for this model in terms of the backward shift operator B is as follows:

$$(1 - \phi_{12} B^{12} - \ldots - \phi_{12P} B^{12P}) W_t = (1 - \theta_{12} B^{12} - \ldots - \theta_{12Q} B^{12Q}) A'_t \ldots$$

$$(6.1)$$

where

$$W_t = (1 - B^{12})^D Z_t,$$

as may be easily verified by multiplying out.

It will usually be reasonable to assume that if similar models are fitted for other months of the year, the parameters contained in the monthly models will be approximately the same for each month. To allow for the fact that observations in different months of the same year will be related in general, the random shocks A'_t in this seasonal model (6.1) are not assumed to form a white noise process, but to be related by means of an ARIMA(p, d, q) model:

$$W_t = \phi_1 W_{t-1} + \ldots + \phi_p W_{t-p} + A_t - \theta_1 A_{t-1} - \ldots - \theta_q A_{t-q}, \qquad (6.2)$$

where

$$W_t = (1 - B)^d A'_t$$

and now the random shocks A_t in (6.2) form a white noise process. An alternative form for this model in terms of the backward shift operator B is as follows:

$$(1 - \phi_1 B - \ldots - \phi_p B^p) W_t = (1 - \theta_1 B - \ldots - \theta_q B^q) A_t, \qquad (6.3)$$

where

$$W_t = (1 - B^d) A'_t.$$

From (6.1) and (6.3) we get the model

$$(1 - \phi_1 B - \ldots - \phi_p B^p)(1 - \phi_{12} B^{12} - \ldots - \phi_{12P} B^{12P}) W_t$$

$$= (1 - \theta_1 B - \ldots - \theta_q B^q)(1 - \theta_{12} B^{12} - \ldots - \theta_{12Q} B^{12Q}) A_t$$

where

$$W_t = (1 - B)^d (1 - B^{12})^D Z_t.$$

As a final generalization, a constant term θ_0 is added to the model, to accommodate the possibility that the variables W_t may have a non-zero mean. The resulting model is given by

$$(1 - \phi_1 B - \ldots - \phi_p B^p)(1 - \phi_{12} B^{12} - \ldots - \phi_{12P} B^{12P}) W_t$$
$$= \theta_0 + (1 - \theta_1 B - \ldots - \theta_q B^q)(1 - \theta_{12} B^{12} - \ldots - \theta_{12Q} B^{12Q}) A_t$$

$$(6.4)$$

where

$$W_t = (1 - B)^d (1 - B^{12})^D Z_t.$$

This model is known as a multiplicate seasonal model of order $(p,d,q) \times (P,D,Q)_{12}$. In this model, the term $(1 - \phi_1 B - \ldots - \phi_p B^p)$ is called a *regular autoregressive operator of order p* and the term $(1 - \phi_{12} B^{12} - \ldots - \phi_{12P} B^{12P})$ is called a *seasonal autoregressive operator of order P*; the term $(1 - \theta_1 B - \ldots - \theta_q B^q)$ is called a *regular moving average operator of order q* and the term $(1 - \theta_{12} B^{12} - \ldots - \theta_{12Q} B^{12Q})$ is called a *seasonal moving average operator of order Q*. Most of the seasonal time series encountered in practice may be adequately represented by particular cases of this multiplicative model. The cases that arise most frequently are the following:

$$(1, d, 0) \times (1, D, 0)_{12},$$

$$(1, d, 0) \times (0, D, 1)_{12},$$

$$(0, d, 1) \times (1, D, 0)_{12},$$

$$(0, d, 1) \times (0, D, 1)_{12},$$

where in each model d and D may take either of the values 0 or 1. The last of these four cases is the one that most frequently arises in practice and it usually occurs in the form $(0, 1, 1) \times (0, 1, 1)_{12}$. In this model, one regular difference and one seasonal difference are required to achieve stationarity and the model includes a regular moving average operator of order 1, the term $(1 - \theta_1 B)$, and a seasonal moving average operator of order 1, the term $(1 - \theta_{12} B^{12})$. When this model is expanded, it can be written in the form:

$$Z_t - Z_{t-1} - Z_{t-12} + Z_{t-13} = \theta_0 + (1 - \theta_1 B)(1 - \theta_{12} B^{12}) A_t$$
$$= \theta_0 + A_t - \theta_1 A_{t-1} - \theta_{12} A_{t-12} + \theta_1 \theta_{12} A_{t-13} \ldots \quad (6.5)$$

This model is a particular case of the *non-multiplicative* model

$$(1 - B)(1 - B^{12}) Z_t = \theta_0 + A_t - \theta_1 A_{t-1} - \theta_{12} A_{t-12} - \theta_{13} A_{t-13} \ldots \quad (6.6)$$

with

$$\theta_{13} = -\theta_1 \theta_{12}.$$

While multiplicative models such as (6.5) provide good models for most of the seasonal time series that occur in practice, non-multiplicative models such as (6.6) are sometimes better. The best-fitting multiplicative model can provide a good starting point from which to construct a better non-multiplicative model. Only multiplicative models will be considered here.

Identification of an appropriate multiplicative seasonal model of the form (6.4) for a given seasonal time series can be quite difficult. Suppose that d regular and D seasonal differences have been taken to achieve stationarity. Then we study the sample ACF and sample PACF of the differenced time series W_t where

$$W_t = (1 - B)^d (1 - B^{12})^D Z_t.$$

We first attempt to determine whether an appropriate model for the time series should contain a regular autoregressive or moving average operator. As mentioned above, it will usually be found that an adequate model need contain either a regular autoregressive operator or a regular moving average operator, but not both. Having determined the type of regular operator to be included, we then determine the order of this regular operator. Then we turn our attention to the seasonal operators and attempt to determine whether a appropriate model should include a seasonal autoregressive operator or a seasonal moving average operator. As mentioned above, it will usually be found that an adequate model need contain either a seasonal autoregressive operator or a seasonal moving average operator, but not both. Having determined the type of seasonal operator to include in the model, we then determine the order of this seasonal operator.

To decide on the type of regular operator, we first study the sample ACF and sample PACF of the differenced time series W_t, disregarding the autocorrelations and partial autocorrelations at the seasonal lags. Thus for a time series for which the sample ACF of w_t has spikes at lags 12, 24, and 36, indicating a seasonal pattern with period 12, for the moment we disregard the sample autocorrelations and sample partial autocorrelations at lags 12, 24, and 36. It often happens that if the sample ACF has spikes at lags 12 and 24, it will also have satellite spikes at lags 11 and 13, 23 and 25, 35 and 37. These spikes will not be as large as the spikes at lags 12, 24, and 36 and are characteristic of realizations of models with both regular and seasonal operators. Since they are associated with the seasonal pattern, such satellite spikes should also be disregarded for the moment. We then use the properties of regular AR(p) and regular MA(q) models to identify the type and order of the regular operator to be included in the model. Thus if the sample ACF tails off towards zero, disregarding the spikes at or near the seasonal lags, and the sample PACF cuts off after lag p, disregarding spikes at or near the seasonal lags, then a regular autoregressive operator of order p should be included in the model. Similarly, if the sample ACF cuts off after lag q, disregarding spikes at or near the seasonal lags, and if the sample PACF tails off towards zero, disregarding spikes at or near the seasonal lags, then a regular moving average operator of order q should be included in the model. Thus in particular, if the sample ACF cuts off after lag 1 and the sample PACF tails off towards zero, apart from spikes at or near the seasonal lags, then a regular moving average operator $(1 - \theta_1 B)$ should be included in the model. To determine the type and order of the seasonal operator, we turn our attention to the spikes at the seasonal lags 12, 24, and 36, disregarding any satellite spikes at lags 11 and 13, 23 and 25, 35 and 37. We then use the characteristic properties of seasonal autoregressive and moving average models to identify the type and order of the regular seasonal operator to be included in the model. If the sample autocorrelations at the seasonal lags 12, 24, and 36 appear to tail off towards zero and the sample partial autocorrelations appear to cut off after lag 12 or lag 24, then a seasonal autoregressive operator of order 1 or 2, respectively, should be included in the model. Similarly if the sample autocorrelations at the seasonal lags appear to cut off after lag 12 or lag 24, and the sample partial autocorrelations at the seasonal lags 12, 24, and 36 appear to tail off towards zero, then a seasonal moving average operator of order 1 or 2, respectively, should be included in the model. In particular, if the sample autocorrelations at the seasonal lags appear to cut off after lag 12, and the sample partial autocorrelations at the seasonal lags 12, 24, and 36 appear to tail off towards zero, then a seasonal moving average operator $(1-\theta_{12}B^{12})$ should be included in the model. These guidelines are derived from the characteristic properties of regular and seasonal operators in multiplicative seasonal models, which are summarized in Table 6.7 at the end of this chapter.

Another problem that arises at the identification stage for seasonal time series is that of deciding if a constant term θ_0 should be included in the multiplicative model (6.4). It may be shown that for a $(p, d, q) \times (P, D, Q)_{12}$ model the constant term θ_0 is related to the mean μ of the variables

$$W_t = (1-B)^d (1-B^{12})^D Z_t$$

as follows:

$$\theta_0 = (1-\phi_1 - \ldots - \phi_p)(1-\phi_{12} - \ldots - \phi_{12P})\,\mu.$$

Thus the constant term θ_0 will be zero if and only if the process mean μ of the variables W_t is zero. This process mean μ is estimated from the sample mean of the differenced time series

$$w_t = (1-B)^d (1-B^{12})^D z_t$$

and only if the sample mean of w_t is large compared with the sample standard deviation should a constant term be included in the model. As in the case of an ARIMA$(p, 1, q)$ model, the presence of a non-zero constant term in a $(p, d, q) \times (P, D, Q)_{12}$ model with $d = 1$ has important implications both for the behaviour of a realization of this model and the behaviour of forecasts produced by this model. If θ_0 is non-zero, a realization of this model will exhibit a linear trend with slope μ, with possibly a seasonal pattern superimposed on this trend and forecasts for this model will follow the same seasonal pattern superimposed on the same linear trend. As was mentioned in Section 5.4, many computer packages, including TSERIES, give the user the option of setting θ_0 equal to zero in calculating forecasts of future values of a time series if it is felt that it is unreasonable to assume that the time series will follow the same trend as in the past.

No new problems are encountered at the estimation stage of fitting a multiplicative seasonal model. It is recommended that, for seasonal time series, back forecasting should always be used where starting value problems arise, rather than setting unknown quantities equal to zero, in order to improve the accuracy of the parameter estimates and of the forecasts produced by the fitted model. When diagnostic checks are applied to the fitted model, the sample ACF and PACF of the residuals may indicate model inadequacies and indicate further operators to be included in the model. For example, if the sample ACF of the residuals has a spike at lag 12, then a seasonal moving average operator of order 1 should be included in the model. Because of the difficulty of identifying an appropriate multiplicate seasonal model for a given time series, it should be expected that several cycles of identification, estimation, and diagnostic checking will be needed before an adequate model is found. Forecasting future values of a time series using a multiplicative seasonal model is easily accomplished by expanding the model as shown in (6.5) and then using the general method of Section 3.8. If the time series has first been transformed to achieve stationarity in the variance, forecasts are first calculated for the transformed time series and then these forecasts are converted into forecasts for the original time series. If the time series is non-stationary in the mean, the width of prediction intervals increases without bound as the lead time increases.

6.4 EXAMPLE 6.1

In this section we analyse time series 6.1 given in Appendix A.3. The plot of time series 6.1 is shown in Figure 6.5 and seems to indicate that the time series is non-stationary in the mean due to an upward trend. The means and standard deviation of subsets of the time series are given in Table 6.8 at the end of the chapter and plotted in Figure 6.6, which indicates that the time series is stationary in the variance. The sample ACF of the time series is given in Figure 6.7 and confirms that the time series is non-stationary, since the sample ACF dies down extremely slowly.

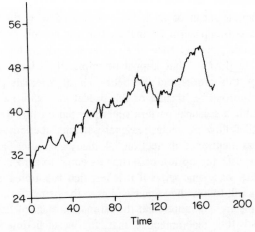

Figure 6.5 Plot of time series 6.1

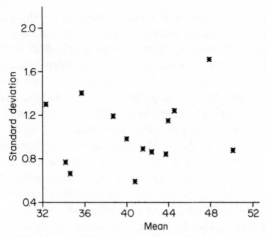

Figure 6.6 Plot of means and standard deviations of subsets of time series 6.1

MEAN AND STANDARD DEVIATION OF THE WORKING SERIES   IDENTIFICATION RUN
MEAN=   0.4096E 02
STANDARD DEVIATION=   0.5109E 01

AUTOCORRELATION FUNCTION OF THE WORKING SERIES   IDENTIFICATION RUN

	VALUE	S.E.	T VALUE	-1.0	0.0	1.0
1	0.978	0.075	13.050	I	******************************	I
2	0.954	0.128	7.459	I	*****************************	I
3	0.931	0.163	5.710	I	****************************	I
4	0.910	0.191	4.772	I	****************************	I
5	0.887	0.214	4.153	I	***************************	I
6	0.867	0.233	3.715	I	**************************	I
7	0.847	0.251	3.376	I	**************************	I
8	0.829	0.256	3.113	I	*************************	I
9	0.809	0.281	2.885	I	*************************	I
10	0.791	0.293	2.696	I	************************	I
11	0.769	0.305	2.522	I	***********************	I
12	0.747	0.316	2.366	I	***********************	I
13	0.719	0.326	2.207	I	**********************	I
14	0.690	0.334	2.064	I	*********************	I
15	0.659	0.342	1.926	I	********************	I
16	0.632	0.349	1.808	I	*******************	I
17	0.607	0.356	1.706	I	******************	I
18	0.586	0.362	1.622	I	*****************	I
19	0.565	0.367	1.539	I	*****************	I
20	0.548	0.372	1.474	I	****************	I
21	0.531	0.376	1.412	I	***************	I
22	0.516	0.380	1.356	I	***************	I
23	0.497	0.384	1.293	I	**************	I
24	0.479	0.388	1.235	I	**************	I
25	0.457	0.391	1.169	I	*************	I
26	0.438	0.394	1.112	I	************	I
27	0.417	0.397	1.050	I	************	I
28	0.399	0.359	0.999	I	***********	I
29	0.381	0.402	0.950	I	***********	I
30	0.369	0.404	0.914	I	**********	I
31	0.357	0.406	0.880	I	**********	I
32	0.348	0.407	0.854	I	**********	I
33	0.338	0.409	0.827	I	*********	I
34	0.330	0.411	0.804	I	*********	I
35	0.320	0.412	0.777	I	*********	I
36	0.311	0.413	0.752	I	*********	I

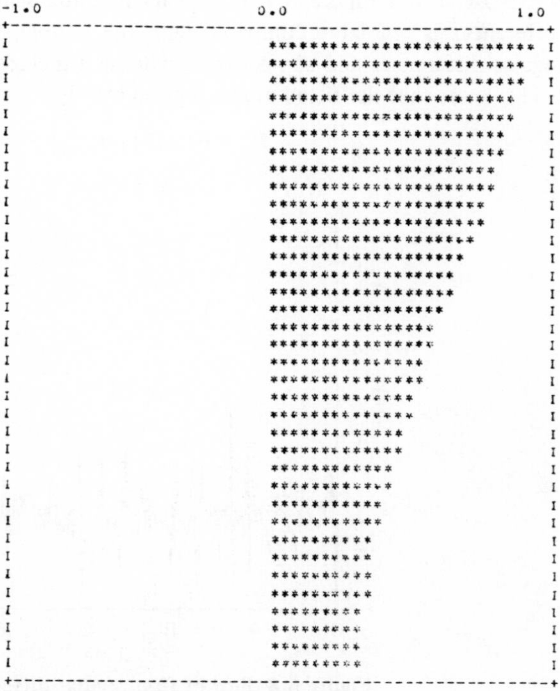

Figure 6.7 Sample ACF for time series 6.1

192

The sample ACF show no evidence of a seasonal pattern, but this may be swamped by the trend. The first regular differences of time series 6.1 are plotted in Figure 6.8 and appear to be stationary in the mean. The sample ACF of the first regular differences is shown in Figure 6.9 and appears to die down quickly towards zero, except for spikes at the seasonal lags 12, 24, and 36. The sample autocorrelation at lag 19 is also significant, but this is probably due to chance. The sample auto-correlations at lags 12 and 24 appear to be dying down towards zero, but this pattern is interrupted by the large sample autocorrelations at lag 36. Assuming that this sample autocorrelation is abnormally large due to sampling error, the sample ACF in Figure 6.9 indicates that the first regular differences are stationary in the mean and no further differencing is necessary. The sample standard deviations of the original time series and its regular and seasonal differences are given in Table 6.10. Since the sample standard deviation is minimum for $d = 1$ and $D = 0$, this confirms that only one regular difference is required for stationarity. The spikes at the seasonal lags 12, 24, and 36 in the sample ACF in Figure 6.9 indicate that a seasonal model is appropriate. The sample PACF for the first regular differences of time series 6.1 is given in Figure 6.10. The sample partial autocorrelations at lags 12, 16, and 20 are significant. Assuming that the large sample partial autocorrelations at lags 16 and 20 are due to chance, the sample PACF appears to cut off after a single spike at lag 12. This, together with the fact that the sample autocorrelations at lags 12, 24, and 36 tail off towards zero, suggests an $\text{SAR}(1)_{12}$ model for the time series of first differences or equivalently a $(0, 1, 0) \times (1, 0, 0)_{12}$ model for time series 6.1. From Figure 6.9, it appears that the sample mean of the first regular differences is not large compared with the sample standard deviation of the first regular differences and so no constant term is included in the model. From Figure 6.11, we see that the fitted model is given by

$$W_t = (0.2771) W_{t-12} + A_t,$$

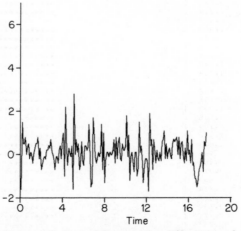

Figure 6.8 Plot of first regular differences of
time series 6.1

```
MEAN AND STANDARD DEVIATION OF THE WORKING SERIES        IDENTIFICATION RUN
MEAN=    0.7853E-01
STANDARD DEVIATION=    0.7044E 00

AUTOCORRELATION FUNCTION OF THE WORKING SERIES   IDENTIFICATION RUN


          VALUE   S.E.   T VALUE  -1.0                    0.0                    1.0
                                  +---------------------------------------------------------------+
   1     -0.039   0.075  -0.522   I                        *                                       I
   2      0.123   0.075   1.632   I                        ****                                    I
   3      0.001   0.076   0.016   I                        *                                       I
   4      0.060   0.076   0.784   I                        **                                      I
   5     -0.040   0.077  -0.522   I                       **                                       I
   6     -0.025   0.077  -0.329   I                        *                                       I
   7     -0.101   0.077  -1.314   I                      ***                                       I
   8      0.069   0.078   0.883   I                        **                                      I
   9     -0.146   0.078  -1.877   I                    ****                                        I
  10      0.098   0.079   1.237   I                        ***                                     I
  11     -0.036   0.080  -0.453   I                        *                                       I
  12      0.234   0.080   2.914   I                        *******                                 I
  13     -0.057   0.084  -0.682   I                       **                                       I
  14      0.143   0.084   1.694   I                        ****                                    I
  15     -0.109   0.086  -1.279   I                      ***                                       I
  16     -0.143   0.086  -1.652   I                    ****                                        I
  17     -0.122   0.088  -1.393   I                    ****                                        I
  18      0.026   0.089   0.289   I                        *                                       I
  19     -0.196   0.089  -2.214   I                   *****                                        I
  20     -0.114   0.091  -1.249   I                     ***                                        I
  21     -0.131   0.092  -1.424   I                    ****                                        I
  22      0.131   0.093   1.406   I                        ****                                    I
  23     -0.073   0.094  -0.773   I                       **                                       I
  24      0.179   0.094   1.896   I                        *****                                   I
  25     -0.111   0.096  -1.157   I                      ***                                       I
  26      0.138   0.097   1.422   I                        ****                                    I
  27     -0.121   0.098  -1.239   I                    ****                                        I
  28     -0.008   0.099  -0.083   I                        *                                       I
  29     -0.153   0.099  -1.550   I                    ****                                        I
  30     -0.005   0.100  -0.049   I                        *                                       I
  31     -0.128   0.100  -1.277   I                    ****                                        I
  32     -0.003   0.101  -0.034   I                        *                                       I
  33     -0.119   0.101  -1.172   I                      ***                                       I
  34      0.049   0.102   0.479   I                        **                                      I
  35     -0.067   0.102  -0.653   I                       **                                       I
  36      0.289   0.102   2.829   I                        ********                                I
                                  +---------------------------------------------------------------+
```

Figure 6.9 Sample ACF for first regular differences of time series 6.1

where

$$W_t = Z_t - Z_{t-1}.$$

When expanded, this model can be written in the form

$$Z_t = Z_{t-1} + (0.2771) Z_{t-12} - (0.2771) Z_{t-13} + A_t,$$

as shown in Figure 6.11. The results of overfitting other multiplicative seasonal models are shown in Table 6.1. This shows that a slightly better fit may be obtained by including an autoregressive operator $(1 - \phi_{12} B^{12})$ in the model, but since the estimate of this parameter ϕ_{12} is $\hat{\phi}_{12} = 0.9943$, which is close to 1, it might be better to take one seasonal difference instead and fit a model of the form $(0, 1, 0) \times (0, 1, 1)_{12}$. The results of this new cycle of identification, estimation, and diagnostic checking will not be presented here for reasons of space. For the simpler $SAR(1)_{12}$ model, the forecasts at origin 178 for the next 12 time periods are given in Figure 6.12 and plotted in Figure 6.13. Note that the width of the prediction intervals increases without bound, as we would expect for a time series which is non-stationary in the mean.

PARTIAL AUTOCORRELATIUN FUNCTION OF THE WORKING SERIES   IDENTIFICATIUN RUN

	VALUE	S.E.	T VALUE	-1.0	0.0	1.0
				+		+
1	-0.039	0.075	-0.522	I	*	I
2	0.122	0.075	1.617	I	****	I
3	0.010	0.075	0.139	I	*	I
4	0.046	0.075	0.614	I	**	I
5	-0.038	0.075	-0.511	I	*	I
6	-0.041	0.075	-0.552	I	**	I
7	-0.097	0.075	-1.291	I	***	I
8	0.069	0.075	0.919	I	**	I
9	-0.118	0.075	-1.565	I	***	I
10	0.084	0.075	1.115	I	***	I
11	0.003	0.075	0.040	I	*	I
12	0.215	0.075	2.862	I	******	I
13	-0.044	0.075	-0.579	I	**	I
14	0.090	0.075	1.194	I	***	I
15	-0.120	0.075	-1.593	I	***	I
16	-0.224	0.075	-2.978	I	******	I
17	-0.097	0.075	-1.286	I	***	I
18	0.044	0.075	0.584	I	**	I
19	-0.108	0.075	-1.435	I	***	I
20	-0.151	0.075	-2.013	I	****	I
21	-0.038	0.075	-0.511	I	*	I
22	0.090	0.075	1.193	I	***	I
23	-0.015	0.075	-0.194	I	*	I
24	0.122	0.075	1.624	I	****	I
25	-0.132	0.075	-1.758	I	****	I
26	0.017	0.075	0.222	I	*	I
27	-0.075	0.075	-0.997	I	**	I
28	0.010	0.075	0.129	I	*	I
29	-0.130	0.075	-1.726	I	****	I
30	-0.005	0.075	-0.064	I	*	I
31	-0.027	0.075	-0.362	I	*	I
32	-0.048	0.075	-0.634	I	**	I
33	-0.027	0.075	-0.360	I	*	I
34	-0.040	0.075	-0.537	I	**	I
35	-0.087	0.075	-1.161	I	***	I
36	0.119	0.075	1.577	I	****	I
				+		+

Figure 6.10 Sample PACF for first regular differences of time series 6.1

ESTIMATION RUN USING (0,1,0)*(1,0,0)12 MODEL

ESTIMATED LAG COEFFICIENTS FOR THE WORKING SERIES

AUTOREGRESSIVE TERMS
         12
       0.2771

ESTIMATED EXPANDED MODEL LAG COEFFICIENTS

AUTOREGRESSIVE TERMS
         1   12   13
       1.0000   0.2771   -0.2771

MOVING AVERAGE TERMS

         NONE

Figure 6.11 The fitted $(0, 1, 0) \times (1, 0, 0)_{12}$ model for
time series 6.1

Table 6.1 Fitted models for time series 6.1

Model type	Fitted model $(W_t = Z_t - Z_{t-1})$	Residual variance	Q statistic
$(0, 1, 0) \times (1, 0, 0)_{12}$	$W_t = (0.2771) W_{t-12} + A_t$ $(t = 3.6002)$	0.4679	27.536
$(1, 1, 0) \times (1, 0, 0)_{12}$	$W_t = -(0.0206) W_{t-1} + (0.2772) W_{t-12} + A_t$ $(t = -0.2703) \quad (t = 3.5825)$	0.4704	29.674
$(0, 1, 1) \times (1, 0, 0)_{12}$	$W_t = (0.2773) W_{t-12} + A_t - (0.0182) A_{t-1}$ $(t = 3.5839) \qquad (t = 0.2383)$	0.4704	29.638
$(0, 1, 0) \times (2, 0, 0)_{12}$	$W_t = (0.2507) W_{t-12} + (0.1735) W_{t-24} + A_t$ $(t = 3.1490) \quad (t = 2.1425)$	0.4530	32.617
$(0, 1, 0) \times (1, 0, 1)_{12}$	$W_t = (0.9943) W_{t-12} + A_t - (0.8824) A_{t-12}$ $(t = 50.9711) \qquad (t = 13.7708)$	0.3853	26.577

ESTIMATION RUN USING (0,1,0)*(1,0,0)12 MODEL

FORECASTS FROM PERIOD 178

PERIOD	FORECAST	95 PERCENT LIMITS	
		LOWER	UPPER
179	44.695	43.354	46.036
180	44.390	42.494	46.287
181	43.975	41.652	46.297
182	43.614	40.932	46.296
183	43.420	40.422	46.419
184	43.254	39.969	46.538
185	43.171	39.623	46.718
186	43.198	39.406	46.991
187	42.977	38.954	46.999
188	43.143	38.903	47.383
189	43.254	38.807	47.701
190	43.531	38.886	48.176

Figure 6.12 Forecasts for time series 6.1 using the
$(0, 1, 0) \times (1, 0, 0)_{12}$ model

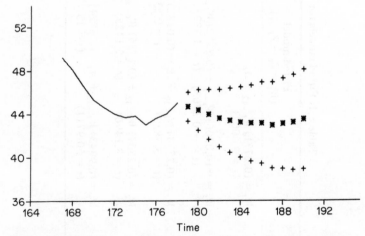

Figure 6.13 Plot of forecasts for time series 6.1 using the $(0, 1, 0) \times$
$(1, 0, 0)_{12}$ model. —— Time series, *** forecasts, +++ 95% prediction limits

6.5 EXAMPLE 6.2

In this section we analyse time series 2.3 given in Appendix A.3. The plot of the
time series is shown in Figure 6.14 and indicates a strong seasonal pattern. There is
constant variability in the seasonal pattern and no apparent trend. The means and
standard deviations of subsets of the time series are given in Table 6.8 and plotted

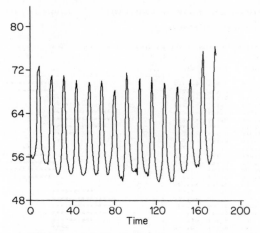

Figure 6.14 Plots of time series 2.3

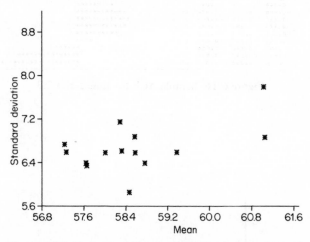

Figure 6.15 Plot of means and standard deviations of
subsets of time series 2.3

in Figure 6.15, which indicates that the time series is stationary in the variance.
The sample ACF of the time series is given in Figure 6.16 and indicates a strong
seasonal pattern because of the spikes at lags 12, 24, and 36, with smaller spikes
of opposite sign at lags 6, 18, and 30. The autocorrelations at these lags appear to
die down extremely slowly towards zero, indicating that seasonal differencing is
required. The first seasonal differences of the time series 2.3 are plotted in Figure
6.17 and appear to be stationary in the mean. The sample ACF of the first seasonal
differences is shown in Figure 6.18 and appears to die down quickly towards zero,
indicating that the first seasonal differences are stationary in the mean and no

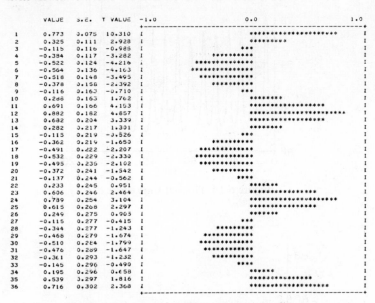

MEAN AND STANDARD DEVIATION OF THE WORKING SERIES   IDENTIFICATION RUN
MEAN=   0.5879E 02
STANDARD DEVIATION=   0.6678E 01

AUTOCORRELATION FUNCTION OF THE WORKING SERIES   IDENTIFICATION RUN

	VALUE	S.E.	T VALUE	-1.0	0.0	1.0
1	0.773	0.075	10.310	I	*********************	I
2	0.325	0.111	2.928	I	*********	I
3	-0.115	0.116	-0.985	I	***	I
4	-0.384	0.117	-3.282	I	**********	I
5	-0.522	0.124	-4.216	I	*************	I
6	-0.564	0.136	-4.163	I	**************	I
7	-0.518	0.148	-3.495	I	*************	I
8	-0.378	0.158	-2.392	I	**********	I
9	-0.116	0.163	-0.710	I	***	I
10	0.288	0.163	1.762	I	********	I
11	0.691	0.166	4.153	I	******************	I
12	0.882	0.182	4.857	I	**********************	I
13	0.682	0.204	3.339	I	*****************	I
14	0.282	0.217	1.301	I	********	I
15	-0.115	0.219	-0.526	I	***	I
16	-0.362	0.219	-1.650	I	**********	I
17	-0.491	0.222	-2.207	I	************	I
18	-0.532	0.229	-2.330	I	**************	I
19	-0.495	0.235	-2.102	I	*************	I
20	-0.372	0.241	-1.542	I	**********	I
21	-0.137	0.244	-0.562	I	****	I
22	0.233	0.245	0.951	I	*******	I
23	0.606	0.246	2.464	I	****************	I
24	0.789	0.254	3.104	I	*******************	I
25	0.615	0.268	2.297	I	****************	I
26	0.249	0.275	0.905	I	*******	I
27	-0.115	0.277	-0.415	I	***	I
28	-0.344	0.277	-1.243	I	*********	I
29	-0.468	0.279	-1.674	I	************	I
30	-0.510	0.284	-1.799	I	*************	I
31	-0.476	0.289	-1.647	I	*************	I
32	-0.361	0.293	-1.232	I	**********	I
33	-0.145	0.296	-0.490	I	****	I
34	0.195	0.296	0.658	I	******	I
35	0.539	0.297	1.816	I	****************	I
36	0.716	0.302	2.368	I	*******************	I

Figure 6.16 Sample ACF for time series 2.3

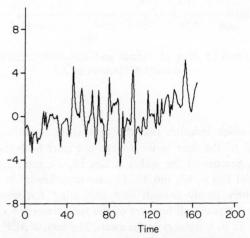

Figure 6.17 Plot of first seasonal differences
of time series 2.3

MEAN AND STANDARD DEVIATION OF THE WORKING SERIES   IDENTIFICATION RUN
MEAN= 0.4759E-01
STANDARD DEVIATION= 0.1721E 01

AUTOCORRELATION FUNCTION OF THE WORKING SERIES   IDENTIFICATION RUN

	VALUE	S.E.	T VALUE
1	0.641	0.078	8.260
2	0.323	0.105	3.081
3	0.168	0.111	1.521
4	0.172	0.112	1.534
5	0.173	0.114	1.523
6	0.168	0.115	1.455
7	0.184	0.117	1.580
8	0.225	0.118	1.902
9	0.285	0.121	2.354
10	0.201	0.125	1.608
11	0.056	0.127	0.440
12	-0.142	0.127	-1.117
13	-0.046	0.128	-0.363
14	0.119	0.128	0.925
15	0.205	0.129	1.595
16	0.210	0.131	1.603
17	0.206	0.133	1.564
18	0.226	0.135	1.679
19	0.171	0.137	1.245
20	0.071	0.138	0.513
21	-0.028	0.138	-0.203
22	0.014	0.139	0.099
23	0.076	0.139	0.549
24	0.075	0.139	0.539
25	-0.019	0.139	-0.136
26	-0.066	0.139	-0.477
27	-0.035	0.139	-0.252
28	0.010	0.139	0.072
29	0.005	0.139	0.032
30	-0.067	0.139	-0.462
31	-0.034	0.139	-0.246
32	0.049	0.140	0.353
33	0.151	0.140	1.083
34	0.120	0.141	0.851
35	-0.028	0.141	-0.199
36	-0.109	0.141	-0.772

Figure 6.18 Sample ACF for first seasonal differences of time series 2.3

further differencing is necessary. The sample standard deviations for time series 2.3 and its regular and seasonal differences are given in Table 6.10. The sample standard deviation is minimum for $d = 1$ and $D = 1$, but this minimum is not much lower than that for $d = 0$ and $D = 1$, which confirms that only one seasonal difference is necessary to achieve stationarity. The sample PACF for the first seasonal differences is given in Figure 6.19. Disregarding the spikes in the sample PACF at or near the seasonal lags 12, 24, and 36, the only significant sample partial autocorrelations occur at lags 1 and 2, so that the sample PACF cuts off after lag 1 or lag 2, suggesting that a regular autoregressive operator of order 1 or 2 should be included in the model. Initially, we may decide to include a regular autoregressive operator of order 1, $(1 - \phi_1 B)$, in our tentative model, with the option of changing this to a regular autoregressive operator of order 2, $(1 - \phi_1 B - \phi_2 B^2)$, if the simpler model is not adequate. Turning our attention to the sample autocorrelations and sample partial autocorrelations at the seasonal lags, we see that the sample partial autocorrelations at these lags appear to tail off towards zero, while the sample autocorrelations at these lags appear to cut off after a non-significant spike at lag 12, indicating that a seasonal moving average operator of order 1, $(1 - \theta_{12} B^{12})$, should be included in the model. Thus our initial tentative model is a $(1, 0, 0) \times (0, 1, 1)_{12}$ model with a regular autoregressive operator of order 1 and a seasonal

PARTIAL AUTOCORRELATION FUNCTION OF THE WORKING SERIES   IDENTIFICATION RUN

	VALUE	S.E.	T VALUE
1	0.641	0.078	8.260
2	-0.150	0.078	-1.929
3	0.046	0.078	0.589
4	0.134	0.078	1.722
5	0.008	0.078	0.107
6	0.053	0.078	0.679
7	0.091	0.078	1.175
8	0.095	0.078	1.224
9	0.133	0.078	1.711
10	-0.117	0.078	-1.511
11	-0.096	0.078	-1.232
12	-0.237	0.078	-3.060
13	0.253	0.078	3.265
14	0.094	0.078	1.213
15	0.040	0.078	0.509
16	0.078	0.078	1.007
17	0.050	0.078	0.639
18	0.065	0.078	0.844
19	-0.043	0.078	-0.552
20	-0.056	0.078	-0.716
21	-0.014	0.078	-0.177
22	0.036	0.078	0.465
23	-0.046	0.078	-0.595
24	-0.200	0.078	-2.578
25	-0.085	0.078	-1.103
26	0.056	0.078	0.723
27	0.059	0.078	0.759
28	0.063	0.078	0.810
29	0.002	0.078	0.021
30	-0.046	0.078	-0.590
31	0.079	0.078	1.022
32	0.017	0.078	0.224
33	0.097	0.078	1.247
34	-0.004	0.078	-0.051
35	-0.182	0.078	-2.341
36	-0.129	0.078	-1.667

Figure 6.19 Sample PACF for first seasonal differences of time series 2.3

moving average operator of order 1. Since the sample mean of the stationary differenced time series is not large compared with the sample standard deviation, no constant term is included in the model. Thus the tentative model has the form:

$$(1 - \phi_1 B)\, W_t = (1 - \theta_{12} B^{12})\, A_t,$$

where

$$W_t = (1 - B^{12})\, Z_t.$$

The fitted model of this type is shown in Table 6.2. None of the diagnostic checks detects any model inadequacies. The results of overfitting other multiplicative models are also shown in this table. These results indicate that a slightly better fit is obtained by including a seasonal autoregressive operator of order 1, $(1 - \phi_{12} B^{12})$, or a seasonal moving average operator of order 2, $(1 - \theta_{12} B^{12} - \theta_{24} B^{24})$, but it seems that the simpler $(1, 0, 0) \times (0, 1, 1)_{12}$ model provides an adequate fit. The forecasts at origin 178 for the next 12 time periods are given in Figure 6.20 and are plotted in Figure 6.21. Note that the forecasts follow the same seasonal pattern as in the 12 previous time periods. The width of the prediction intervals increases without bound as the lead time increases, as we would expect for a non-stationary time series.

Table 6.2 Fitted models for time series 2.3

Model type	Fitted model $(W_t = Z_t - Z_{t-12})$	Residual variance	Q statistic
$(1, 0, 0) \times (0, 1, 1)_{12}$	$W_t = (0.7884)\, W_{t-1} + A_t - (0.7585)\, A_{t-12}$ $(t = 15.9417)$ $(t = 13.8945)$	1.2382	27.967
$(2, 0, 0) \times (0, 1, 1)_{12}$	$W_t = (0.8138)\, W_{t-1} - (0.0350)\, W_{t-2} + A_t - (0.7380)\, A_{t-12}$ $(t = 10.1740)$ $(t = -0.4324)$ $(t = 13.0006)$	1.2479	27.067
$(1, 0, 1) \times (0, 1, 1)_{12}$	$(1 - (0.7635)\, B)\, W_t = (1 + (0.0578)\, B)\,(1 - (0.7324)\, B^{12})\, A_t$ $(t = 11.4267)$ $(t = -0.5639)$ $(t = 12.7814)$	1.2480	26.493
$(1, 0, 0) \times (1, 1, 1)_{12}$	$(1 - (0.7596)\, B)\,(1 - (0.2133)\, B^{12})\, W_t = (1 - (0.9104)\, B^{12})\, A_t$ $(t = 14.1705)$ $(t = 2.1822)$ $(t = 16.2140)$	1.1525	27.285
$(1, 0, 0) \times (0, 1, 2)_{12}$	$W_t = (0.7721)\, W_{t-1} + A_t - (0.7173)\, A_{t-12} - (0.1576)\, A_{t-24}$ $(t = 14.6998)$ $(t = 8.9385)$ $(t = 1.9036)$	1.1461	28.853

ESTIMATION RUN USING (1,0,0)*(0,1,1)12 MODEL

FORECASTS FROM PERIOD 178

PERIOD	FORECAST	95 PERCENT LIMITS LOWER	UPPER
179	57.696	55.515	59.877
180	55.524	52.747	58.302
181	54.196	51.105	57.283
182	53.524	50.253	56.794
133	53.766	50.389	57.144
184	53.872	50.430	57.315
185	54.566	51.084	58.048
186	57.922	54.415	61.428
187	66.836	63.315	70.358
188	72.018	68.487	75.549
139	71.821	68.285	75.358
190	61.931	58.391	65.471

Figure 6.20 Forecasts for time series 2.3 using the $(1, 0, 0) \times (0, 1, 1)_{12}$ model

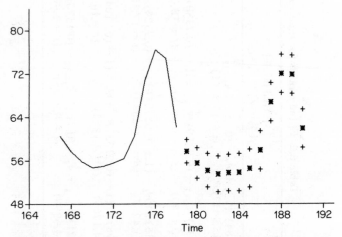

Figure 6.21 Plot of forecasts for time series 2.3 using the $(1, 0, 0) \times (0, 1, 1)_{12}$ model. ——— Time series, *** forecasts, +++ 95% prediction limits

6.6 EXAMPLE 6.3

In this section we analyse time series 2.4 in Appendix A.3. The plot of the time series is shown in Figure 6.22 and indicates a strong seasonal pattern whose variability is increasing with time, superimposed on an upward trend. The means and standard deviations of subsets of the time series are given in Table 6.8 and plotted in Figure 6.23, which indicates that the time series is non-stationary in the variance. The standard deviation is proportional to the mean, since the plot shows a

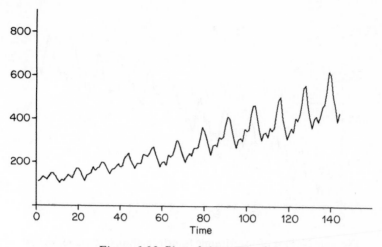

Figure 6.22 Plot of time series 2.4

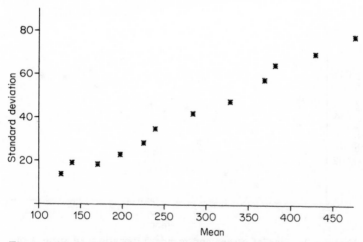

Figure 6.23 Plot of means and standard deviations of subsets of
time series 2.4

random scatter about an upward-sloping straight line which goes through the
origin. As discussed in Section 5.1 the logarithmic transformation

$$z_t^* = \log_e(z_t)$$

is appropriate. A plot of the transformed time series is shown in Figure 6.24 and
indicates that the transformed time series has a seasonal pattern with constant
variability, superimposed on an upward trend. The means and standard deviations
of subsets of the transformed time series are given in Table 6.8 and plotted in

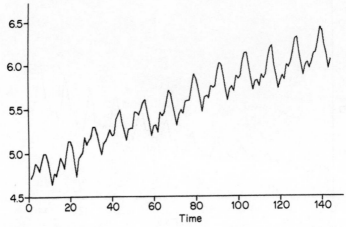

Figure 6.24 Plot of logarithmic transformation of time series 2.4

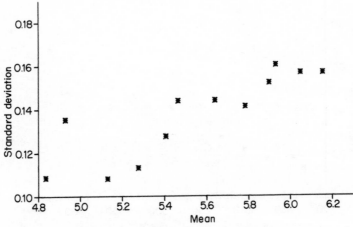

Figure 6.25 Plot of means and standard deviations of subsets of
the logarithmic transformation of time series 2.4

Figure 6.25, which shows that the transformed time series is stationary in the variance. The sample ACF of the transformed time series is given in Figure 6.26. This sample ACF dies down extremely slowly, indicating that the transformed time series is non-stationary in the mean, presumably due to the upward trend. The sample ACF also has small spikes at the seasonal lags 12, 24, and 36, indicating a seasonal pattern in the data. The first regular differences of the transformed series are plotted in Figure 6.27 and exhibit a strong seasonal pattern. The sample ACF of these first regular differences is shown in Figure 6.28 and dies down quickly

MEAN AND STANDARD DEVIATION OF THE WORKING SERIES   IDENTIFICATION RUN
MEAN=   0.5542E 01
STANDARD DEVIATION=   0.4415E 00

AUTOCORRELATION FUNCTION OF THE WORKING SERIES   IDENTIFICATION RUN

	VALUE	S.E.	T VALUE	-1.0	0.0	1.0
1	0.954	0.083	11.445	I	**********************************	I
2	0.899	0.140	6.425	I	********************************	I
3	0.851	0.175	4.848	I	******************************	I
4	0.808	0.202	4.000	I	*****************************	I
5	0.779	0.223	3.486	I	****************************	I
6	0.756	0.242	3.131	I	***************************	I
7	0.738	0.257	2.865	I	**************************	I
8	0.727	0.272	2.676	I	**************************	I
9	0.734	0.285	2.575	I	**************************	I
10	0.744	0.298	2.499	I	***************************	I
11	0.758	0.310	2.442	I	***************************	I
12	0.762	0.323	2.359	I	***************************	I
13	0.717	0.335	2.137	I	**************************	I
14	0.663	0.346	1.918	I	************************	I
15	0.618	0.354	1.744	I	***********************	I
16	0.576	0.362	1.592	I	*********************	I
17	0.544	0.368	1.477	I	********************	I
18	0.519	0.374	1.390	I	*******************	I
19	0.501	0.379	1.322	I	*******************	I
20	0.490	0.383	1.279	I	******************	I
21	0.498	0.388	1.285	I	******************	I
22	0.506	0.392	1.291	I	******************	I
23	0.517	0.397	1.303	I	*******************	I
24	0.521	0.401	1.297	I	*******************	I
25	0.434	0.406	1.191	I	****************	I
26	0.437	0.410	1.067	I	**************	I
27	0.400	0.413	0.969	I	*************	I
28	0.364	0.416	0.876	I	***********	I
29	0.337	0.418	0.806	I	**********	I
30	0.315	0.420	0.750	I	*********	I
31	0.297	0.421	0.704	I	*********	I
32	0.289	0.423	0.682	I	*********	I
33	0.295	0.424	0.696	I	*********	I
34	0.305	0.426	0.715	I	*********	I
35	0.315	0.427	0.738	I	*********	I
36	0.319	0.429	0.745	I	*********	I

Figure 6.26 Sample ACF for logarithmic transformation of time series 2.4

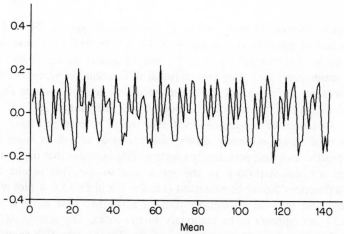

Figure 6.27 Plot of first regular differences of logarithmic transformation of time series 2.4

```
MEAN AND STANDARD DEVIATION OF THE WORKING SERIES        IDENTIFICATION RUN
MEAN=    0.9440E-02
STANDARD DEVIATION=    0.1066E 00

AUTOCORRELATION FUNCTION OF THE WORKING SERIES    IDENTIFICATION RUN


            VALUE    S.E.   T VALUE  -1.0                        0.0                         1.0
                                     +-------------------------------------------------------+
      1     0.200    0.084   2.389   I                         ******                         I
      2    -0.120    0.087  -1.382   I                       ****                             I
      3    -0.151    0.088  -1.712   I                       ****                             I
      4    -0.322    0.090  -3.585   I                  *********                             I
      5    -0.084    0.098  -0.861   I                       ***                              I
      6     0.026    0.098   0.263   I                         *                              I
      7    -0.111    0.098  -1.131   I                       ***                              I
      8    -0.337    0.099  -3.401   I                  **********                            I
      9    -0.116    0.107  -1.083   I                       ***                              I
     10    -0.109    0.108  -1.016   I                       ***                              I
     11     0.206    0.108   1.900   I                         ******                         I
     12     0.841    0.111   7.577   I                         ******************************* I
     13     0.215    0.149   1.442   I                         ******                         I
     14    -0.140    0.151  -0.923   I                       ****                             I
     15    -0.116    0.152  -0.762   I                       ***                              I
     16    -0.279    0.153  -1.826   I                   *******                              I
     17    -0.052    0.156  -0.331   I                       **                               I
     18     0.012    0.156   0.080   I                         *                              I
     19    -0.114    0.156  -0.731   I                       ***                              I
     20    -0.337    0.157  -2.147   I                  *********                             I
     21    -0.107    0.162  -0.663   I                       ***                              I
     22    -0.075    0.162  -0.463   I                       **                               I
     23     0.199    0.163   1.226   I                         ******                         I
     24     0.737    0.164   4.481   I                         ********************            I
     25     0.197    0.186   1.060   I                         ******                         I
     26    -0.124    0.188  -0.660   I                       ****                             I
     27    -0.103    0.188  -0.546   I                       ***                              I
     28    -0.211    0.189  -1.119   I                   ******                               I
     29    -0.065    0.190  -0.344   I                       **                               I
     30     0.016    0.190   0.083   I                         *                              I
     31    -0.115    0.190  -0.606   I                       ***                              I
     32    -0.239    0.191  -1.516   I                   ********                             I
     33    -0.127    0.194  -0.654   I                       ****                             I
     34    -0.041    0.194  -0.209   I                       **                               I
     35     0.147    0.195   0.758   I                         ****                           I
     36     0.657    0.195   3.367   I                         *****************              I
                                     +-------------------------------------------------------+
```

Figure 6.28 Sample ACF for first regular differences of logarithmic transformation of time series 2.4

towards zero, except for large spikes at the seasonal lags 12, 24, and 36, and smaller spikes of opposite sign at lags 4, 8, 16, 20, 28, and 32. The sample auto-correlations at the seasonal lags 12, 24, and 36 appear to die down extremely slowly towards zero, indicating that seasonal differencing is necessary. A plot of the first seasonal differences of the transformed time series is given in Figure 6.29 and exhibits random fluctuations in mean level. The sample ACF of the first seasonal differences of the transformed time series is given in Figure 6.30 and appears to die down extremely slowly towards zero, as well as being first persistently positive and then persistently negative. This indicates that the first seasonal differences are non-stationary in the mean and so the first regular and first seasonal differences should be examined (i.e. $d = 1$ and $D = 1$). A plot of the first regular and first seasonal differences of the transformed time series is shown in Figure 6.31 and appears to be stationary in the mean. The sample ACF of the differenced time series is shown in Figure 6.32. This sample ACF appears to cut off after a spike at lag 12 indicating that the differenced time series is stationary

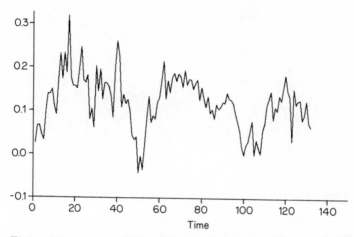

Figure 6.29 Plot of first seasonal differences of logarithmic transformation of time series 2.4

MEAN AND STANDARD DEVIATION OF THE WORKING SERIES   IDENTIFICATION RUN
MEAN=   0.1198E 00
STANDARD DEVIATION=   0.6164E-01

AUTOCORRELATION FUNCTION OF THE WORKING SERIES   IDENTIFICATION RUN

	VALUE	S.E.	T VALUE	-1.0	0.0	1.0
				+--+		
1	0.714	0.087	8.200	I	*******************	I
2	0.623	0.124	5.038	I	*****************	I
3	0.480	0.146	3.301	I	*************	I
4	0.441	0.157	2.809	I	************	I
5	0.387	0.166	2.326	I	**********	I
6	0.319	0.173	1.845	I	*********	I
7	0.242	0.177	1.363	I	*******	I
8	0.194	0.180	1.079	I	******	I
9	0.153	0.181	0.842	I	****	I
10	-0.006	0.182	-0.032	I	*	I
11	-0.115	0.182	-0.630	I	***	I
12	-0.243	0.183	-1.329	I	******	I
13	-0.143	0.185	-0.773	I	****	I
14	-0.141	0.186	-0.756	I	****	I
15	-0.099	0.187	-0.529	I	***	I
16	-0.146	0.187	-0.780	I	****	I
17	-0.096	0.188	-0.512	I	***	I
18	-0.111	0.189	-0.583	I	***	I
19	-0.141	0.189	-0.745	I	****	I
20	-0.158	0.190	-0.832	I	****	I
21	-0.114	0.191	-0.595	I	***	I
22	-0.084	0.191	-0.437	I	***	I
23	0.001	0.192	0.007	I	*	I
24	-0.052	0.192	-0.274	I	**	I
25	-0.103	0.192	-0.538	I	***	I
26	-0.094	0.192	-0.483	I	***	I
27	-0.128	0.193	-0.666	I	****	I
28	-0.145	0.193	-0.752	I	****	I
29	-0.187	0.194	-0.966	I	*****	I
30	-0.196	0.195	-1.003	I	*****	I
31	-0.190	0.197	-0.965	I	*****	I
32	-0.146	0.198	-0.735	I	****	I
33	-0.224	0.199	-1.128	I	******	I
34	-0.226	0.201	-1.126	I	******	I
35	-0.267	0.203	-1.316	I	*******	I
36	-0.223	0.205	-1.086	I	******	I
				+--+		

Figure 6.30 Sample ACF for first seasonal differences of logarithmic transformation of time series 2.4

208

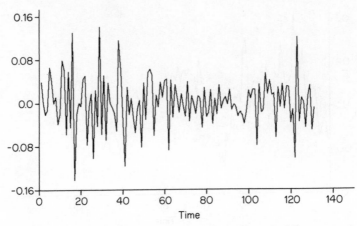

Figure 6.31 Plot of first regular and first seasonal differences of
logarithmic transformation of time series 2.4

MEAN AND STANDARD DEVIATION OF THE WORKING SERIES   IDENTIFICATION RUN
MEAN=   0.2909E-03
STANDARD DEVIATION=   0.4585E-01

AUTOCORRELATION FUNCTION OF THE WORKING SERIES   IDENTIFICATION RUN

```
        VALUE   S.E.   T VALUE  -1.0                    0.0                          1.0
                                 +-----------------------------------------------------+
  1    -0.341   0.087  -3.904   I                  *********       I
  2     0.105   0.097   1.083   I                       ***        I
  3    -0.202   0.098  -2.065   I                  ******          I
  4     0.021   0.101   0.211   I                       *          I
  5     0.056   0.101   0.551   I                       **         I
  6     0.031   0.101   0.304   I                       *          I
  7    -0.056   0.101  -0.548   I                      **          I
  8    -0.001   0.102  -0.007   I                       *          I
  9     0.176   0.102   1.736   I                       *****      I
 10    -0.076   0.104  -0.735   I                      **          I
 11     0.064   0.104   0.617   I                       **         I
 12    -0.387   0.105  -3.695   I                 **********       I
 13     0.152   0.115   1.318   I                       ****       I
 14    -0.058   0.117  -0.494   I                      **          I
 15     0.150   0.117   1.281   I                       ****       I
 16    -0.139   0.118  -1.176   I                   ****           I
 17     0.070   0.119   0.590   I                       **         I
 18     0.016   0.120   0.131   I                       *          I
 19    -0.011   0.120  -0.089   I                       *          I
 20    -0.117   0.120  -0.975   I                   ***            I
 21     0.039   0.121   0.320   I                       **         I
 22    -0.091   0.121  -0.757   I                   ***            I
 23     0.223   0.121   1.841   I                       ******     I
 24    -0.018   0.124  -0.148   I                       *          I
 25    -0.100   0.124  -0.806   I                   ***            I
 26     0.049   0.125   0.389   I                       **         I
 27    -0.030   0.125  -0.242   I                       *          I
 28     0.047   0.125   0.376   I                       **         I
 29    -0.018   0.125  -0.144   I                       *          I
 30    -0.051   0.125  -0.407   I                      **          I
 31    -0.054   0.126  -0.428   I                      **          I
 32     0.196   0.126   1.557   I                       ******     I
 33    -0.122   0.128  -0.956   I                   ****           I
 34     0.078   0.129   0.603   I                       ***        I
 35    -0.152   0.129  -1.180   I                   ****           I
 36    -0.010   0.131  -0.077   I                       *          I
                                 +-----------------------------------------------------+
```

Figure 6.32 Sample ACF for first regular and first seasonal differences of logarithmic
transformation of time series 2.4

in the mean. The sample standard deviations of time series 2.4 and its regular and seasonal differences are given in Table 6.10. Since the sample standard deviation is minimum for $d = 1$ and $D = 1$, this confirms that only one regular and one seasonal difference are needed to achieve stationarity. The sample PACF of the differenced time series is given in Figure 6.33. Disregarding spikes at or near the seasonal lags, the sample PACF appears to tail off towards zero. Disregarding the spikes at or near the seasonal lags, the sample ACF appears to cut off after lag 1, indicating that a regular moving average operator of order 1, $(1 - \theta_1 B)$, should be included in the model. Now we study the spikes in the sample ACF and PACF at or near the seasonal lags 12, 24, and 36. The sample partial autocorrelations at these lags appear to tail off towards zero, while the sample autocorrelations at these lags appear to cut off after lag 12, indicating that a seasonal moving average operator of order 1, $(1 - \theta_{12} B^{12})$, should be included in the model. Thus our initial tentative model is the $(0, 1, 1) \times (0, 1, 1)_{12}$ model with a regular moving average operator of order 1 and a seasonal moving average operator of order 1. Since the sample mean of the stationary differenced time series is not large compared with the standard deviation, no constant term is included in the model. Thus our tentative model is of the form:

```
PARTIAL AUTOCORRELATION FUNCTION OF THE WORKING SERIES   IDENTIFICATION RUN

          VALUE    S.E.   T VALUE   -1.0                    0.0                      1.0
                                     +--------------------------------------------------+
     1   -0.341   0.087   -3.904   I               *********                            I
     2   -0.013   0.087   -0.147   I                       *                             I
     3   -0.193   0.087   -2.205   I                  *****                              I
     4   -0.125   0.087   -1.431   I                   ****                              I
     5    0.033   0.087    0.379   I                       *                             I
     6    0.035   0.087    0.397   I                       *                             I
     7   -0.060   0.087   -0.689   I                      **                             I
     8   -0.020   0.087   -0.231   I                       *                             I
     9    0.226   0.087    2.582   I                       ******                        I
    10    0.043   0.087    0.493   I                       **                            I
    11    0.047   0.087    0.533   I                       **                            I
    12   -0.339   0.087   -3.876   I               *********                             I
    13   -0.109   0.087   -1.249   I                    ***                              I
    14   -0.077   0.087   -0.879   I                     **                              I
    15   -0.022   0.087   -0.249   I                       *                             I
    16   -0.140   0.087   -1.597   I                   ****                              I
    17    0.026   0.087    0.296   I                       *                             I
    18    0.115   0.087    1.314   I                       ***                           I
    19   -0.013   0.087   -0.151   I                       *                             I
    20   -0.167   0.087   -1.916   I                  *****                              I
    21    0.132   0.087    1.515   I                       ****                          I
    22   -0.072   0.087   -0.825   I                     **                              I
    23    0.143   0.087    1.635   I                       ****                          I
    24   -0.067   0.087   -0.771   I                     **                              I
    25   -0.103   0.087   -1.175   I                    ***                              I
    26   -0.010   0.087   -0.115   I                       *                             I
    27    0.044   0.087    0.501   I                       **                            I
    28   -0.090   0.087   -1.029   I                    ***                              I
    29    0.047   0.087    0.537   I                       **                            I
    30   -0.005   0.087   -0.056   I                       *                             I
    31   -0.096   0.087   -1.103   I                    ***                              I
    32   -0.015   0.087   -0.175   I                       *                             I
    33    0.011   0.087    0.132   I                       *                             I
    34   -0.019   0.087   -0.219   I                       *                             I
    35    0.023   0.087    0.264   I                       *                             I
    36   -0.165   0.087   -1.887   I                  *****                              I
                                     +--------------------------------------------------+
```

Figure 6.33 Sample PACF for first regular and first seasonal differences of logarithmic transformation of time series 2.4

Table 6.3 Fitted models for time series 2.4

Model type	Fitted model $W_t = Z_t^* - Z_{t-1}^* - Z_{t-12}^* + Z_{t-13}^*,\ Z_t^* = \log_e Z_t$	Residual variance	Q statistic
$(0, 1, 1) \times (0, 1, 1)_{12}$	$W_t = (1 - (0.3960)B)(1 - (0.6135)B^{12})A_t$ $\quad(t = 4.8938)\qquad\quad(t = 8.1252)$	0.0013	15.831
$(1, 1, 1) \times (0, 1, 1)_{12}$	$(1 - (0.2630)B)\,W_t = (1 - (0.6326)B)(1 - (0.6286)B^{12})\,A_t$ $\quad(t = 1.3596)\qquad\qquad(t = 4.0748)\qquad\quad(t = 8.3020)$	0.0013	21.014
$(0, 1, 2) \times (0, 1, 1)_{12}$	$W_t = (1 - (0.3907)B - (0.0475)B^2)(1 - (0.6164)B^{12})\,A_t$ $\quad(t = 4.4181)\qquad(t = 0.5352)\qquad\quad(t = 8.0926)$	0.0013	21.369
$(0, 1, 1) \times (1, 1, 1)_{12}$	$(1 + (0.1179)B^{12})\,W_t = (1 - (0.4071)B)(1 - (0.5089)B^{12})\,A_t$ $\quad(t = -0.7327)\qquad\qquad(t = 5.0076)\qquad\quad(t = 3.6132)$	0.0014	21.529
$(0, 1, 1) \times (0, 1, 2)_{12}$	$W_t = (1 - (0.4138)B)(1 - (0.6607)B^{12} + (0.0834)B^{24})\,A_t$ $\quad(t = 5.1289)\qquad\quad(t = 7.1660)\qquad\;\;(t = -0.8685)$	0.0013	22.061

$$W_t = (1 - \theta_1 B)(1 - \theta_{12} B^{12}) A_t,$$

where

$$W_t = (1 - B)(1 - B^{12}) Z_t^*$$

and

$$Z_t^* = \log_e(Z_t).$$

The fitted model of this type is shown in Table 6.3. None of the diagnostic checks detects any model inadequacies. The results of overfitting other multiplicative models are also shown in this table. These overfits are rejected and the $(0, 1, 1) \times (0, 1, 1)_{12}$ model is regarded as the best available model for time series 2.4. The forecasts at origin 144 for the next 12 time periods are given in Figure 6.34 and plotted in Figure 6.35. The forecasts follow the same seasonal pattern as for the 12 previous time periods, except for increased seasonal variability and the effect of the

ESTIMATION RUN USING (0,1,1)*(0,1,1)12 MODEL

FORECASTS FROM PERIOD 144

| PERIOD | FORECAST | 95 PERCENT LIMITS | |
		LOWER	UPPER
145	6.110	6.038	6.181
146	6.056	5.972	6.139
147	6.178	6.084	6.272
148	6.199	6.095	6.303
149	6.231	6.119	6.343
150	6.369	6.249	6.489
151	6.505	6.377	6.633
152	6.501	6.366	6.636
153	6.326	6.184	6.467
154	6.208	6.060	6.356
155	6.064	5.910	6.219
156	6.170	6.010	6.330

Figure 6.34 Forecasts for time series 2.4 using the $(0, 1, 1) \times (0, 1, 1)_{12}$ model

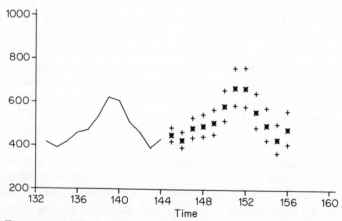

Figure 6.35 Plot of forecasts for time series 2.4 using the $(0, 1, 1) \times (0, 1, 1)_{12}$ model. —— Time series, *** forecasts, +++ 95% prediction limits

upward trend. The width of the prediction intervals increases without bound as the lead time increases, as we would expect for a non-stationary time series. The complete TSERIES program for this example is given as program A.5.4 in Appendix A.5.

6.7 REVIEW OF THE BOX–JENKINS APPROACH TO FORECASTING TIME SERIES

In Section 4.1 the stages in the Box–Jenkins approach to forecasting time series were outlined and in Chapters 4, 5, and 6 the details of the application of this approach have been given for stationary, non-stationary, and seasonal time series, respectively. In the present section, the stages in the Box–Jenkins approach are reviewed and, for each stage of the approach, references are given to the sections in which the appropriate techniques are discussed.

The first step in the analysis of a time series should be to plot the time series and note the obvious features of this plot, such as trend and seasonal pattern as described in Section 2.2. The means and standard deviations of subsets of the time series should then be plotted, as described in Section 2.4, to see if the time series is stationary in the variance. If not, an appropriate transformation should be chosen, as described in Section 5.1. The sample ACF of the transformed time series should then be examined to see if the transformed time series is stationary in the mean, as described in Section 2.6. Evidence of a seasonal pattern should also be sought in the sample ACF, as described in Sections 2.6 and 6.1. If the transformed time series is non-stationary in the mean, regular and/or seasonal differences should be taken until the differenced time series is stationary in the mean, as described in Sections 5.2 and 6.1. This will determine the appropriate class of models from which to select a model for the stationary differenced time series: ARMA, ARIMA, or multiplicative seasonal models. A tentative model from within the chosen class of models is then identified by studying the sample ACF and sample PACF of the stationary differenced time series, using the characteristic properties of these models, which are summarized in Tables 3.3, 5.7, and 6.7, respectively. A constant term should be included in the model if the sample mean of the stationary differenced time series is large compared with the sample standard deviation. The parameters of the tentative model are then estimated using the method of least squares, as described in Section 4.3. Diagnostic checks are applied to the tentative model. These involve a study of the sample ACF and sample PACF of the residuals of the fitted model as described in Section 4.4. The Q statistic is used as a test of model adequacy. Diagnostic checking also involves over-fitting more complex models, as described in Section 4.4. The residual variance is used to compare the fit of different models. If the diagnostic checks indicate model inadequacies or if a more complex model appears to give a better fit, a new cycle of model identification, estimation, and diagnostic checking is begun and this continues until an adequate model is obtained. This model is then used to forecast future values of the time series, using the general method of Section 3.8. As further observations of the time series become available, updated forecasts incorporating this information are easily derived using this method. However, this assumes that the underlying stochastic process is not changing with time and that the previously fitted model is still adequate. This assumption will not remain valid indefinitely and so after several new observations have been obtained it is advisable to fit a new model to the extended data, or at least to re-estimate the parameters in the previously fitted model.

As well as the Exercises in Section 6.8, revision exercises are also given in Section 6.9. These involve stationary, non-stationary, and seasonal time series. Readers with access to computer packages using the Box–Jenkins approach are recommended to find appropriate models for the time series in these exercises. In Appendix A.4, a table is given showing the types of models that have been fitted to these time series. However, other types of models besides those given there may give equally good fits. References to textbooks and case studies using the Box–Jenkins approach are given in Appendix A.1. A brief description of the TSERIES package appears in Appendix A.5 and some other computer packages are reviewed in Appendix A.6.

6.8 EXERCISES

6.8.1 Time series 6.2, 6.3, and 6.4 are given in Appendix A.3. Figures 6.36 to 6.71 provide relevant information for these time series, as do Tables 6.4, 6.5, 6.6, 6.9, and 6.10. For each time series, complete the following exercises:

    (a) Determine if the time series is stationary in the variance and, if not, find an appropriate transformation.

    (b) Find the appropriate number of regular and seasonal differences required to reduce the time series to stationarity.

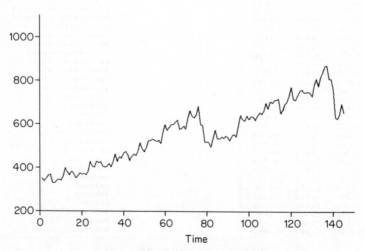

Figure 6.36 Plot of time series 6.2

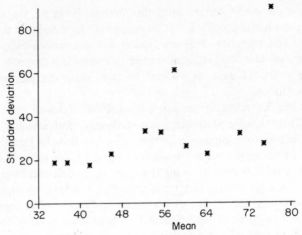

Figure 6.37 Plot of means and standard deviations of subsets of time series 6.2

MEAN AND STANDARD DEVIATION OF THE WORKING SERIES   IDENTIFICATION RUN
MEAN= 0.5639E 03
STANDARD DEVIATION= 0.1388E 03

AUTOCORRELATION FUNCTION OF THE WORKING SERIES   IDENTIFICATION RUN

	VALUE	S.E.	T VALUE	-1.0	0.0	1.0
				+----	-----------------	----+
1	0.971	0.083	11.723	I	*****************************.*****	I
2	0.939	0.141	6.663	I	**********************************	I
3	0.917	0.178	5.140	I	*********************************	I
4	0.894	0.208	4.291	I	********************************	I
5	0.869	0.233	3.731	I	*******************************	I
6	0.842	0.254	3.312	I	******************************	I
7	0.814	0.273	2.936	I	*****************************	I
8	0.790	0.289	2.735	I	*****************************	I
9	0.761	0.303	2.510	I	****************************	I
10	0.732	0.316	2.314	I	***************************	I
11	0.713	0.328	2.176	I	**************************	I
12	0.697	0.338	2.063	I	**************************	I
13	0.665	0.348	1.913	I	*************************	I
14	0.632	0.356	1.773	I	************************	I
15	0.606	0.364	1.666	I	***********************	I
16	0.579	0.371	1.561	I	**********************	I
17	0.551	0.377	1.461	I	*********************	I
18	0.526	0.382	1.375	I	********************	I
19	0.502	0.387	1.297	I	*******************	I
20	0.481	0.392	1.229	I	******************	I
21	0.459	0.396	1.160	I	*****************	I
22	0.435	0.399	1.088	I	****************	I
23	0.421	0.403	1.046	I	****************	I
24	0.412	0.406	1.015	I	***************	I
25	0.387	0.408	0.947	I	***************	I
26	0.362	0.411	0.880	I	**************	I
27	0.342	0.413	0.828	I	*************	I
28	0.320	0.415	0.771	I	************	I
29	0.300	0.417	0.719	I	***********	I
30	0.283	0.418	0.677	I	***********	I
31	0.263	0.420	0.626	I	**********	I
32	0.245	0.421	0.583	I	*********	I
33	0.228	0.422	0.541	I	********	I
34	0.210	0.423	0.496	I	*******	I
35	0.199	0.423	0.471	I	******	I
36	0.191	0.424	0.450	I	*****	I
				+----	-----------------	----+

Figure 6.38 Sample ACF for time series 6.2

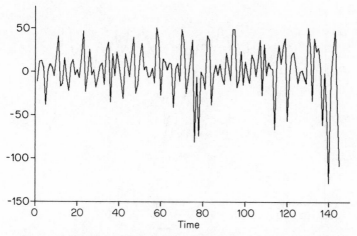

Figure 6.39 Plot of first regular differences of time series 6.2

MEAN AND STANDARD DEVIATION OF THE WORKING SERIES   IDENTIFICATION RUN
MEAN=   0.1372E 01
STANDARD DEVIATION=   0.2680E 02

AUTOCORRELATION FUNCTION OF THE WORKING SERIES   IDENTIFICATION RUN

```
        VALUE    S.E.   T VALUE   -1.0                        0.0                         1.0
                                  +-------------------------------------------------------------------+
  1     0.032    0.083   0.381    I                            *                                      I
  2    -0.195    0.083  -2.345    I                       *****                                       I
  3     0.053    0.086   0.617    I                            **                                     I
  4     0.012    0.086   0.138    I                            *                                      I
  5     0.006    0.086   0.070    I                            *                                      I
  6     0.022    0.086   0.251    I                            *                                      I
  7    -0.069    0.087  -0.799    I                          **                                       I
  8     0.104    0.087   1.200    I                            ***                                    I
  9     0.021    0.088   0.241    I                            *                                      I
 10    -0.235    0.088  -2.674    I                      ******                                       I
 11    -0.017    0.092  -0.188    I                            *                                      I
 12     0.360    0.092   3.907    I                            ***********                            I
 13    -0.014    0.101  -0.138    I                            *                                      I
 14    -0.150    0.101  -1.477    I                        ****                                       I
 15     0.026    0.103   0.253    I                            *                                      I
 16    -0.045    0.103  -0.440    I                          **                                       I
 17    -0.058    0.103  -0.566    I                          **                                       I
 18    -0.010    0.103  -0.094    I                            *                                      I
 19    -0.072    0.103  -0.698    I                          **                                       I
 20     0.023    0.104   0.221    I                            *                                      I
 21     0.045    0.104   0.431    I                            **                                     I
 22    -0.239    0.104  -2.309    I                      ******                                       I
 23    -0.017    0.107  -0.160    I                            *                                      I
 24     0.319    0.107   2.970    I                            *********                              I
 25    -0.002    0.114  -0.020    I                            *                                      I
 26    -0.087    0.114  -0.764    I                          ***                                      I
 27     0.038    0.114   0.328    I                            *                                      I
 28    -0.035    0.114  -0.303    I                            *                                      I
 29    -0.123    0.114  -1.076    I                        ****                                       I
 30     0.069    0.115   0.601    I                            **                                     I
 31    -0.070    0.116  -0.609    I                          **                                       I
 32     0.019    0.116   0.166    I                            *                                      I
 33     0.001    0.116   0.009    I                            *                                      I
 34    -0.147    0.116  -1.271    I                        ****                                       I
 35     0.012    0.117   0.104    I                            *                                      I
 36     0.293    0.117   2.503    I                            ********                               I
                                  +-------------------------------------------------------------------+
```

Figure 6.40 Sample ACF for first regular differences of time series 6.2

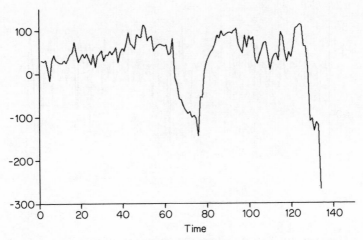

Figure 6.41 Plot of first seasonal differences of time series 6.2

MEAN AND STANDARD DEVIATION OF THE WORKING SERIES   IDENTIFICATION RUN
MEAN=   0.3401E 02
STANDARD DEVIATION=   0.6288E 02

AUTOCORRELATION FUNCTION OF THE WORKING SERIES   IDENTIFICATION RUN

	VALUE	S.E.	T VALUE	-1.0	0.0	1.0
1	0.811	0.086	9.389	I	*******************.	I
2	0.713	0.131	5.424	I	*******************	I
3	0.612	0.158	3.879	I	****************	I
4	0.481	0.175	2.757	I	*************	I
5	0.364	0.184	1.978	I	*********	I
6	0.226	0.189	1.195	I	******	I
7	0.143	0.191	0.750	I	****	I
8	0.085	0.192	0.441	I	***	I
9	0.004	0.193	0.022	I	*	I
10	-0.042	0.193	-0.216	I	**	I
11	-0.081	0.193	-0.422	I	***	I
12	-0.138	0.193	-0.716	I	****	I
13	-0.137	0.194	-0.707	I	****	I
14	-0.164	0.194	-0.846	I	****	I
15	-0.201	0.195	-1.027	I	*****	I
16	-0.224	0.197	-1.136	I	******	I
17	-0.245	0.199	-1.234	I	******	I
18	-0.275	0.201	-1.370	I	*******	I
19	-0.260	0.204	-1.274	I	*******	I
20	-0.226	0.206	-1.094	I	******	I
21	-0.222	0.208	-1.066	I	******	I
22	-0.233	0.210	-1.109	I	******	I
23	-0.226	0.212	-1.066	I	******	I
24	-0.218	0.214	-1.021	I	******	I
25	-0.222	0.215	-1.029	I	******	I
26	-0.211	0.217	-0.973	I	******	I
27	-0.178	0.218	-0.817	I	*****	I
28	-0.151	0.220	-0.689	I	****	I
29	-0.134	0.220	-0.606	I	****	I
30	-0.108	0.221	-0.487	I	***	I
31	-0.117	0.221	-0.528	I	***	I
32	-0.120	0.222	-0.540	I	***	I
33	-0.095	0.222	-0.427	I	***	I
34	-0.064	0.223	-0.288	I	**	I
35	-0.055	0.223	-0.246	I	**	I
36	-0.059	0.223	-0.264	I	**	I

Figure 6.42 Sample ACF for first seasonal differences of time series 6.2

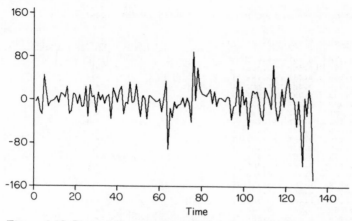

Figure 6.43 Plot of first regular and first seasonal differences of
time series 6.2

MEAN AND STANDARD DEVIATION OF THE WORKING SERIES   IDENTIFICATION RUN
MEAN=   -0.2241E 01
STANDARD DEVIATION=   0.2853E 02

AUTOCORRELATION FUNCTION OF THE WORKING SERIES   IDENTIFICATION RUN

```
            VALUE    S.E.   T VALUE   -1.0                      0.0                           1.0
                                       +--------------------------------------------------------+
    1      -0.036   0.087   -0.418   I                          *                               I
    2       0.033   0.087    0.374   I                          *                               I
    3       0.083   0.087    0.958   I                         ***                              I
    4       0.009   0.088    0.103   I                          *                               I
    5       0.087   0.088    0.989   I                         ***                              I
    6       0.073   0.088    0.823   I                         **                               I
    7       0.021   0.089    0.240   I                          *                               I
    8       0.110   0.089    1.239   I                         ***                              I
    9      -0.034   0.090   -0.376   I                          *                               I
   10      -0.023   0.090   -0.254   I                          *                               I
   11       0.070   0.090    0.785   I                         **                               I
   12      -0.294   0.090   -3.261   I                  ********                                 I
   13       0.021   0.097    0.213   I                          *                               I
   14      -0.023   0.097   -0.234   I                          *                               I
   15      -0.035   0.097   -0.359   I                          *                               I
   16      -0.069   0.097   -0.703   I                        **                                I
   17       0.102   0.098    1.042   I                         ***                              I
   18      -0.121   0.098   -1.229   I                      ****                                 I
   19      -0.061   0.100   -0.612   I                        **                                I
   20      -0.038   0.100   -0.380   I                          *                               I
   21       0.116   0.100    1.159   I                         ****                             I
   22      -0.095   0.101   -0.936   I                       ***                                I
   23      -0.038   0.102   -0.373   I                          *                               I
   24      -0.015   0.102   -0.143   I                          *                               I
   25       0.032   0.102    0.313   I                          *                               I
   26      -0.028   0.102   -0.271   I                          *                               I
   27       0.021   0.102    0.202   I                          *                               I
   28       0.001   0.102    0.009   I                          *                               I
   29      -0.081   0.102   -0.796   I                       ***                                I
   30       0.119   0.102    1.165   I                         ****                             I
   31      -0.009   0.103   -0.086   I                          *                               I
   32       0.011   0.103    0.107   I                          *                               I
   33      -0.047   0.103   -0.454   I                        **                                I
   34       0.128   0.104    1.231   I                         ****                             I
   35      -0.009   0.105   -0.083   I                          *                               I
   36       0.018   0.105    0.172   I                          *                               I
                                       +--------------------------------------------------------+
```

Figure 6.44 Sample ACF for first regular and first seasonal differences of time
series 6.2

PARTIAL AUTOCORRELATION FUNCTION OF THE WORKING SERIES   IDENTIFICATION RUN

	VALUE	S.E.	T VALUE	-1.0	0.0	1.0
1	-0.036	0.087	-0.418	I	*	I
2	0.031	0.087	0.360	I	*	I
3	0.086	0.087	0.983	I	***	I
4	0.014	0.087	0.165	I	*	I
5	0.083	0.087	0.953	I	***	I
6	0.073	0.087	0.836	I	**	I
7	0.021	0.087	0.239	I	*	I
8	0.096	0.087	1.104	I	***	I
9	-0.040	0.087	-0.460	I	*	I
10	-0.045	0.087	-0.513	I	**	I
11	0.042	0.087	0.489	I	**	I
12	-0.305	0.087	-3.515	I	*******	I
13	-0.022	0.087	-0.256	I	*	I
14	-0.032	0.087	-0.373	I	*	I
15	0.004	0.087	0.044	I	*	I
16	-0.075	0.087	-0.870	I	**	I
17	0.173	0.087	2.000	I	*****	I
18	-0.069	0.087	-0.797	I	**	I
19	-0.049	0.087	-0.567	I	**	I
20	0.025	0.087	0.284	I	*	I
21	0.150	0.087	1.733	I	****	I
22	-0.133	0.087	-1.534	I	****	I
23	0.002	0.087	0.019	I	*	I
24	-0.108	0.087	-1.250	I	***	I
25	0.039	0.087	0.453	I	**	I
26	-0.057	0.087	-0.663	I	**	I
27	0.074	0.087	0.851	I	**	I
28	-0.086	0.087	-0.996	I	***	I
29	0.022	0.087	0.258	I	*	I
30	0.092	0.087	1.060	I	***	I
31	-0.001	0.087	-0.010	I	*	I
32	-0.029	0.087	-0.332	I	*	I
33	0.064	0.087	0.743	I	**	I
34	0.050	0.087	0.572	I	**	I
35	-0.013	0.087	-0.144	I	*	I
36	-0.026	0.087	-0.304	I	*	I

Figure 6.45 Sample PACF for first regular and first seasonal differences of time series 6.2

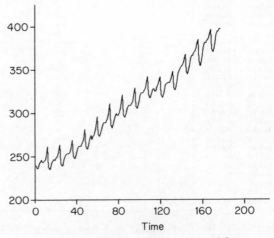

Figure 6.46 Plot of time series 6.3

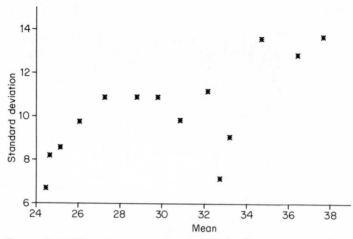

Figure 6.47 Plot of means and standard deviations of subsets of time series 6.3

MEAN AND STANDARD DEVIATION OF THE WORKING SERIES   IDENTIFICATION RUN
MEAN=   0.3075E 03
STANDARD DEVIATION=   0.4678E 02

AUTOCORRELATION FUNCTION OF THE WORKING SERIES   IDENTIFICATION RUN

```
         VALUE    S.E.    T VALUE   -1.0                    0.0                                   1.0
                                    +-----------------------------------------------------------------+
 1       0.971    0.075   12.955    I                       ***********************************  I
 2       0.941    0.127    7.391    I                       *********************************** I
 3       0.916    0.162    5.660    I                       ***********************************  I
 4       0.899    0.189    4.764    I                       ***********************************  I
 5       0.884    0.211    4.185    I                       **********************************   I
 6       0.871    0.231    3.770    I                       *********************************    I
 7       0.854    0.249    3.431    I                       ********************************     I
 8       0.839    0.265    3.165    I                       ********************************     I
 9       0.826    0.279    2.956    I                       *******************************      I
10       0.819    0.293    2.799    I                       *******************************      I
11       0.813    0.305    2.660    I                       *******************************      I
12       0.807    0.317    2.544    I                       ******************************       I
13       0.777    0.329    2.364    I                       ****************************         I
14       0.746    0.339    2.203    I                       ***************************          I
15       0.720    0.348    2.070    I                       **************************           I
16       0.702    0.356    1.971    I                       *************************            I
17       0.687    0.364    1.888    I                       *************************            I
18       0.673    0.371    1.813    I                       ************************             I
19       0.655    0.378    1.734    I                       ***********************               I
20       0.640    0.384    1.665    I                       ***********************               I
21       0.627    0.390    1.608    I                       **********************                I
22       0.620    0.396    1.567    I                       **********************                I
23       0.611    0.401    1.523    I                       *********************                 I
24       0.604    0.406    1.486    I                       *********************                 I
25       0.574    0.411    1.396    I                       ********************                  I
26       0.545    0.416    1.309    I                       *******************                   I
27       0.519    0.420    1.236    I                       ******************                    I
28       0.502    0.424    1.184    I                       *****************                     I
29       0.487    0.427    1.141    I                       *****************                     I
30       0.473    0.430    1.100    I                       ****************                      I
31       0.456    0.433    1.053    I                       ****************                      I
32       0.440    0.436    1.010    I                       ***************                       I
33       0.427    0.438    0.974    I                       **************                        I
34       0.419    0.440    0.951    I                       **************                        I
35       0.410    0.443    0.927    I                       *************                         I
36       0.404    0.445    0.907    I                       *************                         I
                                    +-----------------------------------------------------------------+
```

Figure 6.48 Sample ACF for time series 6.3

220

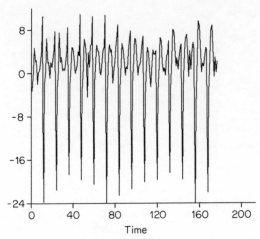

Figure 6.49 Plot of first regular differences of
time series 6.3

MEAN AND STANDARD DEVIATION OF THE WORKING SERIES   IDENTIFICATION RUN
MEAN=   0.9028E 00
STANDARD DEVIATION=   0.7244E 01

AUTOCORRELATION FUNCTION OF THE WORKING SERIES   IDENTIFICATION RUN

	VALUE	S.E.	T VALUE	-1.0	0.0	1.0
1	0.023	0.075	0.305	I	*	I
2	-0.193	0.075	-2.563	I	****	I
3	-0.315	0.078	-4.037	I	********	I
4	-0.121	0.085	-1.425	I	****	I
5	0.002	0.086	0.027	I	*	I
6	0.238	0.086	2.779	I	*******	I
7	-0.004	0.089	-0.046	I	*	I
8	-0.102	0.089	-1.146	I	***	I
9	-0.304	0.090	-3.370	I	********	I
10	-0.177	0.096	-1.850	I	*****	I
11	0.040	0.098	0.407	I	**	I
12	0.898	0.098	9.201	I	*************************	I
13	0.015	0.137	0.111	I	*	I
14	-0.186	0.137	-1.358	I	*****	I
15	-0.293	0.138	-2.122	I	********	I
16	-0.115	0.141	-0.816	I	***	I
17	0.003	0.142	0.023	I	*	I
18	0.221	0.142	1.553	I	******	I
19	0.001	0.144	0.006	I	*	I
20	-0.092	0.144	-0.642	I	***	I
21	-0.274	0.144	-1.900	I	*******	I
22	-0.158	0.147	-1.074	I	****	I
23	0.030	0.148	0.200	I	*	I
24	0.813	0.148	5.467	I	**********************	I
25	0.002	0.172	0.012	I	*	I
26	-0.172	0.172	-1.004	I	*****	I
27	-0.265	0.172	-1.533	I	*******	I
28	-0.116	0.175	-0.665	I	***	I
29	0.014	0.175	0.080	I	*	I
30	0.210	0.175	1.196	I	******	I
31	-0.003	0.177	-0.016	I	*	I
32	-0.033	0.177	-0.469	I	***	I
33	-0.258	0.177	-1.456	I	*******	I
34	-0.141	0.179	-0.790	I	****	I
35	0.034	0.180	0.188	I	*	I
36	0.752	0.180	4.188	I	*********************	I

Figure 6.50 Sample ACF for first regular differences of time series 6.3

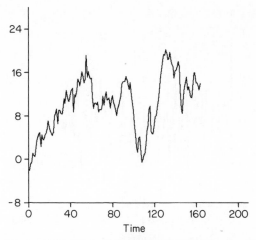

Figure 6.51 Plot of first seasonal differences of
time series 6.3

```
MEAN AND STANDARD DEVIATION OF THE WORKING SERIES      IDENTIFICATION RUN
MEAN=    0.1038E 02
STANDARD DEVIATION=    0.5052E 01

AUTOCORRELATION FUNCTION OF THE WORKING SERIES    IDENTIFICATION RUN


          VALUE    S.E.   T VALUE   -1.0                    0.0                    1.0
                                    +------------------------------------------------+
    1     0.933    0.078   12.019   I                       ************************* I
    2     0.863    0.128    6.716   I                       *********************** I
    3     0.793    0.160    4.968   I                       ********************* I
    4     0.730    0.182    4.014   I                       ******************* I
    5     0.676    0.199    3.402   I                       ****************** I
    6     0.616    0.212    2.907   I                       ****************** I
    7     0.554    0.223    2.487   I                       *************** I
    8     0.500    0.231    2.165   I                       ************** I
    9     0.435    0.237    1.836   I                       ************ I
   10     0.370    0.242    1.529   I                       ********** I
   11     0.305    0.245    1.244   I                       ******** I
   12     0.231    0.248    0.935   I                       ******* I
   13     0.196    0.249    0.788   I                       ***** I
   14     0.159    0.250    0.637   I                       ***** I
   15     0.125    0.250    0.497   I                       **** I
   16     0.087    0.251    0.346   I                       *** I
   17     0.039    0.251    0.155   I                       ** I
   18    -0.000    0.251   -0.002   I                       * I
   19    -0.027    0.251   -0.106   I                       * I
   20    -0.058    0.251   -0.230   I                      ** I
   21    -0.082    0.251   -0.327   I                      *** I
   22    -0.111    0.251   -0.443   I                      *** I
   23    -0.144    0.252   -0.570   I                     **** I
   24    -0.173    0.252   -0.686   I                     ***** I
   25    -0.187    0.253   -0.741   I                     ***** I
   26    -0.195    0.254   -0.767   I                     ***** I
   27    -0.201    0.255   -0.788   I                    ****** I
   28    -0.204    0.255   -0.797   I                    ****** I
   29    -0.197    0.256   -0.769   I                     ***** I
   30    -0.196    0.257   -0.763   I                     ***** I
   31    -0.195    0.258   -0.756   I                     ***** I
   32    -0.186    0.259   -0.719   I                     ***** I
   33    -0.168    0.260   -0.647   I                     ***** I
   34    -0.142    0.261   -0.546   I                     **** I
   35    -0.122    0.261   -0.467   I                     **** I
   36    -0.102    0.261   -0.391   I                      *** I
                                    +------------------------------------------------+
```

Figure 6.52 Sample ACF for first seasonal differences of time series 6.3

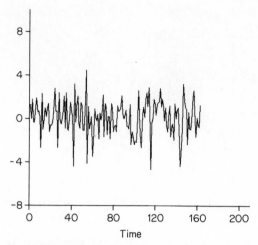

Figure 6.53 Plot of first regular and first seasonal differences of time series 6.3

```
MEAN AND STANDARD DEVIATION OF THE WORKING SERIES          IDENTIFICATION RUN
MEAN=    0.8727E-01
STANDARD DEVIATION=    0.1576E 01

AUTOCORRELATION FUNCTION OF THE WORKING SERIES    IDENTIFICATION RUN

            VALUE   S.E.   T VALUE   -1.0                    0.0                         1.0
                                     +--------------------------------------------------------+
      1     0.063   0.078    0.807   I                        **                             I
      2    -0.008   0.078   -0.106   I                        *                              I
      3    -0.013   0.078   -0.162   I                        *                              I
      4    -0.112   0.078   -1.432   I                       ***                             I
      5     0.043   0.079    0.548   I                        **                             I
      6     0.065   0.079    0.825   I                        **                             I
      7    -0.043   0.080   -0.542   I                        **                             I
      8     0.118   0.080    1.480   I                        ****                           I
      9     0.045   0.081    0.554   I                        **                             I
     10     0.009   0.081    0.111   I                        *                              I
     11     0.007   0.081    0.088   I                        *                              I
     12    -0.333   0.081   -4.117   I                ********                               I
     13    -0.022   0.089   -0.250   I                        *                              I
     14    -0.022   0.089   -0.250   I                        *                              I
     15     0.048   0.089    0.535   I                        **                             I
     16     0.114   0.089    1.276   I                        ***                            I
     17    -0.057   0.090   -0.638   I                        **                             I
     18    -0.087   0.090   -0.965   I                       ***                             I
     19     0.028   0.091    0.306   I                        *                              I
     20    -0.093   0.091   -1.028   I                       ***                             I
     21     0.014   0.091    0.158   I                        *                              I
     22    -0.003   0.091   -0.037   I                        *                              I
     23    -0.016   0.091   -0.175   I                        *                              I
     24    -0.068   0.091   -0.743   I                        **                             I
     25    -0.051   0.092   -0.556   I                        **                             I
     26     0.007   0.092    0.071   I                        *                              I
     27    -0.107   0.092   -1.170   I                       ***                             I
     28    -0.038   0.093   -0.411   I                        *                              I
     29     0.051   0.093    0.555   I                        **                             I
     30    -0.021   0.093   -0.227   I                        *                              I
     31    -0.101   0.093   -1.084   I                       ***                             I
     32    -0.066   0.094   -0.710   I                        **                             I
     33    -0.017   0.094   -0.185   I                        *                              I
     34     0.022   0.094    0.234   I                        *                              I
     35     0.075   0.094    0.800   I                        **                             I
     36     0.039   0.094    0.417   I                        **                             I
                                     +--------------------------------------------------------+
```

Figure 6.54 Sample ACF for first regular and first seasonal differences of time series 6.3

PARTIAL AUTOCORRELATION FUNCTION OF THE WORKING SERIES   IDENTIFICATION RUN

	VALUE	S.E.	T VALUE	-1.0	0.0	1.0
1	0.063	0.078	0.807	I	**	I
2	-0.012	0.078	-0.158	I	*	I
3	-0.011	0.078	-0.146	I	*	I
4	-0.111	0.078	-1.426	I	***	I
5	0.058	0.078	0.746	I	**	I
6	0.058	0.078	0.739	I	**	I
7	-0.053	0.078	-0.685	I	**	I
8	0.116	0.078	1.495	I	****	I
9	0.042	0.078	0.535	I	**	I
10	0.015	0.078	0.197	I	*	I
11	-0.008	0.078	-0.108	I	*	I
12	-0.319	0.078	-4.096	I	*******	I
13	0.030	0.078	0.383	I	*	I
14	-0.052	0.078	-0.667	I	**	I
15	0.060	0.078	0.767	I	**	I
16	0.045	0.078	0.572	I	**	I
17	-0.056	0.078	-0.724	I	**	I
18	-0.042	0.078	-0.543	I	**	I
19	0.014	0.078	0.179	I	*	I
20	-0.024	0.078	-0.307	I	*	I
21	0.031	0.078	0.396	I	*	I
22	-0.011	0.078	-0.144	I	*	I
23	0.012	0.078	0.149	I	*	I
24	-0.229	0.078	-2.942	I	******	I
25	-0.033	0.078	-0.420	I	*	I
26	0.010	0.078	0.127	I	*	I
27	-0.101	0.078	-1.295	I	***	I
28	0.032	0.078	0.415	I	*	I
29	0.024	0.078	0.310	I	*	I
30	-0.055	0.078	-0.701	I	**	I
31	-0.134	0.078	-1.727	I	****	I
32	-0.100	0.078	-1.282	I	***	I
33	0.086	0.078	1.110	I	***	I
34	-0.002	0.078	-0.030	I	*	I
35	0.099	0.078	1.273	I	***	I
36	-0.054	0.078	-0.693	I	**	I

Figure 6.55 Sample PACF for first regular and first seasonal differences of time series 6.3

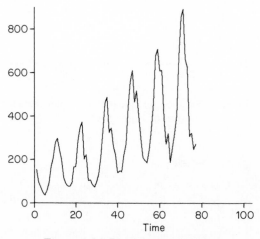

Figure 6.56 Plot of time series 6.4

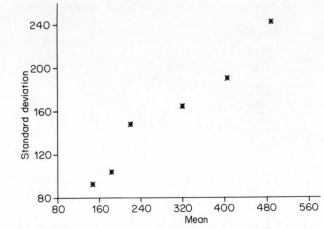

Figure 6.57 Plot of means and standard deviations of subsets of time series 6.4

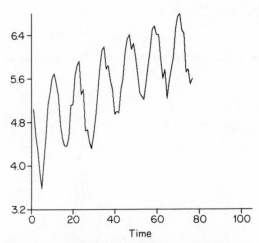

Figure 6.58 Plot of logarithmic transformation of time series 6.4

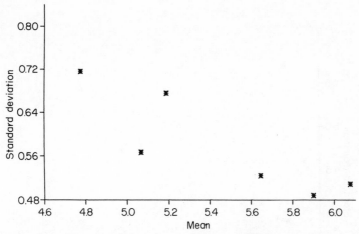

Figure 6.59 Plot of means and standard deviations of subsets of logarithmic transformation of time series 6.4

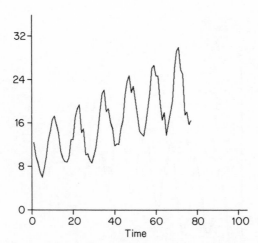

Figure 6.60 Plot of square root transformation of time series 6.4

226

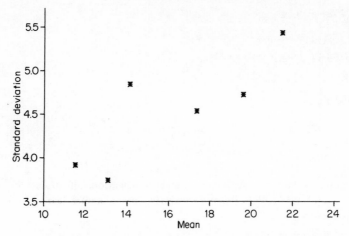

Figure 6.61 Plot of means and standard deviations of subsets of square root transformation of time series 6.4

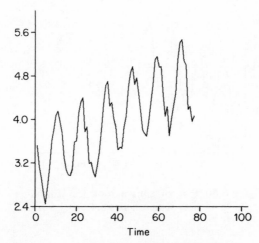

Figure 6.62 Plot of fourth root transformation of time series 6.4

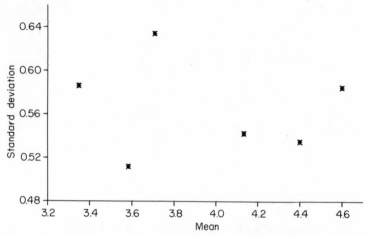

Figure 6.63 Plot of means and standard deviations of subsets of fourth root transformation of time series 6.4

MEAN AND STANDARD DEVIATION OF THE WORKING SERIES   IDENTIFICATION RUN
MEAN=   0.3984E 01
STANDARD DEVIATION=   0.6983E 00

AUTOCORRELATION FUNCTION OF THE WORKING SERIES   IDENTIFICATION RUN

```
        VALUE   S.E.   T VALUE   -1.0                    0.0                         1.0
                                  +-------------------------------------------------------+
    1   0.893   0.114   7.834    I                        ********************************    I
    2   0.712   0.184   3.879    I                        ***********************         I
    3   0.445   0.216   2.054    I                        ***********             I
    4   0.137   0.228   0.822    I                        *****                   I
    5  -0.014   0.230  -0.062    I                        *                       I
    6  -0.093   0.230  -0.403    I                     ***                        I
    7  -0.066   0.231  -0.287    I                      **                        I
    8   0.079   0.231   0.340    I                        ***                     I
    9   0.279   0.231   1.208    I                        ********                I
   10   0.480   0.235   2.037    I                        ************            I
   11   0.632   0.248   2.549    I                        ****************        I
   12   0.688   0.268   2.567    I                        ******************      I
   13   0.614   0.290   2.118    I                        ****************        I
   14   0.460   0.306   1.500    I                        ************            I
   15   0.247   0.315   0.783    I                        *******                 I
   16   0.033   0.318   0.103    I                        *                       I
   17  -0.136   0.318  -0.427    I                     ****                       I
   18  -0.212   0.318  -0.666    I                   ******                       I
   19  -0.193   0.320  -0.602    I                    *****                       I
   20  -0.065   0.322  -0.263    I                      ***                       I
   21   0.072   0.322   0.223    I                        **                      I
   22   0.243   0.322   0.753    I                        *******                 I
   23   0.365   0.325   1.125    I                        **********              I
   24   0.424   0.330   1.284    I                        ************            I
   25   0.379   0.337   1.123    I                        **********              I
   26   0.265   0.342   0.773    I                        *******                 I
   27   0.034   0.345   0.239    I                        **                      I
   28  -0.097   0.345  -0.280    I                     ***                        I
   29  -0.258   0.346  -0.745    I                  *******                       I
   30  -0.343   0.348  -0.985    I                *********                       I
   31  -0.356   0.353  -1.010    I                *********                       I
   32  -0.291   0.357  -0.815    I                 ********                       I
   33  -0.178   0.360  -0.495    I                    *****                       I
   34  -0.040   0.361  -0.110    I                        *                       I
   35   0.069   0.361   0.190    I                        **                      I
   36   0.136   0.362   0.375    I                        ****                    I
                                  +-------------------------------------------------------+
```

Figure 6.64 Sample ACF for fourth root transformation of time series 6.4

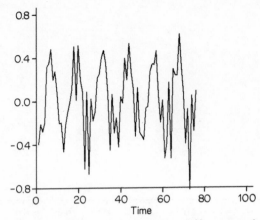

Figure 6.65 Plot of first regular differences of
fourth root transformation of time series 6.4

```
MEAN AND STANDARD DEVIATION OF THE WORKING SERIES        IDENTIFICATION RUN
MEAN=   0.7084E-02
STANDARD DEVIATION=   0.3209E 00

AUTOCORRELATION FUNCTION OF THE WORKING SERIES    IDENTIFICATION RUN
```

	VALUE	S.E.	T VALUE	-1.0	0.0	1.0
1	0.329	0.115	2.871	I	****×**×*×	I
2	0.399	0.127	3.156	I	********×**×	I
3	-0.065	0.142	-0.460	I	**	I
4	-0.290	0.143	-2.033	I	*******××	I
5	-0.573	0.150	-3.819	I	*****************	I
6	-0.490	0.177	-2.775	I	*************	I
7	-0.539	0.194	-2.782	I	***************×	I
8	-0.255	0.212	-1.198	I	*******	I
9	0.024	0.216	0.112	I	*	I
10	0.238	0.217	1.098	I	*******	I
11	0.451	0.220	2.051	I	**********×**	I
12	0.613	0.232	2.647	I	**************×***×	I
13	0.354	0.252	1.405	I	*********×**	I
14	0.268	0.259	1.036	I	******×	I
15	-0.006	0.262	-0.022	I	*	I
16	-0.227	0.262	-0.867	I	******	I
17	-0.435	0.265	-1.641	I	***********	I
18	-0.434	0.274	-1.582	I	***********	I
19	-0.426	0.283	-1.506	I	***********	I
20	-0.197	0.291	-0.677	I	*****	I
21	-0.053	0.293	-0.182	I	**	I
22	0.239	0.293	0.817	I	*******	I
23	0.273	0.296	0.923	I	*******×	I
24	0.502	0.299	1.679	I	**************×××	I
25	0.288	0.310	0.930	I	********	I
26	0.290	0.313	0.926	I	********×	I
27	0.037	0.317	0.116	I	*	I
28	-0.131	0.317	-0.412	I	****	I
29	-0.350	0.318	-1.100	I	*********	I
30	-0.337	0.323	-1.045	I	*********	I
31	-0.350	0.327	-1.070	I	*********	I
32	-0.200	0.332	-0.602	I	******	I
33	-0.097	0.334	-0.289	I	***	I
34	0.152	0.334	0.455	I	****	I
35	0.175	0.335	0.523	I	*****	I
36	0.387	0.336	1.152	I	**********	I

Figure 6.66 Sample ACF for first regular differences of fourth root transformation
of time series 6.4

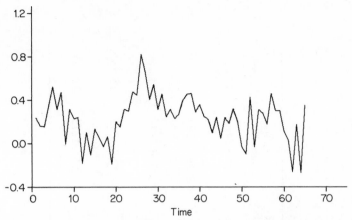

Figure 6.67 Plot of first seasonal differences of fourth root transformation of time series 6.4

```
MEAN AND STANDARD DEVIATION OF THE WORKING SERIES        IDENTIFICATION RUN
MEAN=   0.2321E 00
STANDARD DEVIATION=    0.2103E 00

AUTOCORRELATION FUNCTION OF THE WORKING SERIES     IDENTIFICATION RUN


          VALUE    S.E.   T VALUE   -1.0                    0.0                     1.0
                                    +-----------------------------------------------------+
    1     0.396    0.124    3.194   I                      *******+*+**               I
    2     0.537    0.142    3.775   I                      ********+*+*+*+*            I
    3     0.225    0.171    1.320   I                      ******                     I
    4     0.192    0.175    1.097   I                      *+***                      I
    5     0.070    0.178    0.391   I                      **                         I
    6     0.042    0.179    0.236   I                      **                         I
    7    -0.130    0.179   -0.727   I                    ****                         I
    8    -0.101    0.180   -0.562   I                     ***                         I
    9    -0.057    0.181   -0.317   I                      **                         I
   10    -0.141    0.181   -0.777   I                    ****                         I
   11     0.087    0.183    0.473   I                      ***                        I
   12    -0.222    0.184   -1.207   I                   ******                        I
   13    -0.098    0.188   -0.521   I                     ***                         I
   14    -0.215    0.189   -1.138   I                   ******                        I
   15    -0.136    0.192   -0.706   I                    ****                         I
   16    -0.118    0.194   -0.607   I                     ***                         I
   17    -0.056    0.195   -0.287   I                      **                         I
   18    -0.105    0.195   -0.537   I                     ***                         I
   19    -0.037    0.196   -0.190   I                      *                          I
   20    -0.035    0.196   -0.178   I                      *                          I
   21    -0.021    0.196   -0.107   I                      *                          I
   22    -0.057    0.196   -0.291   I                     **                          I
   23    -0.138    0.196   -0.701   I                    ****                         I
   24    -0.202    0.198   -1.023   I                   ******                        I
   25    -0.170    0.201   -0.846   I                    *****                        I
   26    -0.078    0.203   -0.382   I                     **                          I
   27    -0.094    0.204   -0.464   I                     ***                         I
   28     0.013    0.204    0.064   I                      *                          I
   29     0.001    0.204    0.005   I                      *                          I
   30     0.058    0.204    0.282   I                      **                         I
   31     0.099    0.205    0.483   I                      ***                        I
   32     0.097    0.205    0.475   I                      ***                        I
   33    -0.003    0.206   -0.014   I                      *                          I
   34    -0.012    0.206   -0.060   I                      *                          I
   35    -0.128    0.206   -0.622   I                    ****                         I
   36    -0.143    0.207   -0.691   I                    ****                         I
                                    +-----------------------------------------------------+
```

Figure 6.68 Sample ACF for first seasonal differences of fourth root transformation of time series 6.4

Table 6.4 Fitted models for time series 6.2

Model type	Fitted model $(W_t = Z_t - Z_{t-1} - Z_{t-12} + Z_{t-13})$	Residual variance	Q statistic
$(0, 1, 0) \times (0, 1, 1)_{12}$	$W_t = A_t - (0.8962)\, A_{t-12}$ $(t = 10.6523)$	545.9482	12.001
$(1, 1, 0) \times (0, 1, 1)_{12}$	$W_t = (0.0109)\, W_{t-1} + A_t - (0.8962)\, A_{t-12}$ $(t = 0.1122) \qquad\qquad (t = 10.6169)$	549.9597	12.580
$(0, 1, 1) \times (0, 1, 1)_{12}$	$W_t = (1 + (0.0062)B)\,(1 - (0.9369)B^{12})\, A_t$ $(t = -0.0642) \qquad (t = 14.4787)$	536.6121	11.107
$(0, 1, 0) \times (1, 1, 1)_{12}$	$W_t = -(0.0594)\, W_{t-12} + A_t - (0.8723)\, A_{t-12}$ $(t = -0.4297) \qquad\qquad (t = 9.7556)$	558.3005	15.451
$(0, 1, 0) \times (0, 1, 2)_{12}$	$W_t = A_t - (1.1083)\, A_{t-12} + (0.2283)\, A_{t-24}$ $(t = 9.0559) \qquad\quad (t = -1.7842)$	551.2275	12.851

Table 6.5 Fitted models for time series 6.3

Model type	Fitted model $(W_t = Z_t - Z_{t-1} - Z_{t-12} + Z_{t-13})$	Residual variance	Q statistic
$(0, 1, 1) \times (0, 1, 1)_{12}$	$W_t = (1 + (0.0948)B)(1 - (0.5519)B^{12})A_t$ $\qquad\qquad (t = -1.2166) \qquad (t = 8.1094)$	2.0069	9.101
$(1, 1, 1) \times (0, 1, 1)_{12}$	$(1 - (0.2494)B)W_t = (1 - (0.1521)B)(1 - (0.5569)B^{12})A_t$ $(t = 0.3320) \qquad\qquad (t = 0.1986) \qquad (t = 8.1534)$	2.0177	9.433
$(0, 1, 2) \times (0, 1, 1)_{12}$	$W_t = (1 + (0.0962)B + (0.0229)B^2)(1 - (0.5567)B^{12})A_t$ $\qquad (t = -1.2241)(t = -0.2916) \qquad (t = 8.1539)$	2.0177	9.436
$(0, 1, 1) \times (1, 1, 1)_{12}$	$(1 - (0.2157)B^{12})W_t = (1 + (0.0964)B)(1 - (0.7146)B^{12})A_t$ $\qquad (t = 1.4446) \qquad\qquad (t = -1.2349) \qquad (t = 6.0268)$	1.9903	10.523
$(0, 1, 1) \times (0, 1, 2)_{12}$	$W_t = (1 + (0.0950)B)(1 - (0.4975)B^{12} - (0.1253)B^{24})A_t$ $\qquad\qquad (t = -1.2166) \qquad (t = 6.3210) \qquad (t = 1.4588)$	1.9905	10.638

Table 6.6 Fitted models for time series 6.4

Model type	Fitted model $(W_t = Z_t^* - Z_{t-1}^* - Z_{t-12}^* + Z_{t-13}^*,\ Z_t^* = (Z_t)^{0.25})$	Residual variance	Q statistic
$(1, 1, 0) \times (0, 1, 1)_{12}$	$W_t = -(0.5082)\,W_{t-1} + A_t - (0.7995)\,A_{t-12}$ $\quad\quad (t = -4.4934) \quad\quad\quad (t = 6.4344)$	0.0211	21.468
$(2, 1, 0) \times (0, 1, 1)_{12}$	$W_t = -(0.4780)\,W_{t-1} + (0.0618)\,W_{t-2} + A_t - (0.7996)\,A_{t-12}$ $\quad\quad (t = -3.5545) \quad (t = 0.4699) \quad\quad\quad (t = 6.2523)$	0.0213	20.985
$(1, 1, 1) \times (0, 1, 1)_{12}$	$(1 + (0.6494)\,B)\,W_t = (1 + (0.2178)\,B)\,(1 - (0.8401)\,B^{12})\,A_t$ $\quad\quad (t = -3.3249) \quad\quad (t = -0.8695) \quad (t = 7.1769)$	0.0203	20.305
$(1, 1, 0) \times (1, 1, 1)_{12}$	$(1 + (0.5162)\,B)\,(1 - (0.0010)\,B^{12})\,W_t = (1 - (0.8376)\,B^{12})\,A_t$ $\quad\quad (t = -4.2234) \quad (t = 0.0052) \quad\quad\quad (t = 5.5713)$	0.0206	20.933
$(1, 1, 0) \times (0, 1, 2)_{12}$	$W_t = -(0.6023)\,W_{t-1} + A_t - (0.4824)\,A_{t-12} - (0.2964)\,A_{t-24}$ $\quad\quad (t = -5.2005) \quad\quad\quad (t = 2.9676) \quad\quad (t = 1.6174)$	0.0227	19.823

Table 6.7 Characteristic properties of regular and seasonal operators in multiplicative seasonal models

Operator	Theoretical ACF of stationary differenced time series	Theoretical PACF of stationary differenced time series
Regular autoregressive of order 1 $(1 - \phi_1 B)$	Tails off towards zero	Cuts off after lag 1
Regular autoregressive of order 2 $(1 - \phi_1 B - \phi_2 B^2)$	Tails off towards zero	Cuts off after lag 2
Regular moving average of order 1 $(1 - \theta_1 B)$	Cuts off after lag 1	Tails off towards zero
Regular moving average of order 2 $(1 - \theta_1 B - \theta_2 B^2)$	Cuts off after lag 2	Tails off towards zero
Seasonal autoregressive of order 1 $(1 - \phi_{12} B^{12})$	Autocorrelations at lags 12, 24, 36 tail off towards zero	Partial autocorrelations at lags 12, 24, 36 cut off after lag 12
Seasonal autoregressive of order 2 $(1 - \phi_{12} B^{12} - \phi_{24} B^{24})$	Autocorrelations at lags 12, 24, 36 tail off towards zero	Partial autocorrelations at lags 12, 24, 36 cut off after lag 24
Seasonal moving average of order 1 $(1 - \theta_{12} B^{12})$	Autocorrelations at lags 12, 24, 36 cut off after lag 12	Partial autocorrelations at lags 12, 24, 36 tail off towards zero
Seasonal moving average of order 2 $(1 - \theta_{12} B^{12} - \theta_{24} B^{24})$	Autocorrelations at lags 12, 24, 36 cut off after lag 24	Partial autocorrelations at lags 12, 24, 36 tail off towards zero

Table 6.8 Means and standard deviations of subsets of the time series used in the examples in this chapter

| | Time series 6.1 | | | Time series 2.3 | |
Subset	Mean	Standard deviation	Subset	Mean	Standard deviation
1–12	32.3	1.3	1–12	61.0	6.9
13–24	34.1	0.8	13–24	59.4	6.6
25–36	34.6	0.7	25–36	58.6	6.9
37–48	35.7	1.4	37–48	58.0	6.6
49–60	38.7	1.2	49–60	58.3	6.6
61–72	40.0	1.0	61–72	58.6	6.6
73–84	40.8	0.6	73–84	58.5	5.9
85–96	41.5	0.9	85–96	58.3	7.1
97–108	44.6	1.2	97–108	57.6	6.4
109–120	43.8	0.8	109–120	57.7	6.3
121–132	42.4	0.9	121–132	57.2	6.7
133–144	44.0	1.2	133–144	57.3	6.6
145–156	47.9	1.7	145–156	58.8	6.4
157–168	50.1	0.9	157–168	61.0	7.8
1–178	41.0	5.1	1–178	58.8	6.7

	Time series 2.4			Time series 2.4 (logarithmic transformation)	
1–12	126.7	13.7	1–12	4.8	0.1
13–24	139.7	19.1	13–24	4.9	0.1
25–36	170.2	18.4	25–36	5.1	0.1
37–48	197.0	23.0	37–48	5.3	0.1
49–60	225.0	28.5	49–60	5.4	0.1
61–72	238.9	34.9	61–72	5.5	0.1
73–84	284.0	42.1	73–84	5.6	0.1
85–96	328.3	47.9	85–96	5.8	0.1
97–108	368.4	57.9	97–108	5.9	0.2
109–120	381.0	64.5	109–120	5.9	0.2
121–132	428.3	69.8	121–132	6.0	0.2
133–144	476.2	77.7	133–144	6.2	0.2
1–144	280.3	120.0	1–144	5.5	0.4

Table 6.9 Means and standard deviations of subsets of the time series used in the exercises in this chapter

	Time series 6.2			Time series 6.3			Time series 6.4	
Subset	Mean	Standard deviation	Subset	Mean	Standard deviation	Subset	Mean	Standard deviation
1–12	351.4	18.9	1–12	244.7	6.7	1–12	146.8	92.7
13–24	376.3	18.8	13–24	246.4	8.2	13–24	183.8	104.1
25–36	418.8	17.5	25–36	251.3	8.6	25–36	220.7	148.1
37–48	459.7	22.6	37–48	260.5	9.8	37–48	320.3	164.4
49–60	524.3	33.2	49–60	272.6	10.9	49–60	405.8	190.0
61–72	601.4	26.1	61–72	288.0	10.9	61–72	489.0	242.1
73–84	579.9	61.2	73–84	298.0	10.9			
85–96	554.1	32.7	85–96	308.6	9.8	1–77	298.4	198.4
97–108	641.9	22.6	97–108	321.6	11.2			
109–120	703.3	32.0	109–120	327.4	7.2			
121–132	749.1	27.1	121–132	332.1	9.1			
133–144	763.5	90.0	133–144	346.9	13.6			
			145–156	364.4	12.9			
			157–168	376.6	13.7			
1–144	560.9	138.8	1–178	307.5	46.8			

	Time series 6.4 (logarithmic transformation)			Time series 6.4 (square root transformation)			Time series 6.4 (fourth root transformation)	
Subset	Mean	Standard deviation	Subset	Mean	Standard deviation	Subset	Mean	Standard deviation
1–12	4.8	0.7	1–12	11.5	3.9	1–12	3.3	0.6
13–24	5.1	0.6	13–24	13.1	3.7	13–24	3.6	0.5
25–36	5.2	0.7	25–36	14.1	4.8	25–36	3.7	0.6
37–48	5.6	0.5	37–48	17.4	4.5	37–48	4.1	0.5
49–60	5.9	0.5	49–60	19.6	4.7	49–60	4.4	0.5
61–72	6.1	0.5	61–72	21.5	5.4	61–72	4.6	0.6
1–77	5.5	0.7	1–77	16.4	5.6	1–77	4.0	0.7

236

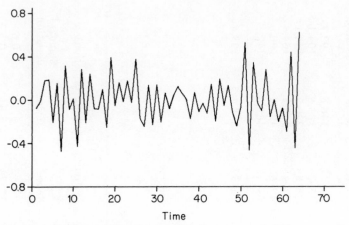

Figure 6.69 Plot of first regular and first seasonal differences of fourth root transformation of time series 6.4

MEAN AND STANDARD DEVIATION OF THE WORKING SERIES   IDENTIFICATION RUN
MEAN=   0.1804E-02
STANDARD DEVIATION=   0.2326E 00

AUTOCORRELATION FUNCTION OF THE WORKING SERIES   IDENTIFICATION RUN

         VALUE   S.E.   T VALUE   -1.0   0.0   1.0
                                      +---+
   1   -0.597   0.125   -4.773   I   ***************   I
   2   0.360   0.164   2.202   I   **********   I
   3   -0.216   0.176   -1.231   I   ******   I
   4   0.064   0.180   0.356   I   **   I
   5   -0.081   0.180   -0.451   I   ***   I
   6   0.113   0.181   0.626   I   ***   I
   7   -0.166   0.182   -0.916   I   *****   I
   8   -0.019   0.184   -0.103   I   *   I
   9   0.116   0.184   0.632   I   ****   I
  10   -0.262   0.185   -1.417   I   *******   I
  11   0.445   0.191   2.331   I   ************* I
  12   -0.348   0.206   -1.684   I   *********   I
  13   0.184   0.215   0.853   I   *****   I
  14   -0.144   0.218   -0.662   I   ****   I
  15   0.048   0.219   0.220   I   **   I
  16   -0.045   0.220   -0.203   I   **   I
  17   0.087   0.220   0.398   I   ***   I
  18   -0.092   0.220   -0.417   I   ***   I
  19   0.052   0.221   0.234   I   **   I
  20   -0.003   0.221   -0.012   I   *   I
  21   0.034   0.221   0.156   I   *   I
  22   0.042   0.221   0.191   I   **   I
  23   -0.018   0.221   -0.081   I   *   I
  24   -0.082   0.221   -0.370   I   ***   I
  25   -0.054   0.222   -0.244   I   **   I
  26   0.094   0.222   0.422   I   ***   I
  27   -0.109   0.223   -0.490   I   ***   I
  28   0.099   0.223   0.445   I   ***   I
  29   -0.055   0.224   -0.243   I   **   I
  30   0.017   0.224   0.076   I   *   I
  31   0.037   0.224   0.166   I   *   I
  32   0.079   0.224   0.354   I   ***   I
  33   -0.073   0.225   -0.325   I   **   I
  34   0.081   0.225   0.359   I   ***   I
  35   -0.079   0.226   -0.350   I   **   I
  36   -0.084   0.226   -0.373   I   ***   I
                                      +---+

Figure 6.70 Sample ACF for first regular and first seasonal differences of fourth root transformation of time series 6.4

PARTIAL AUTOCORRELATION FUNCTION OF THE WORKING SERIES   IDENTIFICATION RUN

	VALUE	S.E.	T VALUE	−1.0	0.0	1.0
1	−0.597	0.125	−4.773	I	****************	I
2	0.006	0.125	0.052	I	*	I
3	0.002	0.125	0.016	I	*	I
4	−0.102	0.125	−0.816	I	***	I
5	−0.127	0.125	−1.020	I	****	I
6	0.063	0.125	0.502	I	**	I
7	−0.101	0.125	−0.809	I	***	I
8	−0.311	0.125	−2.485	I	********	I
9	0.039	0.125	0.313	I	**	I
10	−0.224	0.125	−1.790	I	******	I
11	0.229	0.125	1.832	I	******	I
12	0.051	0.125	0.410	I	**	I
13	−0.159	0.125	−1.276	I	****	I
14	−0.119	0.125	−0.950	I	***	I
15	−0.150	0.125	−1.203	I	****	I
16	−0.050	0.125	−0.397	I	**	I
17	−0.062	0.125	−0.497	I	**	I
18	0.015	0.125	0.117	I	*	I
19	0.049	0.125	0.395	I	**	I
20	−0.108	0.125	−0.861	I	***	I
21	0.142	0.125	1.133	I	****	I
22	−0.093	0.125	−0.741	I	***	I
23	0.022	0.125	0.176	I	*	I
24	−0.109	0.125	−0.873	I	***	I
25	−0.287	0.125	−2.296	I	********	I
26	0.110	0.125	0.877	I	***	I
27	−0.122	0.125	−0.974	I	****	I
28	−0.036	0.125	−0.287	I	*	I
29	0.008	0.125	0.066	I	*	I
30	−0.097	0.125	−0.780	I	***	I
31	0.091	0.125	0.731	I	***	I
32	−0.079	0.125	−0.634	I	**	I
33	0.076	0.125	0.609	I	**	I
34	−0.041	0.125	−0.330	I	**	I
35	0.050	0.125	0.401	I	**	I
36	−0.047	0.125	−0.379	I	**	I

Figure 6.71 Sample PACF for first regular and first seasonal differences of fourth root transformation of time series 6.4

(c) Identify a tentative multiplicative seasonal model for the time series.

(d) Choose the most appropriate fitted model for the time series from those given in Tables 6.4, 6.5, and 6.6.

6.8.2 (This exercise is intended for readers with access to computer packages using the Box–Jenkins approach and the only information provided about each time series is the time series itself.) Identify tentative models for time series 6.5, 6.8, 6.10, and 6.14 in Appendix A.3.

6.9 REVISION EXERCISES

(These exercises are intended for readers with access to computer packages using the Box–Jenkins approach and the only information provided about each time series is the time series itself. In Appendix A.4, a table is given showing the types of models that have been fitted to those time series. However, other types of models may give equally good fits.)

6.9.1 Time series 6.5 to 6.14 are given in Appendix A.3. For each time series, use the Box–Jenkins approach to fit an appropriate model to the time series and forecast the next twelve observations.

Table 6.10 Standard deviations of the time series and their differences used in this chapter

Time series 6.1

		D	
d	0	1	2
0	5.1	2.5	3.4
1	0.7	0.8	1.4
2	1.0	1.2	2.1

Time series 2.3

		D	
d	0	1	2
0	6.9	1.7	2.6
1	4.5	1.4	2.4
2	4.5	2.0	3.5

Time series 2.4
(logarithmic transformation)

		D	
d	0	1	2
0	0.44	0.06	0.10
1	0.11	0.05	0.08
2	0.14	0.08	0.13

Time series 6.2

		D	
d	0	1	2
0	138.8	62.9	89.4
1	28.8	28.5	44.0
2	39.2	39.2	63.3

Time series 6.3

		D	
d	0	1	2
0	46.8	5.1	5.9
1	7.2	1.6	2.6
2	10.2	2.2	3.6

Time series 6.4
(fourth root transformation)

		D	
d	0	1	2
0	0.70	0.21	0.34
1	0.32	0.23	0.38
2	0.37	0.41	0.68

Appendix A.1

References

BOOKS

Anderson, O. D. (1976). *Time Series Analysis and Forecasting: the Box–Jenkins Approach*, Butterworths, London.

Bowerman, B. L., and O'Connell, R. T. (1979). *Time Series and Forecasting: an Applied Approach*, Duxbury Press, North Scituate, Massachusetts.

Box, G. E. P., and Jenkins, G. M. (1976). *Time Series Analysis: Forecasting and Control*, Holden-Day, San Francisco.

Chatfield, C. (1980). *The Analysis of Time Series: an Introduction*, Chapman and Hall, London.

Cook, T. D., and Campbell, D. T. (1979). *Quasi-Experimentation: Design and Analysis Issues for Field Settings*, Rand McNally, Chicago.

Gilchrist, W. (1976). *Statistical Forecasting*, Wiley, Chichester.

Glass, G. V., Willson, V. L., and Gottman, J. M. (1975). *Design and Analysis of Time-Series Experiments*, Colorado Associated University Press, Boulder, Colorado.

Granger, C. W. J. (1980). *Forecasting in Business and Economics*, Academic Press, New York.

Granger, C. W. J., and Newbold, P. (1977). *Forecasting Economic Time Series*, Academic Press, New York.

Jenkins, G. M. (1979). *Practical Experiences with Modelling and Forecasting Time Series*, Gwilym Jenkins and Partners (Overseas) Ltd, Jersey, Channel Islands.

Mabert, V. A. (1975). *An Introduction to Short Term Forecasting using the Box–Jenkins Methodology*, American Institute of Industrial Engineers, Inc., Norcross, Georgia.

Makridakis, S., and Wheelwright, S. C. (1978). *Forecasting: Methods and Applications*, Wiley, New York.

Makridakis, S., and Wheelwright, S. C. (1978). *Interactive Forecasting: Univariate and Multivariate Methods*, Holden-Day, San Francisco.

McCleary, R., and Hay, R. A., Jr. (1980). *Applied Time Series Analysis for the Social Sciences*, Sage Publications, Beverly Hills, California.

Miller, R. B., and Wichern, D. W. (1977). *Intermediate Business Statistics: Analysis of Variance, Regression and Time Series*, Holt, Rinehart, and Winston, New York.

Montgomery, D. C., and Johnson, L. A. (1976). *Forecasting and Time Series Analysis*, McGraw-Hill, New York.

Nelson, C. R. (1973). *Applied Time Series for Managerial Forecasting*, Holden-Day, San Francisco.

Pindyck, R. S., and Rubinfeld, D. L. (1976). *Econometric Models and Economic Forecasts*, McGraw-Hill, New York.

Thomopoulos, N. T. (1980). *Applied Forecasting Methods*, Prentice-Hall, Englewood Cliffs, New Jersey.

Wheelwright, S. C., and Makridakis, S. (1980). *Forecasting Methods for Management*, Wiley, New York.

CASE STUDIES

Bhattacharyya, M. N. (1974). 'Forecasting the demand for telephones in Australia.' *Appl. Statist.*, **23**, 1–10.

Brubacher, S. R., and Wilson, G. T. (1976). 'Interpolating time series with application to the estimation of holiday effects on electricity demand.' *Appl. Statist.*, **25**, 107–116.

Chatfield, C., and Prothero, D. L. (1973). 'Box–Jenkins seasonal forecasting: problems in a case-study.' *J. R. Statist. Soc., A*, **136**, 295–336.

Cramer, R. H., and Miller, R. B. (1973). 'Development of a deposit forecasting procedure for use in bank financial management.' *J. Bank Research*, **4**, 122–138.

Christ, C. F. (1975). 'Judging the performance of econometric models of the U.S. economy.' *Int. Econ. Review*, **16**, 54–74.

Cooper, R. L. (1972). 'The predictive performance of quarterly econometric models of the United States.' In B. G. Hickman (Ed.), *Econometric Models of Cyclical Behaviour*, Columbia University Press, New York. pp. 813–874.

Cooper, J. P., and Nelson, C. R. (1975). 'The ex ante prediction performance of the St. Louis and FBR–MIT–PENN econometric models and some results on composite predictors.' *J. Money, Credit and Banking*, **7**, 1–32.

Hirsh, A. A., Grimm, B. T., and Narasimham, G. V. L. (1974). 'Some multiplier and error characteristics of the BEA quarterly model.' *Int. Econ. Review*, **15**, 616–631.

Kyle, P. W. (1978). 'Lydia Pinkham Revisited: A Box–Jenkins Approach.' *J. Advertising Research*, **19**, 31–39.

Leuthold, R. M., MacCormick, A. J. A., Schmitz, A., and Watts, D. G. (1970). 'Forecasting daily hog prices and quantities: a study of alternative forecasting techniques.' *J. Am. Statist. Assoc.*, **65**, 90–107.

Mabert, V. A., and Radcliffe, R. C. (1974). 'A forecasting methodology as applied to financial time series.' *Accounting Rev.*, **49**, 61–75.

Makridakis, S., and Wheelwright, S. (1972). 'The Box–Jenkins method of forecasting.' *Eur. Mktng. Rev.*, **7**, 1–18.

Naylor, T. H., Seaks, T. G., and Wichern, D. W. (1972). 'Box–Jenkins Methods: an alternative to econometric models.' *Int. Statist. Rev.*, **40**, 123–137.

Nelson, C. R. (1972). 'The predictive performance of the FRB–MIT–PENN model of the U.S. Economy.' *Am. Econ. Rev.*, **62**, 902–917.

Prothero, D. L., and Wallis, K. F. (1976). 'Modelling macroeconomic time series.' *J. R. Statist. Soc., A*, **139**, 468–500.

Rausser, G. C., and Oliveira, R. A. (1976). 'The econometric analysis of wilderness area use.' *J. Am. Statist. Assoc.*, **71**, 276–285.

Thompson, H. E., and Tiao, G. C. (1971). 'Analysis of telephone data: a case study of forecasting seasonal time series,' *Bell J. Econ. Manag. Sci.*, **2**, 515–541.

Tomasek, O. (1972). 'Statistical forecasting of telephone time series.' *Telecommunication J.*, **39**, 725–731.

Trivedi, P. K. (1973). 'Retail inventory investment behaviour.' *J. Econometrics*, **1**, 61–80.

Vigderhous, G. (1978). 'Forecasting sociological phenomena: application of Box–Jenkins methodology to suicide rates.' In K. F. Schuessler (Ed.), *Sociological Methodology 1978*, Jossey–Bass, San Francisco. pp. 20–51.

Zellner, A., and Palm, F. (1974). 'Time series analysis and simultaneous equation econometric models.' *J. Econometrics*, **2**, 17–54.

Appendix A.2
Statistical tables

Table A.2.1 Standardized normal distribution. (The table plots the cumulative probability $Z \geqslant z$)

z	0.00	0.01	0.02	0.03	0.04	0.05	0.06	0.07	0.08	0.09
0.0	0.5000	0.4960	0.4920	0.4880	0.4840	0.4801	0.4761	0.4721	0.4681	0.4641
0.1	0.4602	0.4562	0.4522	0.4483	0.4443	0.4404	0.4364	0.4325	0.4686	0.4247
0.2	0.4207	0.4168	0.4129	0.4090	0.4052	0.4013	0.3974	0.3936	0.3897	0.3859
0.3	0.3821	0.3873	0.3745	0.3707	0.3669	0.3632	0.3594	0.3557	0.3520	0.3483
0.4	0.3446	0.3409	0.3372	0.3336	0.3300	0.3264	0.3228	0.3192	0.3156	0.3121
0.5	0.3085	0.3050	0.3015	0.2981	0.2946	0.2912	0.2877	0.2843	0.2810	0.2776
0.6	0.2743	0.2709	0.2676	0.2643	0.2611	0.2578	0.2546	0.2514	0.2483	0.2451
0.7	0.2420	0.2389	0.2358	0.2327	0.2296	0.2266	0.2236	0.2206	0.2217	0.2148
0.8	0.2119	0.2090	0.2061	0.2033	0.2005	0.1977	0.1949	0.1922	0.1894	0.1867
0.9	0.1841	0.1814	0.1788	0.1762	0.1736	0.1711	0.1685	0.1660	0.1635	0.1611
1.0	0.1587	0.1562	0.1539	0.1515	0.1492	0.1469	0.1446	0.1423	0.1401	0.1379
1.1	0.1357	0.1335	0.1314	0.1292	0.1271	0.1251	0.1230	0.1210	0.1190	0.1170
1.2	0.1151	0.1131	0.1112	0.1093	0.1075	0.1056	0.1038	0.1020	0.1003	0.0985
1.3	0.0968	0.0951	0.0934	0.0918	0.0901	0.0885	0.0869	0.0853	0.0838	0.0823
1.4	0.0808	0.0793	0.0778	0.0764	0.0749	0.0735	0.0721	0.0708	0.0694	0.0681
1.5	0.0668	0.0655	0.0643	0.0630	0.0618	0.0606	0.0594	0.0582	0.0571	0.0559
1.6	0.0548	0.0537	0.0526	0.0516	0.0505	0.0495	0.0485	0.0475	0.0465	0.0455
1.7	0.0446	0.0436	0.0427	0.0418	0.0409	0.0401	0.0392	0.0384	0.0375	0.0367
1.8	0.0359	0.0351	0.0344	0.0366	0.0329	0.0322	0.0314	0.0307	0.0301	0.0294
1.9	0.0287	0.0281	0.0274	0.0268	0.0262	0.0256	0.0250	0.0244	0.0239	0.0233
2.0	0.0228	0.0222	0.0217	0.0212	0.0207	0.0202	0.0197	0.0192	0.0188	0.0183
2.1	0.0179	0.0174	0.0170	0.0166	0.0162	0.0158	0.0154	0.0150	0.0146	0.0143
2.2	0.0139	0.0136	0.0132	0.0129	0.0125	0.0122	0.0119	0.0116	0.0113	0.0110
2.3	0.0107	0.0104	0.0102	0.0099	0.0096	0.0094	0.0091	0.0089	0.0087	0.0084
2.4	0.0082	0.0080	0.0078	0.0075	0.0073	0.0071	0.0069	0.0068	0.0066	0.0064
2.5	0.0062	0.0060	0.0059	0.0057	0.0055	0.0054	0.0052	0.0051	0.0049	0.0048
2.6	0.0047	0.0045	0.0044	0.0043	0.0041	0.0040	0.0039	0.0038	0.0037	0.0036
2.7	0.0035	0.0034	0.0033	0.0032	0.0031	0.0030	0.0029	0.0028	0.0027	0.0026
2.8	0.0026	0.0025	0.0024	0.0023	0.0023	0.0022	0.0021	0.0020	0.0020	0.0019
2.9	0.0019	0.0018	0.0018	0.0017	0.0016	0.0016	0.0015	0.0015	0.0014	0.0014
3.0	0.0013	0.0013	0.0013	0.0012	0.0012	0.0011	0.0011	0.0010	0.0011	0.0010

Table A.2.2 Percentiles of the chi-square distribution

Df	Percent									
	0.5	1	2.5	5	10	90	95	97.5	99	99.5
1	—	—	—	0.0039	0.0158	2.71	3.84	5.02	6.63	7.88
2	0.0100	0.0201	0.0506	0.1026	0.2107	4.61	5.99	7.38	9.21	10.60
3	0.0717	0.115	0.216	0.352	0.584	6.25	7.81	9.35	11.34	12.84
4	0.207	0.297	0.484	0.711	1.064	7.78	9.49	11.14	13.28	14.86
5	0.412	0.554	0.831	1.15	1.61	9.24	11.07	12.83	15.09	16.75
6	0.676	0.872	1.24	1.64	2.20	10.64	12.59	14.45	16.81	18.55
7	0.989	1.24	1.69	2.17	2.83	12.02	14.07	16.01	18.48	20.28
8	1.34	1.65	2.18	2.73	3.49	13.36	15.51	17.53	20.09	21.96
9	1.73	2.09	2.70	3.33	4.17	14.68	16.92	19.02	21.67	23.59
10	2.16	2.56	3.25	3.94	4.87	15.99	18.31	20.48	23.21	25.19
11	2.60	3.05	3.82	4.57	5.58	17.28	19.68	21.92	24.73	26.76
12	3.07	3.57	4.40	5.23	6.30	18.55	21.03	23.34	26.22	28.30
13	3.57	4.11	5.01	5.89	7.04	19.81	22.36	24.74	27.69	29.82
14	4.07	4.66	5.63	6.57	7.79	21.06	23.68	26.12	29.14	31.32
15	4.60	5.23	6.26	7.26	8.55	22.31	25.00	27.49	30.58	32.80
16	5.14	5.81	6.91	7.96	9.31	23.54	26.30	28.85	32.00	34.27
18	6.26	7.01	8.23	9.39	10.86	25.99	28.87	31.53	34.81	37.16
20	7.43	8.26	9.59	10.85	12.44	28.41	31.41	34.17	37.57	40.00
24	9.89	10.86	12.40	13.85	15.66	33.20	36.42	39.36	42.98	45.56
30	17.79	14.95	16.79	18.49	20.60	40.26	43.77	47.98	50.89	53.67
40	20.71	22.16	24.43	26.51	29.05	51.81	55.76	59.34	63.69	66.77
60	35.53	37.48	40.48	43.19	46.46	74.40	79.08	83.30	88.38	91.95
120	83.85	86.92	91.58	95.70	100.62	140.23	146.57	152.21	158.95	163.64

Appendix A.3

Collection of time series

All time series are read from left to right, top to bottom.

Time series 2.1 Consecutive yields from a batch chemical process (70 observations). (From Box, G. E. P., and Jenkins, G. M. (1976). *Times Series Analysis: Forecasting and Control.* Reproduced by permission of Holden-Day Inc.)

47	64	23	71	38	64	55	41	59	48	71	35	57	40	58
44	80	55	37	74	51	57	50	60	45	57	50	45	25	59
50	71	56	74	50	58	45	54	36	54	48	55	45	57	50
62	44	64	43	52	38	59	55	41	53	49	34	35	54	45
68	38	50	60	39	59	40	57	54	23					

Time series 2.2 U.S. Expenditures on Producers' Durables (EDP) in billions of current dollars, quarterly 1947-01 through 1966-04 (80 observations). (From Nelson, C. R. (1973). *Applied Time Series for Managerial Forecasting.* Reproduced by permission of Holden-Day Inc.)

15.5	15.7	15.6	16.7	18.0	17.4	17.9	18.8	17.6	17.0
16.1	15.7	15.9	17.9	20.3	20.4	20.2	20.5	20.9	20.9
21.1	21.4	18.2	20.1	21.4	21.3	21.9	21.3	20.4	20.4
20.7	20.7	20.9	23.0	24.9	26.5	25.6	26.1	27.0	27.2
28.1	28.0	29.1	28.3	25.7	24.5	24.4	25.5	27.0	28.7
29.1	29.0	29.6	31.2	30.6	29.8	27.6	27.7	29.0	30.3
31.0	32.1	33.5	33.2	33.2	33.8	35.5	36.8	37.9	39.0
41.0	41.6	43.7	44.4	46.6	48.3	50.2	32.1	54.0	56.0

Time series 2.3 Monthly numbers of employees involved in the production of food and kindred products in the State of Wisconsin from January 1961 through October 1975. All values are given in units of 1000 employees (178 observations). (From *Intermediate and Business Statistics: Analysis of Variance, Regression and Time Series* by Robert B. Miller and Dean W. Wichern. Copyright © 1977 by Holt, Rinehart and Winston. Reprinted by permission of Holt, Rinehart and Winston, CBS College Publishing.)

Year	Jan.	Feb.	Mar.	Apr.	May	June	July	Aug.	Sept.	Oct.	Nov.	Dec.
1961	56.3	55.7	55.8	56.3	57.2	59.1	71.5	72.2	72.7	61.5	57.4	56.9
1962	55.3	54.9	54.9	54.9	54.6	57.7	68.2	70.6	71.0	60.0	56.0	54.4
1963	53.3	52.8	53.0	53.4	54.3	58.2	67.4	71.0	69.8	59.4	55.6	54.6
1964	53.4	53.0	53.0	53.2	54.2	58.0	67.5	70.1	68.2	56.6	54.9	54.0
1965	52.9	52.6	52.8	53.0	53.6	56.1	66.1	69.8	69.3	61.2	57.5	54.9
1966	53.4	52.7	53.0	52.9	55.4	58.7	67.9	70.0	68.7	59.3	56.4	54.5
1967	52.8	52.8	53.2	55.3	55.8	58.2	65.3	67.9	68.3	61.7	56.4	53.9
1968	52.6	52.1	52.4	51.6	52.7	57.3	65.1	71.5	69.9	61.9	57.3	55.1
1969	53.6	53.4	53.5	53.3	53.9	52.7	61.0	69.9	70.4	59.4	56.3	54.3
1970	53.5	53.0	53.2	52.5	53.4	56.5	65.3	70.7	66.9	58.2	55.3	53.4
1971	52.1	51.5	51.5	52.4	53.3	55.5	64.2	69.6	69.3	58.5	55.3	53.6
1972	52.3	51.5	51.7	51.5	52.2	57.1	63.6	68.8	68.9	60.1	55.6	53.9
1973	53.3	53.1	53.5	53.5	53.9	57.1	64.7	69.4	70.3	62.6	57.9	55.8
1974	54.8	54.2	54.6	54.3	54.8	58.1	68.1	73.3	75.5	66.4	60.5	57.7
1975	55.8	54.7	55.0	55.6	56.4	60.6	70.8	76.4	74.8	62.2		

Time series 2.4 International airline passengers: monthly totals (in thousands of passengers), January 1949 through December 1960 (144 observations). (From Box, G. E. P., and Jenkins, G. M. (1976). *Time Series Analysis: Forecasting and Control*. Reproduced by permission of Holden-Day Inc.)

Year	Jan.	Feb.	Mar.	Apr.	May	June	July	Aug.	Sept.	Oct.	Nov.	Dec.
1949	112	118	132	129	121	135	148	148	136	119	104	118
1950	115	126	141	135	125	149	170	170	158	133	114	140
1951	145	150	178	163	172	178	199	199	184	162	146	166
1952	171	180	193	181	183	218	230	242	209	191	172	194
1953	196	196	236	235	229	243	264	272	237	211	180	201
1954	204	188	235	227	234	264	302	293	259	229	203	229
1955	242	233	267	269	270	315	364	347	312	274	237	278
1956	284	277	317	313	318	374	413	405	355	306	271	306
1957	315	301	356	348	355	422	465	467	404	347	305	336
1958	340	318	362	348	363	435	491	505	404	359	310	337
1959	360	342	406	396	420	472	548	559	463	407	362	405
1960	417	391	419	461	472	535	622	606	508	461	390	432

Time series 2.5 Purse snatchings in the Hyde Park neighbourhood of Chicago over 71 twenty-eight day periods from January 1969 to September 1973 (71 observations). (Reprinted from Richard McCleary and Richard A. Hay Jr, *Applied Time Series Analysis for the Social Sciences*, p. 315, © 1980 Sage Publications, Inc., with permission.)

10	15	10	10	12	10	7	17	10	14	8	17
14	18	3	9	11	10	6	12	14	10	25	29
33	33	12	19	16	19	19	12	34	15	36	29
26	21	17	19	13	20	24	12	6	14	6	12
9	11	17	12	8	14	14	12	5	8	10	3
16	8	8	7	66	6	10	8	10	5	7	

Time series 4.1 Consecutive readings from a batch chemical process (70 observations). (From *Intermediate Business Statistics: Analysis of Variance, Regression and Time Series* by Robert B. Miller and Dean W. Wichern. Copyright © 1977 by Holt, Rinehart and Winston. Reprinted by permission of Holt, Rinehart and Winston, CBS College Publishing.)

40	54	48	52	41	52	38	56	48	45
66	17	62	50	38	59	51	55	48	51
50	52	44	65	40	65	41	64	53	48
53	43	66	48	52	42	44	56	44	58
41	54	51	56	38	56	49	52	33	52
59	34	57	39	60	40	52	44	65	43
48	44	49	44	49	69	40	54	58	49

Time series 4.2 Simulation of MA(1) process (100 observations). (From Anderson, O. D. (1976). *Time Series Analysis and Forecasting*. Reproduced by permission of Butterworth and Co.)

-1.23	0.03	-0.10	-0.50	0.26	1.62	-1.21	-0.57	1.34	-1.75
-0.23	0.63	0.48	-0.83	-0.03	1.31	0.86	-1.28	0.00	-0.63
0.08	-1.30	1.48	-0.28	-0.79	1.86	0.07	0.09	-0.20	-0.21
0.91	-0.36	0.48	0.61	-1.38	-0.04	0.90	1.79	-0.37	0.40
-1.19	0.98	-1.51	0.90	-1.56	2.18	-1.93	1.87	-0.97	0.46
2.12	-2.11	0.70	0.69	-0.24	0.34	0.60	0.15	-0.02	0.46
-0.54	0.89	1.07	0.20	-0.97	0.83	-0.33	0.91	-1.13	2.22
0.80	-1.95	2.61	0.59	0.71	-0.84	-0.11	1.27	-0.80	-0.76
1.58	-0.38	0.10	-0.62	2.27	-0.62	0.74	-0.16	1.34	-1.83
0.31	1.13	-0.87	1.45	-1.95	-0.51	-0.41	0.49	1.54	-0.69

Time series 4.3 Simulation of white noise process (100 observations). (From Anderson, O. D. (1976). *Time Series Analysis and Forecasting*. Reproduced by permission of Butterworth and Co.)

0.40	-0.26	1.06	-0.52	1.79	-0.09	-0.80	-0.98	-0.35	0.59
-0.31	-1.13	0.00	-0.36	0.55	0.56	1.67	-0.84	-1.14	0.63
-0.29	-1.04	-0.87	-0.26	0.02	-0.34	-0.19	-0.25	0.80	1.02
0.52	0.79	0.01	-0.38	-0.07	0.57	-0.23	0.53	0.65	0.64
0.84	0.05	-1.04	0.35	0.21	-1.26	-0.77	-0.42	-0.64	0.88
0.52	-1.16	0.89	-0.45	-0.99	-0.81	-2.51	-1.45	-1.98	1.78
1.10	-0.34	-0.48	0.21	-0.85	-1.12	-0.86	0.47	-0.97	-0.10
-1.20	2.00	-0.65	2.57	-1.55	0.71	-0.33	0.24	0.67	1.20
-0.78	0.15	0.51	0.12	-1.72	0.01	-1.48	-0.75	0.13	0.38
-1.32	0.74	-1.48	-0.06	-0.31	0.90	0.47	0.21	-0.27	-1.96

Time series 4.4 Second differences of chemical process temperatures (224 observations). (From Box, G. E. P., and Jenkins, G. M. (1976). *Time Series Analysis: Forecasting and Control*. Reproduced by permission of Holden-Day Inc.)

−0.3	−0.1	0.0	0.0	−0.2	0.1	0.0	−0.2
−0.1	0.2	0.0	−0.2	0.2	−0.2	0.0	0.2
−0.1	0.0	0.0	0.1	0.1	0.0	0.0	−0.1
0.0	0.0	0.0	−0.2	−0.1	−0.1	0.3	0.3
0.2	0.0	0.0	0.0	0.0	0.1	0.0	−0.2
−0.1	0.1	0.0	0.0	−0.1	0.0	0.2	0.0
0.1	0.1	−0.1	0.0	0.0	0.1	0.2	0.7
−0.7	−0.5	−0.2	0.3	0.3	0.1	−0.1	0.3
0.0	0.0	−0.3	0.0	−0.3	0.1	0.3	−0.2
−0.1	−0.1	0.0	0.0	0.0	−0.2	−0.1	−0.1
0.0	0.1	0.1	0.0	0.0	0.0	0.3	0.2
−0.1	0.0	0.0	0.1	0.1	−0.1	−0.1	0.0
0.0	0.1	−0.2	0.2	−0.1	0.1	−0.1	0.1
0.0	0.0	0.0	−0.1	−0.1	−0.1	0.0	−0.1
−0.1	0.0	0.0	0.1	0.0	0.0	0.1	0.0
0.0	−0.2	−0.1	0.1	0.2	0.1	0.0	0.0
0.1	0.2	0.2	−0.1	0.0	−0.2	−0.1	0.1
0.1	0.0	0.0	0.0	−0.2	0.1	0.0	0.2
0.0	0.0	−0.3	0.1	0.1	−0.2	0.2	−0.2
−0.3	0.2	0.0	0.1	0.0	−0.1	−0.1	0.0
0.0	0.0	0.1	−0.2	0.2	0.0	0.0	0.0
0.0	−0.1	−0.1	0.0	0.1	0.0	0.1	−0.1
0.1	0.0	0.1	0.0	0.1	−0.1	0.1	−0.1
0.2	−0.2	0.1	−0.1	−0.1	−0.1	−0.1	0.0
0.1	0.0	0.1	−0.1	−0.1	0.1	0.2	−0.1
−0.1	0.0	−0.1	0.1	−0.1	0.0	0.0	−0.2
−0.1	0.0	−0.1	0.1	0.1	0.2	0.1	−0.1

Time series 4.5 Simulation of ARMA(1, 1) process (100 observations). (From Anderson, O. D. (1976). *Time Series Analysis and Forecasting*. Reproduced by permission of Butterworth and Co.)

−1.40	−2.59	−1.38	−0.27	−0.75	0.63	1.09	0.88	0.95	0.98
−0.77	−0.33	−2.15	−2.50	−1.36	−0.48	−2.05	1.46	1.13	2.85
2.67	2.71	1.30	0.88	0.07	1.47	−1.04	−1.02	2.03	2.54
0.23	−0.49	0.87	−0.61	−0.20	−0.98	−0.78	−0.80	−0.86	−1.72
−0.15	1.15	2.46	0.37	−0.80	−0.49	−0.50	−0.07	−1.92	−1.00
−2.16	−0.04	−1.91	−0.43	0.32	0.48	0.13	2.26	0.73	−0.10
1.47	0.89	0.53	0.20	0.70	0.27	−0.39	0.07	−0.89	−0.37
0.75	1.24	0.62	0.54	0.23	−1.05	0.66	−0.25	0.63	−0.91
0.21	−0.24	−0.05	−0.85	−1.55	−0.40	−1.82	−0.81	−0.28	−1.06
−0.82	0.51	−0.80	−0.24	−0.51	1.21	0.81	−0.75	−1.29	−2.26

Time series 5.1 I.C.I. closing stock prices (new pence), 25 August 1972–19 January 1973 (107 observations). (Reproduced by permission of the *Financial Times*)

304	303	307	299	296	293	301	293	301	295
284	286	286	287	284	282	278	281	278	277
279	278	270	268	272	273	279	279	280	275
271	277	278	279	283	284	282	283	279	280
280	279	278	283	278	270	275	273	273	272
275	273	273	272	273	272	273	271	272	271
273	277	274	274	272	280	282	292	295	295
294	290	291	288	288	290	293	288	289	291
293	293	290	288	287	289	292	288	288	285
282	286	286	287	284	283	286	282	287	286
287	292	292	294	291	288	289			

Time series 5.2   Chemical process temperature readings: every minute (226 observations). (From Box, G. E. P., and Jenkins, G. M. (1976). *Time Series: Forecasting and Control*. Reproduced by permission of Holden-Day Inc.)

26.6	27.0	27.1	27.1	27.1	27.1	26.9	26.8	26.7	26.4	26.0	25.8	25.6	25.2	25.0	24.6
24.2	24.0	23.7	23.4	23.1	22.9	22.8	22.7	22.6	22.4	22.2	22.0	21.8	21.4	20.9	20.3
19.7	19.4	19.3	19.2	19.1	19.0	18.9	18.9	19.2	19.3	19.3	19.4	19.5	19.6	19.6	19.6
19.6	19.6	19.7	19.9	20.0	20.1	20.2	20.3	20.6	21.6	21.9	21.7	21.3	21.2	21.4	21.7
22.2	23.0	23.8	24.6	25.1	25.6	25.8	26.1	26.3	26.3	26.2	26.0	25.8	25.6	25.4	25.2
24.9	24.7	24.5	24.4	24.4	24.4	24.4	24.4	24.3	24.4	24.4	24.4	24.4	24.4	24.5	24.5
24.4	24.3	24.2	24.2	24.0	23.9	23.7	23.6	23.5	23.5	23.5	23.5	23.5	23.7	23.8	23.8
23.9	23.9	23.8	23.7	23.6	23.4	23.2	23.0	22.8	22.6	22.4	22.0	21.6	21.3	21.2	21.2
21.1	21.0	20.9	21.0	21.0	21.1	21.2	21.1	20.9	20.8	20.8	20.8	20.8	20.9	20.8	20.8
20.7	20.7	20.8	20.9	21.2	21.4	21.7	21.8	21.9	22.2	22.5	22.8	23.1	23.4	23.8	24.1
24.6	24.9	24.9	25.1	25.0	25.0	25.0	25.0	24.9	24.8	24.7	24.6	24.5	24.5	24.5	24.5
24.5	24.5	24.5	24.4	24.4	24.2	24.2	24.1	24.1	24.0	24.0	24.0	23.9	23.8	23.8	23.7
23.7	23.6	23.7	23.6	23.6	23.6	23.5	23.5	23.4	23.3	23.3	23.3	23.4	23.4	23.3	23.2
23.3	23.3	23.2	23.1	22.9	22.8	22.6	22.4	22.2	21.8	21.3	20.8	20.2	19.7	19.3	19.1
19.0	18.8														

Time series 5.3 Chemical process concentration readings: every two hours (197 observations). (From Box, G. E. P., and Jenkins, G. M. (1976). *Time Series Analysis: Forecasting and Control*. Reproduced by permission of Holden-Day Inc.)

17.0	16.6	16.3	16.1	17.1	16.9	16.8	17.4	17.1	17.0
16.7	17.4	17.2	17.4	17.4	17.0	17.3	17.2	17.4	16.8
17.1	17.4	17.4	17.5	17.4	17.6	17.4	17.3	17.0	17.8
17.5	18.1	17.5	17.4	17.4	17.1	17.6	17.7	17.4	17.8
17.6	17.5	16.5	17.8	17.3	17.3	17.1	17.4	16.9	17.3
17.6	16.9	16.7	16.8	16.8	17.2	16.8	17.6	17.2	16.6
17.1	16.9	16.6	18.0	17.2	17.3	17.0	16.9	17.3	16.8
17.3	17.4	17.7	16.8	16.9	17.0	16.9	17.0	16.6	16.7
16.8	16.7	16.4	16.5	16.4	16.6	16.5	16.7	16.4	16.4
16.2	16.4	16.3	16.4	17.0	16.9	17.1	17.1	16.7	16.9
16.5	17.2	16.4	17.0	17.0	16.7	16.2	16.6	16.9	16.5
16.6	16.6	17.0	17.1	17.1	16.7	16.8	16.3	16.6	16.8
16.9	17.1	16.8	17.0	17.2	17.3	17.2	17.3	17.2	17.2
17.5	16.9	16.9	16.9	17.0	16.5	16.7	16.8	16.7	16.7
16.6	16.5	17.0	16.7	16.7	16.9	17.4	17.1	17.0	16.8
17.2	17.2	17.4	17.2	16.9	16.8	17.0	17.4	17.2	17.2
17.1	17.1	17.1	17.4	17.2	16.9	16.9	17.0	16.7	16.9
17.3	17.8	17.8	17.6	17.5	17.0	17.0	17.1	17.2	17.4
17.5	17.9	17.0	17.0	17.0	17.2	17.3	17.4	17.4	17.0
18.0	18.2	17.6	17.8	17.7	17.4				

Time series 5.4 Weekly sales of a plastic container (300 observations). (From Johnson L., and Montgomery, D. (1974). *Operations Research in Production Planning, Scheduling and Inventory Control*. Reproduced by permission of John Wiley and Sons, Inc.)

592	1 204	1 864	2 508	3 160	3 792	4 419	5 023	5 626	6 250
6 903	7 564	8 223	8 900	9 569	10 226	10 823	11 304	11 785	12 252
12 724	13 339	13 940	14 514	15 102	15 648	16 212	16 725	17 217	17 839
18 463	19 094	19 718	20 342	20 966	21 563	22 167	22 802	23 431	24 044
24 562	25 131	25 676	26 242	26 718	27 215	27 767	28 389	28 974	29 502
30 022	30 542	31 044	31 556	32 092	32 636	33 196	33 772	34 347	34 915
35 502	36 078	36 643	37 219	37 804	38 381	38 974	39 513	40 044	40 634
41 237	41 853	42 430	42 977	43 529	44 081	44 657	45 277	45 917	46 517
47 100	47 692	48 241	48 802	49 399	49 992	50 601	51 214	51 855	52 499
53 127	53 763	54 387	54 979	55 591	56 219	56 843	57 491	58 127	58 767
59 264	59 777	60 298	60 779	61 348	61 942	62 521	63 041	63 576	64 082
64 550	65 074	65 594	66 168	66 664	67 204	67 711	68 272	68 837	69 414
70 012	70 617	71 211	71 701	72 214	72 740	73 283	73 889	74 509	75 115
75 743	76 351	76 971	77 585	78 169	78 745	79 309	79 918	80 563	81 184
81 761	82 318	82 855	83 384	83 921	84 476	85 028	85 647	86 275	86 889
87 493	88 097	88 737	89 361	90 017	90 668	91 313	91 938	92 575	93 156
93 669	94 182	94 695	95 184	95 679	96 183	96 783	97 397	97 989	98 603
99 223	99 839	100 478	101 095	101 724	102 333	102 902	103 516	104 157	104 784
105 411	106 026	106 626	107 214	107 806	108 418	109 048	109 688	110 321	110 961
111 586	112 211	112 828	113 437	114 038	114 663	115 288	115 604	116 519	117 121
117 688	118 280	118 916	119 548	120 130	120 647	121 210	121 773	122 350	122 947
123 540	124 102	124 705	125 255	125 769	126 325	126 893	127 501	128 133	128 769
129 402	129 994	130 491	130 996	131 565	132 142	132 719	133 280	133 863	134 435
134 997	135 587	136 187	136 812	137 424	138 024	138 648	139 272	139 909	140 534
141 171	141 768	142 329	142 878	143 423	144 000	144 585	145 168	145 738	146 294
146 832	147 364	147 920	148 520	149 128	149 744	150 342	150 902	151 407	151 895
152 396	152 885	153 390	153 939	154 520	155 129	155 742	156 374	157 006	157 648
158 295	158 951	159 655	160 339	161 039	161 723	162 410	163 050	163 698	164 366
165 031	165 680	166 321	166 934	167 559	168 193	168 882	169 580	170 277	170 954
171 602	172 220	172 952	173 500	174 136	174 764	175 364	175 956	176 560	177 197

Time series 5.5 Daily dry bulb temperatures (°F) at noon on Ben Nevis, 1 February–18 August, 1884 (200 observations). (From Buchan, A. (1980). 'Metrology of Ben Nevis', *Trans. R. Soc. Edinb.*, **34**. Reproduced by permission of The Royal Society of Edinburgh)

22.9	13.8	31.4	30.1	31.8	31.0	18.3	23.8	31.6	18.9
18.8	31.8	31.1	27.0	23.0	19.9	21.5	23.8	22.8	24.8
20.4	25.8	24.3	22.9	23.2	23.8	19.2	18.2	14.5	22.6
20.1	18.6	24.9	25.2	30.1	29.4	23.3	20.4	17.6	14.7
24.5	32.4	32.0	33.4	37.3	36.7	31.3	26.6	23.8	21.9
26.9	25.0	25.8	30.5	25.1	21.7	20.7	21.2	22.4	24.2
25.8	29.1	35.6	32.2	29.9	30.5	32.6	29.0	33.2	35.4
32.8	27.4	25.3	27.6	29.3	26.7	24.5	23.2	30.7	26.5
23.9	24.6	24.4	28.1	26.0	27.3	27.7	27.7	27.0	24.2
26.3	25.7	25.3	27.9	27.5	25.0	23.6	31.6	35.7	35.2
38.8	31.2	32.5	32.0	33.1	31.8	35.0	27.7	31.1	26.7
30.9	38.7	41.8	45.6	36.0	38.5	46.1	46.0	42.5	35.3
36.8	33.2	34.5	39.5	38.7	32.5	33.0	33.0	30.9	30.7
37.0	36.8	34.7	35.7	31.7	32.0	37.9	42.4	38.2	35.3
38.4	40.9	39.1	34.1	41.9	32.1	41.9	45.7	56.5	49.4
46.3	50.9	47.1	50.9	53.9	50.9	45.9	43.1	45.0	48.3
48.6	40.9	41.6	45.7	40.6	40.6	37.0	36.1	33.9	32.1
34.1	34.2	41.9	39.8	35.1	31.9	34.9	39.8	39.0	42.9
44.4	42.7	45.2	41.0	37.0	37.5	41.0	45.0	47.9	56.5
55.6	54.2	52.5	52.4	44.9	40.9	41.1	44.8	46.7	49.4

Time series 5.6 Dow Jones utilities index, 28 August–18 December, 1972 (78 observations). (Reprinted by permission of *The Wall Street Journal*)

110.94	110.69	110.43	110.56	110.75	110.84	110.46	110.56	110.46	110.05
109.60	109.31	109.31	109.25	109.02	108.54	108.77	109.02	109.44	109.38
109.53	109.89	110.56	110.56	110.72	111.23	111.48	111.58	111.90	112.19
112.06	111.96	111.68	111.36	111.42	112.00	112.22	112.70	113.15	114.36
114.65	115.06	115.86	116.40	116.44	116.88	118.07	118.51	119.28	119.79
119.70	119.28	119.66	120.14	120.97	121.13	121.55	121.96	122.26	123.79
124.11	124.14	123.37	123.02	122.86	123.02	123.11	123.05	123.05	122.83
123.18	122.67	122.73	122.86	122.67	111.09	122.00	121.23		

Time series 6.1 Monthly numbers of employees involved in the production of fabricated metals in the State of Wisconsin from January 1961 through October 1975. All values are given in units of 1000 employees (178 observations). (From *Intermediate Business Statistics: Analysis of Variance, Regression and Time Series* by Robert B. Miller and Dean W. Wichern. Copyright © 1977 by Holt, Rinehart and Winston. Reprinted by permission of Holt, Rinehart and Winston, CBS College Publishing.)

Year	Jan.	Feb.	Mar.	Apr.	May	June	July	Aug.	Sept.	Oct.	Nov.	Dec.
1961	31.1	29.5	31.0	31.5	32.0	32.8	32.8	33.1	33.6	33.4	33.5	33.5
1962	33.1	33.1	33.4	33.9	34.4	35.2	35.0	35.3	34.6	34.1	33.9	33.8
1963	33.6	33.8	34.0	34.4	34.7	35.4	35.5	35.5	35.2	34.5	34.4	34.3
1964	33.9	34.1	34.5	34.3	35.0	36.0	35.0	37.2	37.4	36.9	37.2	37.3
1965	37.2	37.6	36.0	38.8	38.8	39.5	39.6	40.1	39.4	38.9	39.5	39.2
1966	38.7	39.1	39.5	39.7	40.0	41.4	41.3	39.8	38.5	40.2	41.0	40.9
1967	40.5	40.3	40.4	40.3	40.4	41.8	41.1	42.1	40.8	40.5	40.6	40.7
1968	40.6	40.7	40.7	40.7	40.9	41.6	41.2	42.0	41.8	42.3	43.1	42.9
1969	42.6	43.1	43.3	43.5	43.9	45.7	45.6	46.5	45.3	45.2	45.3	45.0
1970	44.2	44.3	44.4	42.4	42.8	44.3	44.4	44.8	44.4	43.1	42.6	42.4
1971	42.2	41.8	40.1	42.0	42.4	43.1	42.4	43.1	43.2	42.8	43.0	42.8
1972	42.5	42.6	42.3	42.9	43.6	44.7	44.5	45.0	44.8	44.9	45.2	45.2
1973	45.0	45.5	46.2	46.8	47.5	48.3	48.3	49.1	48.9	49.4	50.0	50.0
1974	49.6	49.6	49.6	50.7	50.7	50.9	50.5	51.2	50.7	50.3	50.0	48.1
1975	46.6	45.3	44.6	44.0	43.7	43.8	43.0	43.6	44.0	45.0		

Time series 6.2 Average daily calls to Directory Assistance, Cincinatti, Ohio; monthly observations from January 1962 through February 1974 (146 observations). (Reprinted from Richard McCleary and Richard A. Hay, Jr., *Applied Time Series Analysis for the Social Sciences*, p. 316, © 1980 Sage Publications, Inc., with permission.)

Year	Jan.	Feb.	Mar.	Apr.	May	June	July	Aug.	Sept.	Oct.	Nov.	Dec.
1962	350	339	351	364	369	331	331	340	346	341	357	398
1963	381	367	383	375	353	361	375	371	373	366	382	429
1964	406	403	429	425	427	409	402	409	419	404	429	463
1965	428	449	444	467	474	463	432	453	462	456	474	514
1966	489	475	492	525	527	533	527	522	526	513	564	599
1967	572	587	599	601	611	620	579	582	592	581	630	663
1968	638	631	645	682	601	595	521	521	516	496	538	575
1969	537	534	542	538	547	540	526	548	555	545	594	643
1970	625	616	640	625	637	634	621	641	654	649	662	699
1971	672	704	700	711	715	718	652	664	695	704	733	772
1972	716	712	732	755	761	748	748	750	744	731	782	810
1973	777	816	840	868	872	811	810	762	634	626	649	697
1974	657	549										

Time series 6.3 Monthly numbers of employees involved in wholesale and retail trade in the State of Wisconsin from January 1961 through October 1975. All values are given in units of 1000 employees (178 observations). (From *Intermediate Business Statistics: Analysis of Variance, Regression and Time Series* by Robert B. Miller and Dean W. Wichern. Copyright © by Holt, Rinehart and Winston. Reprinted by permission of Holt, Rinehart and Winston, CBS College publishing.)

Year	Jan.	Feb.	Mar.	Apr.	May	June	July	Aug.	Sept.	Oct.	Nov.	Dec.
1961	239.6	236.4	236.8	241.5	243.7	246.1	244.1	244.2	244.8	246.6	250.9	261.4
1962	237.6	235.7	236.1	242.6	244.5	246.6	245.7	247.7	248.9	251.4	255.9	263.7
1963	242.2	239.3	239.7	247.2	249.3	252.3	252.8	253.6	254.2	256.1	260.3	268.8
1964	250.1	247.9	249.0	253.8	258.3	261.3	261.3	261.9	263.3	267.3	270.6	281.5
1965	261.9	258.6	259.7	266.0	271.1	274.4	274.0	273.8	274.9	280.0	285.4	295.9
1966	275.4	273.6	275.9	281.1	285.2	289.1	289.2	288.9	291.1	295.3	300.2	310.9
1967	286.9	283.0	286.2	291.5	295.4	299.7	297.9	298.1	300.2	304.8	311.9	320.9
1968	298.3	295.5	297.2	302.7	306.7	309.1	308.7	309.9	310.8	314.7	321.2	329.0
1969	307.6	305.5	308.0	314.4	320.5	323.4	323.0	324.4	326.1	329.3	335.0	341.9
1970	321.8	317.3	318.6	323.4	327.1	327.9	325.3	325.7	330.0	333.5	337.1	341.3
1971	321.6	318.2	319.6	326.2	332.3	334.2	334.5	335.5	335.1	338.2	341.9	347.9
1972	329.5	326.4	329.1	337.2	344.6	349.9	351.0	353.8	354.5	357.4	362.1	367.5
1973	347.9	345.0	348.9	355.3	362.4	366.6	366.0	370.2	370.9	374.5	380.2	384.6
1974	360.6	354.4	357.4	367.0	375.7	381.0	381.2	383.0	384.3	387.0	391.7	396.0
1975	374.0	370.4	373.2	381.1	389.9	394.6	394.0	397.0	397.2	399.4		

Time series 6.4 Sales of Company X, January 1965–May 1971 (77 observations). (Reproduced by permission of Dr C. Chatfield)

Year	Jan.	Feb.	Mar.	Apr.	May	June	July	Aug.	Sept.	Oct.	Nov.	Dec.
1965	154	96	73	49	36	59	95	169	210	278	298	245
1966	200	118	90	79	78	91	167	169	289	347	375	203
1967	223	104	107	85	75	99	135	211	335	460	488	326
1968	346	261	224	141	148	145	223	272	445	560	612	467
1969	518	404	300	210	196	186	247	343	464	680	711	610
1970	613	392	273	322	189	257	324	404	677	858	895	664
1971	628	308	324	248	272							

Time series 6.5 Mean monthly air temperature (°F) at Nottingham Castle, January 1920–December 1939 (240 observations). (Reproduced by permission of City of Nottingham Museum and Art Gallery)

40.6	40.8	44.4	46.7	54.1	58.5	57.7	56.4	54.3	50.5
42.9	39.8	44.2	39.8	45.1	47.0	54.1	58.7	66.3	59.9
57.0	54.2	39.7	42.8	37.5	38.7	39.5	42.1	55.7	57.8
56.8	54.3	54.3	47.1	41.8	41.7	41.8	40.1	42.9	45.8
49.2	52.7	64.2	59.6	54.4	49.2	36.6	37.6	39.3	37.5
38.3	45.5	53.2	57.7	60.8	58.2	56.4	49.8	44.4	43.6
40.0	40.5	40.8	45.1	53.8	59.4	63.5	61.0	53.0	50.0
38.1	36.3	39.2	43.4	43.4	48.9	50.6	56.8	62.5	62.0
57.5	46.7	41.6	39.8	39.4	38.5	45.3	47.1	51.7	55.0
60.4	60.5	54.7	50.3	42.3	35.2	40.8	41.1	42.8	47.3
50.9	56.4	62.2	60.5	55.4	50.2	43.0	37.3	34.8	31.3
41.0	43.9	53.1	56.9	62.5	60.3	59.8	49.2	42.9	41.9
41.6	37.1	41.2	46.9	51.2	60.4	60.1	61.6	57.0	50.9
43.0	38.8	37.1	38.4	38.4	46.5	53.5	58.4	60.6	58.2
53.8	46.6	45.5	40.6	42.4	38.4	40.3	44.6	50.9	57.0
62.1	63.5	56.2	47.3	43.6	41.8	36.2	39.3	44.5	48.7
54.2	60.8	65.5	64.9	60.1	50.2	42.1	35.6	39.4	38.2
40.4	46.9	53.4	59.6	66.5	60.4	59.2	51.2	42.8	45.8
40.4	42.6	43.5	47.1	50.0	60.5	64.6	64.0	56.8	48.6
44.2	36.4	37.3	35.0	44.0	43.9	52.7	58.6	60.0	61.1
58.1	49.6	41.6	41.3	40.8	41.0	38.4	47.4	54.1	58.6
61.4	61.8	56.3	50.9	41.4	37.1	42.1	41.2	47.3	46.6
52.4	59.0	59.6	60.4	57.0	50.7	47.8	39.2	39.4	40.9
42.4	47.8	52.4	58.0	60.7	61.8	58.2	46.7	46.6	37.8

Time series 6.6 Simulation of AR(1) process (100 observations). (From Anderson, O. D. (1976). *Time Series Analysis and Forecasting*. Reproduced by permission of Butterworth and Co.)

-0.26	1.32	2.56	2.08	1.81	1.40	1.17	1.33	0.14	0.45
0.17	0.43	-2.42	-0.68	-1.52	-2.38	-2.48	-2.16	-3.42	-1.31
-1.66	-2.30	-1.52	0.06	-1.18	-0.84	0.82	1.22	2.65	4.55
5.99	4.84	6.04	6.23	5.75	5.74	3.71	1.78	-0.24	-0.76
1.67	3.09	4.97	3.67	3.08	2.84	2.49	3.32	3.41	2.55
2.33	1.34	1.03	1.10	1.61	1.18	0.67	-0.21	-0.37	-0.78
-1.32	-1.37	-2.21	-1.43	0.49	0.44	-0.22	-1.72	-1.96	-2.77
-3.27	-4.19	-3.03	-2.55	-2.53	-1.57	-3.01	-2.17	-1.96	-3.81
-3.70	-2.47	-4.30	-3.40	-1.75	-1.53	-1.74	-1.39	-0.51	-0.69
1.50	1.98	2.22	1.98	3.05	2.92	1.99	1.78	0.46	0.54

Time series 6.7 Weekly demand for a plastic container (100 observations). (From Montgomery, D. C., and Johnson, L. A. (1976). *Forecasting and Time Series Analysis*. Reproduced by permission of McGraw-Hill Book Company)

5000	4965	4496	4491	4566	4585	4724	4951	4917	4888
5087	5082	5039	5054	4940	4913	4871	4901	4864	4750
4856	4959	5004	5415	5550	5657	6010	6109	6052	6391
6798	6740	6778	7005	7045	7279	7367	6934	6506	6374
6066	6102	6204	6138	5938	5781	5813	5811	5818	5982
6132	6111	5948	6056	6342	6626	6591	6302	6132	5837
5572	5744	6005	6239	6523	6652	6585	6622	6754	6712
6675	6882	7011	7140	7197	7411	7233	6958	6960	6927
6814	6757	6765	6870	6954	6551	6022	5974	6052	6033
6030	5944	5543	5416	5571	5571	5627	5679	5455	5443

Time series 6.8 Monthly hotel room averages* from January 1963 through December 1976 (168 observations). (From Bowerman, B. L., and O'Connell, R. T. (1979). *Time Series and Forecasting: An Applied Approach*. Reproduced by permission of Duxbury Press)

Year	Jan.	Feb.	Mar.	Apr.	May	June	July	Aug.	Sept.	Oct.	Nov.	Dec.
1963	501	488	504	578	545	632	728	725	585	542	480	530
1964	518	489	528	599	572	659	739	758	602	587	497	558
1965	555	523	532	623	598	683	774	780	609	604	531	592
1966	578	543	565	648	615	697	785	830	645	643	551	606
1967	585	553	576	665	656	720	826	838	652	661	584	644
1968	623	553	599	657	680	759	878	881	705	684	577	656
1969	645	593	617	686	679	773	906	934	713	710	600	676
1970	645	602	601	709	706	817	930	983	745	735	620	698
1971	665	626	649	740	729	824	937	994	781	759	643	728
1972	691	649	656	735	748	837	995	1040	809	793	692	763
1973	723	655	658	761	768	885	1067	1038	812	790	692	782
1974	758	709	715	788	794	893	1046	1075	812	822	714	802
1975	748	731	748	827	788	937	1076	1125	840	864	717	813
1976	811	732	745	844	833	935	1110	1124	868	860	762	877

* A 'monthly hotel room average' is found by totalling the number of occupied rooms per day over all the days in the month and dividing this total by the number of days in the month.

Time series 6.9 Viscosity of a chemical product (100 observations). (From Montgomery, D. C., and Johnson, L. A. (1976). *Forecasting and Time Series Analysis*. Reproduced by permission of McGraw-Hill Book Company)

29.33	19.98	25.76	29.00	31.03	32.68	33.56	27.50	26.75	30.55
28.94	28.50	28.19	26.13	27.79	27.63	29.89	28.18	26.65	30.01
30.80	30.45	36.61	31.40	30.83	33.22	30.15	27.08	33.66	36.58
29.04	28.08	30.28	29.35	33.60	30.29	20.11	17.51	23.71	24.22
32.43	32.44	29.39	23.45	23.62	28.12	29.94	30.56	32.30	31.58
27.99	24.13	29.20	34.30	26.41	28.78	21.28	21.71	21.47	24.71
33.61	36.54	35.70	33.68	29.29	25.12	27.23	30.61	29.06	28.48
32.01	31.89	31.72	29.02	31.92	24.28	22.69	26.60	28.86	28.27
28.17	28.58	30.76	30.62	20.84	16.57	25.23	31.79	32.52	30.28
26.14	19.03	24.34	31.53	31.95	31.68	29.10	23.15	26.74	32.44

Time series 6.10 Monthly numbers of reported armed robberies in Boston, Massachusetts, from January 1966 through October 1975 (118 observations). (Reprinted from Richard McCleary and Richard A. Hay, Jr., *Applied Time Series Analysis for the Social Sciences*, p. 315, © 1980 Sage Publications, Inc., with permission.)

Year	Jan.	Feb.	Mar.	Apr.	May	June	July	Aug.	Sept.	Oct.	Nov.	Dec.
1966	41	39	50	40	43	38	44	35	39	35	29	49
1967	50	59	63	32	39	47	53	60	57	52	70	90
1968	74	62	55	84	94	70	108	139	120	97	126	149
1969	158	124	140	109	114	77	120	133	110	92	97	78
1970	99	107	112	90	98	125	155	190	236	189	174	178
1971	136	161	171	149	184	155	276	224	213	279	268	287
1972	238	213	257	293	212	246	353	339	308	247	257	322
1973	298	278	312	249	286	279	309	401	309	328	353	354
1974	327	324	285	243	241	287	355	460	364	487	452	391
1975	500	451	375	372	302	316	398	394	431	431		

Time series 6.11 Paris IBM closing prices (in Francs) from April 30 through October 28, 1976 (130 observations). (From Makridakis, S., and Wheelwright, S. C. (1978). *Interactive Forecasting: Univariate and Multivariate Methods.* Reproduced by permission of Holden-Day Inc.)

1186	1187	1169	1190	1172	1181	1185	1223	1212
1217	1211	1190	1200	1213	1200	1227	1208	1195
1187	1196	1205	1229	1219	1218	1220	1220	1212
1214	1200	1200	1213	1221	1233	1233	1241	1263
1260	1275	1278	1293	1301	1304	1299	1305	1317
1305	1309	1317	1312	1320	1326	1342	1350	1348
1345	1353	1358	1336	1322	1329	1356	1353	1360
1343	1351	1352	1344	1350	1350	1361	1372	1378
1380	1391	1399	1402	1404	1406	1407	1403	1378
1360	1379	1362	1350	1334	1340	1340	1352	1377
1378	1377	1377	1383	1371	1361	1370	1375	1355
1355	1386	1396	1392	1408	1401	1383	1391	1413
1400	1383	1412	1397	1392	1368	1370	1398	1370
1373	1354	1358	1308	1317	1323	1318	1302	1270
1262	1300	1315	1337					

Time series 6.12 Annual Swedish population increases per thousand population from 1750 through 1849 (100 observations). (Reprinted from Richard McCleary and Richard A. Hay, Jr., *Applied Time Series Analysis for the Social Sciences*, p. 318, © 1980 Sage Publications, Inc., with permission.)

9	12	8	12	10	10	8	2	0	7	10	9
4	1	7	5	8	9	5	5	6	4	−9	−27
12	10	10	8	8	8	14	7	4	1	1	2
6	7	7	−2	−1	7	12	10	10	4	9	10
9	5	4	3	7	7	6	8	3	4	−5	−14
1	6	3	2	6	1	13	10	10	6	9	10
13	16	14	16	12	8	7	6	9	4	7	12
8	14	11	5	5	5	10	11	11	9	12	13
8	6	10	13								

Time series 6.13 U.S. Gross National Product (GNP) in billions of current dollars, quarterly 1947-01 through 1966-04 (80 observations). (From Nelson, C. R. (1973). *Applied Time Series for Managerial Forecasting.* Reproduced by permission of Holden-Day Inc.)

224	228	232	242	248	256	263	264	259	255
257	255	266	275	293	305	318	326	333	337
340	339	346	358	364	368	366	361	361	360
365	373	386	394	403	409	411	416	421	430
437	440	446	442	435	438	451	464	474	487
484	491	503	505	504	503	504	515	524	538
548	557	564	572	577	584	595	606	618	628
639	645	663	676	691	710	730	743	756	771

Time series 6.14 Monthly industry sales (thousands of Francs) for printing and writing paper in France from 1963 through 1972 (120 observations). (From Makridakis, S., and Wheelwright, S. C. (1978). *Interactive Forecasting: Univariate and Multivariate Methods*. Reproduced by permission of Holden-Day Inc.)

Year	Jan.	Feb.	Mar.	Apr.	May	June	July	Aug.	Sept.	Oct.	Nov.	Dec.
1963	56.27	59.90	66.85	59.78	57.99	66.82	49.92	21.52	55.58	58.69	54.61	57.11
1964	63.47	63.93	71.22	62.16	62.10	67.60	50.13	22.03	56.07	60.25	62.64	60.55
1965	64.68	65.84	71.29	68.77	72.39	70.72	62.90	23.75	61.33	73.04	73.49	65.18
1966	67.62	74.82	81.07	72.94	70.11	79.01	59.46	23.07	61.72	69.14	70.11	70.58
1967	74.76	77.34	81.38	76.67	72.89	74.92	68.10	24.14	68.02	70.83	69.42	77.21
1968	79.53	78.84	89.00	79.74	75.10	82.13	69.16	29.07	72.71	86.84	81.24	79.96
1969	84.30	84.70	94.20	80.43	84.03	87.15	65.63	37.05	74.20	84.72	73.17	89.85
1970	77.81	85.61	93.88	81.30	78.34	82.81	65.73	31.00	78.00	86.00	78.00	80.80
1971	89.52	85.61	89.33	87.50	83.51	93.46	83.25	30.00	79.14	90.00	78.17	88.00
1972	87.50	99.30	97.68	96.87	87.17	100.69	83.20	34.56	84.95	91.39	86.87	99.37

Appendix A.4

Table of fitted models for time series used in examples and exercises

Time series	Fitted model
2.1	AR(2)
2.2	IMA(1, 1)
2.3	$(1, 0, 0) \times (0, 1, 1)_{12}$
2.4	$(0, 1, 1) \times (0, 1, 1)_{12}$ (logarithmic transformation)
4.1	AR(1)
4.2	MA(1)
4.3	White noise
4.4	MA(2)
4.5	ARMA(1, 1)
5.1	Random walk
5.2	ARI(1, 1)
5.3	IMA(1, 1)
5.4	ARI(2, 1)
5.5	IMA(1, 2)
5.6	ARIMA(1, 1, 1)
6.1	$(0, 1, 0) \times (1, 0, 0)_{12}$
6.2	$(0, 1, 0) \times (0, 1, 1)_{12}$
6.3	$(0, 1, 1) \times (0, 1, 1)_{12}$
6.4	$(1, 1, 0) \times (0, 1, 1)_{12}$ (fourth root transformation)
6.5	$(0, 0, 0) \times (1, 1, 0)_{12}$
6.6	AR(1)
6.7	IMA(1, 1)
6.8	$(1, 0, 0) \times (0, 1, 1)_{12}$ (logarithmic transformation)
6.9	AR(2)
6.10	$(0, 1, 1) \times (0, 0, 1)_{12}$ (logarithmic transformation)
6.11	Random walk
6.12	MA(1)
6.13	ARI(1, 1)
6.14	$(0, 1, 1) \times (0, 1, 1)_{12}$

Appendix A.5

TSERIES—a user-oriented computer program for time series exercises

(The TSERIES computer package was devised by William Q. Meeker, Jr, Statistical Laboratory, Iowa State University, Ames, Iowa 50011. Professor Meeker is the author of the following brief outline of the TSERIES package, which appeared in *American Statistician*, August 1978, **32**, No. 3, pp. 111–112, from which it is reprinted with permission. Figures A.5.1–A.5.5 illustrate the application of this package in the analysis of time series 2.1, 5.3, and 2.4.)

TSERIES is a computer program which was written to perform Box–Jenkins type analyses for univariate time series data. The program is capable of performing the analyses described in the first nine chapters of Box and Jenkins (1976) and it follows the general outline given there. TSERIES is both versatile and easy to use. Input is accomplished through a series of simple, compact commands, only a small number of which are needed for standard analyses. However, there is a large number of additional commands that can be used to modify standard assumptions and invoke special options. It is easy to learn to use the program. As a result, it has been very useful in practical applications as well as for giving students 'hands-on' experience in courses on applied time series analysis.

```
C     PROGRAM A.5.1 IDENTIFICATION RUN FOR TIME SERIES 2.1
C
C
C
DATA 70 READ SEVENTY OBSERVATIONS
47 64   23 71 38 64 55 41 59 48 71 35 57 40 58
44 80 55 37 74 51 57 50 60 45 57 50 45 25 59
50 71 56 74 50 58 45 54 36 54 48 55 45 57 50
62 44 64 43 52 38 59 55 41 53 49 34 35 54 45
68 38 50 60 39 59 40 57 54 23
C
C
C
HEAD IDENTIFICATION RUN
IDEN PERFORM IDENTIFICATION RUN
STOP END OF PROGRAM
```

Figure A.5.1 Program A.5.1. (Identification run for time series 2.1)

269

```
C    PROGRAM A.5.2 COMPLETE PROGRAM FOR TIME SERIES 2.1
C
C
C
DATA 70
47 64   23 71 38 64 55 41 59 48 71 35 57 40 58
44 80 55 37 74 51 57 50 60 45 57 50 45 25 59
50 71 56 74 50 58 45 54 36 54 48 55 45 57 50
62 44 64 43 52 38 59 55 41 53 49 34 35 54 45
68 38 50 60 39 59 40 57 54 23
C
C
C
HEAD IDENTIFICATION RUN
IDEN
C
C
C
HEAD ESTIMATION RUN USING AR(1) MODEL
MEAN 2 INCLUDE CONSTANT TERM IN MODEL
RART 1 INCLUDE REGULAR AUTOREGRESSIVE TERM OF ORDER ONE IN MODEL
ESTI PERFORM ESTIMATION RUN
C
C
C
HEAD GRID RUN USING AR(2) MODEL
NEWM SPECIFY NEW MODEL
MEAN 2
RART 1 -0.4 SPECIFY VALUE OF REGULAR AUTOREGRESSIVE TERM OF ORDER ONE
RART 2 0 SPECIFY VALUE OF REGULAR AUTOREGRESSIVE TERM OF ORDER TWO
GRID 1 0.1 2 0.1 PERFORM GRID RUN USING SPECIFIED INCREMENTS OF TWO PARAMETERS
C
C
C
HEAD ESTIMATION RUN USING AR(2) MODEL
NEWM
MEAN 2
RART 1
RART 2 INCLUDE REGULAR AUTOREGRESSIVE TERM OF ORDER TWO IN MODEL
FORE 10 CALCULATE FORECASTS FOR TEN FUTURE TIME PERIODS
ESTI
C
C
C
HEAD OVERFIT AR(3) MODEL
NEWM
MEAN 2
RART 1
RART 2
RART 3 INCLUDE REGULAR AUTOREGRESSIVE TERM OF ORDER THREE IN MODEL
ESTI
C
C
C
HEAD OVERFIT ARMA(1,2) MODEL
NEWM
MEAN 2
RART 1
RART 2
RMAT 1 INCLUDE REGULAR MOVING AVERAGE TERM OF ORDER ONE IN MODEL
ESTI
STOP
```

Figure A.5.2 Program A.5.2. (Complete program for time series 2.1)

```
C     PROGRAM A.5.3 COMPLETE PROGRAM FOR TIME SERIES 5.3
C
C
C
DATA 197
17.0 16.6 16.3 16.1 17.1 16.9 16.8 17.4 17.1 17.0
16.7 17.4 17.2 17.4 17.4 17.0 17.3 17.2 17.4 15.8
17.1 17.4 17.4 17.5 17.4 17.6 17.4 17.3 17.0 17.8
17.5 18.1 17.5 17.4 17.4 17.1 17.6 17.7 17.4 17.8
17.6 17.5 16.5 17.8 17.3 17.3 17.1 17.4 16.9 17.3
17.6 16.9 16.7 16.8 16.8 17.2 16.8 17.6 17.2 16.6
17.1 16.9 16.6 18.0 17.2 17.3 17.0 16.9 17.3 16.8
17.3 17.4 17.7 16.8 16.9 17.0 16.9 17.0 16.6 16.7
16.8 16.7 16.4 16.5 16.4 16.6 16.5 16.7 16.4 16.4
16.2 16.4 16.3 16.4 17.0 16.9 17.1 17.1 16.7 16.9
16.5 17.2 16.4 17.0 17.0 16.7 16.2 16.6 16.9 16.5
16.6 16.6 17.0 17.1 17.1 16.7 16.8 16.3 16.6 16.8
16.9 17.1 16.8 17.0 17.2 17.3 17.2 17.3 17.2 17.2
17.5 16.9 16.9 16.9 17.0 16.5 16.7 16.8 16.7 16.7
16.6 16.5 17.0 16.7 16.7 16.9 17.4 17.1 17.0 16.8
17.2 17.2 17.4 17.2 16.9 16.8 17.0 17.4 17.2 17.2
17.1 17.1 17.1 17.4 17.2 16.9 16.9 17.0 16.7 16.9
17.3 17.8 17.8 17.6 17.5 17.0 16.9 17.1 17.2 17.4
17.5 17.9 17.0 17.0 17.0 17.2 17.3 17.4 17.4 17.0
18.0 18.2 17.6 17.8 17.7 17.2 17.4
C
C
C
HEAD IDENTIFICATION RUN
IDEN
NRDF 1 PERFORM ONE REGULAR DIFFERENCE
IDEN
C
C
C
HEAD ESTIMATION RUN USING IMA(1,1) MODEL
MEAN 0 NO CONSTANT TERM IS INCLUDED IN MODEL
RMAT 1
FORE 10
ESTI
C
C
C
HEAD OVERFIT ARIMA(1,1,1) MODEL
NEWM
MEAN 0
RART 1
RMAT 1
ESTI
C
C
C
HEAD OVERFIT IMA(1,2) MODEL
NEWM
MEAN 0
RMAT 1
RMAT 2 INCLUDE REGULAR MOVING AVERAGE TERM OF ORDER TWO IN MOCEL
ESTI
C
C
C
HEAD CHECK FOR OVERDIFFERENCING
NRDF 2 PERFORM TWO REGULAR DIFFERENCES
IDEN
STOP
```

Figure A.5.3   Program A.5.3. (Complete program for time series 5.3)

```
C     PROGRAM A.5.4 COMPLETE PROGRAM FOR TIME SERIES 2.4
C
C
C
DATA 144
112   118   132   129   121   135   148   148   136   119   104   118
115   126   141   135   125   149   170   170   158   133   114   140
145   150   178   163   172   178   199   199   184   162   146   166
171   180   193  ·181   183   218   230   242   209   191   172   194
196   196   236   235   229   243   264   272   237   211   180   201
204   188   235   227   234   264   302   293   259   229   203   229
242   233   267   269   270   315   364   347   312   274   237   278
284   277   317   313   318   374   413   405   355   306   271   306
315   301   356   348   355   422   465   467   404   347   305   336
340   318   362   348   363   435   491   505   404   359   310   337
360   342   406   396   420   472   548   559   463   407   362   405
417   391   419   461   472   535   622   606   508   461   390   432
C
C
C
HEAD IDENTIFICATION RUN
NACR 36 CALCULATE THIRTY SIX SAMPLE AUTOCORRELATIONS
NPAC 36 CALCULATE THIRTY SIX SAMPLE PARTIAL AUTOCORRELATIONS
IDEN
TRAN 0 0 PERFORM LOGARITHMIC TRANSFORMATION
IDEN
NRDF 1 PERFORM ONE REGULAR DIFFERENCE
IDEN
NRDF 0
NSDF 1 12 PERFORM ONE SEASONAL DIFFERENCE OF PERIOD TWELVE
IDEN
NRDF 1 PERFORM ONE REGULAR AND ONE SEASONAL DIFFERENCE OF PERIOD TWELVE
IDEN
C
C
C
HEAD ESTIMATION RUN USING (0,1,1)*(0,1,1)12 MODEL
MEAN 0
RMAT 1
SMAT 12 INCLUDE SEASONAL MOVING AVERAGE TERM OF ORDER ONE AND PERIOD TWELVE
FORE 12
ESTI
```

Figure A.5.4 Program A.5.4. (Complete program for time series 2.4)

One of the important features of TSERIES is its easy-to-use free field command structure which was patterned after two other popular statistical packages, OMNITAB and MINITAB. For example, the following commands would be sufficient to produce outputs for identification of a time series model for a stationary time series of length 200:

DATA 200

> Any number of cards containing the
> 200 observations in free field format.

IDEN
STOP

If first differences of the time series had been desired for the evaluations, an NRDF 1 command could have been inserted before the IDEN command.

The commands to estimate the parameters of an ARIMA model are equally simple. Suppose that a first-order autoregressive model has been identified for an example. The following TSERIES commands would fit the model, provide outputs for diagnostic checking, and provide forecasts for ten periods following the last observation:

```
C
C
C
HEAD OVERFIT (1,1,1)*(0,1,1)12 MODEL
NEWM
MEAN 0
RART 1
RMAT 1
SMAT 12
ESTI
C
C
C
HEAD OVERFIT (0,1,2)*(0,1,1)12 MODEL
NEWM
MEAN 0
RMAT 1
RMAT 2
SMAT 12
ESTI
C
C
C
HEAD OVERFIT (0,1,1)*(1,1,1)12 MODEL
NEWM
MEAN 0
RMAT 1
SART 12 INCLUDE SEASONAL AUTOREGRESSIVE TERM OF ORDER ONE AND PERIOD TWELVE
SMAT 12
ESTI
C
C
C
HEAD OVERFIT (0,1,1)*(0,1,2)12 MODEL
NEWM
MEAN 0
RMAT 1
SMAT 12
SMAT 24 INCLUDE SEASONAL MOVING AVERAGE TERM OF ORDER TWO AND PERIOD TWELVE
ESTI
STOP
```

Figure A.5.5 Continuation of Program A.5.4

```
DATA 200
         Any number of cards containing the
         200 observations in free field format.
RART 1
FORE 10
ESTI
STOP
```

The examples illustrate only seven of the TSERIES commands. Thirty other commands are available to specify other models and to request or control various user options, some of which are indicated below. The TSERIES commands are described in detail in the TSERIES users' manual (Meeker 1977).

TSERIES provides outputs for identification, fitting, and forecasting of ARIMA time series models. For identification, TSERIES provides the sample mean and variance of the (possibly transformed and differenced) time series as well as the sample autocorrelation and partial autocorrelation functions. Estimation output includes progress of the Marquardt nonlinear least squares algorithm, the final estimates and their standard errors, and the variance–covariance and correlation matrices of the estimated parameters. A number of outputs for diagnostic checking of the model is also available, including the autocorrelation function, a normalized

274

cumulative periodogram, a normal probability plot, and various other functions of the residuals. If requested, forecasts from the fitted model are also provided. As a special option, the user can request printing of a grid of sum of squares values for specified increments of two selected parameter values. This can be used, for example, to assess the characteristics of the likelihood function and to determine if the Marquardt algorithm converged properly.

Some other features of TSERIES are:

1. optional preliminary estimation of the model parameters;
2. least squares (i.e. approximate maximum likelihood) estimation, employing 'back forecasting';
3. an extensive error checking facility;
4. file-handling capabilities for reading and writing of time series data or residuals.

TSERIES also allows the user to easily:

1. transform and/or difference the inputted time series;
2. suppress printing of unwanted outputs;
3. change the control parameters of the Marquardt algorithm;
4. analyse many time series in one program run.

TSERIES is written in ANSI FORTRAN IV and is reasonably machine-independent. To date, it has been run on Burroughs, Honeywell, Univac, and IBM computers in the batch mode, and in a slightly modified form (with respect to input/output) on the General Electric Mark III and IBM TSO time-sharing systems. As currently dimensioned (300 observations and ten parameters), the program requires approximately $128k$ bytes ($32k$ words) of memory on an IBM 360/65. The program can be redimensioned to handle larger problems. TSERIES should be able to run on any medium-to-large-scale system with little or no modification.

The TSERIES user's manual (Meeker 1977) assumes some familiarity with Box–Jenkins methodology. Box and Jenkins (1976) give a comprehensive account of and Nelson (1973) provides a good introduction to the necessary material. In addition to instructions on how to use TSERIES, the user's manual contains a detailed example which employs most of the frequently used TSERIES commands and a complete description of the program input and output. Nine appendices treat topics of special interest such as computational details, explanation of error messages, and instructions for installation of the program. Copies of the TSERIES user's manual and/or a magnetic tape of the source program and example data can be obtained from the author for a nominal charge to cover costs.

REFERENCES

Box, G. E. P., and Jenkins, G. M. (1976). *Time Series Analysis: Forecasting and Control*, revised ed., Holden-Day, San Francisco.
Meeker, W. Q., Jr (1977), 'TSERIES User's Manual,' available from the author, Statistical Laboratory, Iowa State University, Ames, IA 50011.
Nelson, C. R. (1973). *Applied Time Series Analysis for Managerial Forecasting*, Holden-Day, San Francisco.

Appendix A.6

Some computer packages for time series analysis using the Box–Jenkins approach

Table A.6.1

Distributor	Package name	Program name	Univariate Box–Jenkins	Transfer function or multivariate Box–Jenkins	Academic License Fee Initial	Academic License Fee Renewal
SAS Institute Inc., SAS Circle, Box 8000, Cary, NC 275 11	SAS	SAS/ETS	X	X	$2000 p.a.	$1000 p.a.
SPSS, Inc., Suite 3300, 444 N. Michigan Avenue, Chicago, IL 60611	IDA		X	—	$1000 p.a.	$1000 p.a.
BMDP Statistical Software, Department of Biomathematics, University of California, Los Angeles, CA 90024	BMDP	BMDP2T	X	X	$500 p.a.	$500 p.a.
Professor Thomas A. Ryan, Minitab Project, 215 Pond Laboratory, University Park, PA 16802	MINITAB		X	—	$500 p.a.	$500 p.a.
Gwilym Jenkins and Partners, 8501 South Pennsylvania, Oklahoma City, OK 73159	JENASYS	UNISTOC	X	—	$1250	—
		UNITRAN	—	X	$1250	—
		MULTISTOC	—	X	$1500	—
		MULTITRAN	—	X	$1500	—

Organization	Product	Routines			Price	
Applied Decision Systems, 33 Hayden Avenue, Lexington, MA 02173	SYBIL/RUNNER	SR1	X	—	$1000	—
		SR2	—	X	$1000	—
Charles R. Nelson Associates, Inc., 4921 Northeast 39th Street, Seattle, WA 98015		IDENT, ESTIMATE and FORECAST	X	—	$500	—
		CROSSCORR, TRANSEST and TRANSFOR	—	X	$1000	—
Automatic Forecasting Systems, Inc., P.O. Box 563, Hatboro, PA 19040	PACK		X	X	$175	—
Professor G. C. Tiao, Department of Statistics, 1210 West Dayton Street, Maidison, WI 53706	WMTS-1		—	X	$100	—
Professor William Q. Meeker, Jr, Statistical Laboratory, Iowa State University, Ames, IA 50011	TSERIES		X	—	$50	—

Index

Accuracy, 3, 5, 9
ACF, 32, 34
AR(1) model, 53, 91, 94, 116, 182, 267
  ACF for, 54, 73–74, 79–80, 94
  estimated standard error for, 86
  forecasts for, 57, 75, 103, 139
  least squares estimates for, 96
  mean of, 53, 74
  PACF for, 55, 73–74, 79–80, 94
  stationarity conditions for, 54, 73, 100
  starting value problem, 96
  sum of squares for, 96
  variance of, 54, 74
  variance of forecast error for, 57, 75
AR(2) model, 59, 116, 267
  ACF for, 59, 73–74, 79
  estimated standard error for, 86
  forecasts for, 75
  mean of, 74
  PACF for, 60, 73–74, 79
  stationarity conditions for, 59, 73
  variance of, 74
variance of forecast error for, 75
AR(p) model, 79
  sum of squares for, 97
ARI(1, 1) model, 138, 149, 267
  forecasts for, 139
ARI(2, 1) model, 138, 267
ARI(p, d) model, 138
ARIMA(1, 1, 1) model, 141, 267
ARIMA(p, 1, q) model, 141
ARIMA(p, d, q) model, 141
ARMA models, 4, 79
ARMA(1, 1) model, 70–71, 91, 267
  ACF for, 71, 73–74, 79
  estimated standard error for, 86

forecasts for, 75
invertibility condition for, 71, 73
mean for, 74
non-stationary, 139
PACF for, 71, 73–74, 79
stationarity condition for, 71, 73
variance of, 74
variance of forecast error for, 75
ARMA(2, 1) model, 120
ARMA(p, q) model, 72, 79, 83, 85
Autocorrelation coefficient, 31–32
Autocorrelation function, 31–32
Autoregression coefficient, 53, 59
Autoregressive integrated moving
  average model, 138–142
Autoregressive model, 53–62
  regular, 182
Autoregressive moving average model, 4,
  70–75
Autoregressive term, 131

Back forecasting, 69, 96, 109
Bayesian forecasting, 4, 11, 19
Box–Jenkins method, ix, 4, 7–11, 77,
  212
  advantages and disadvantages, ix
  multivariate, 5, 7–12
  stages in, 77
  univariate, 5
Box–Pierce chi-square statistic, 90, 101,
  212

Causal models, 4, 8, 11, 13
Census X.11, 4
Chance significance, 82, 89, 100
Chi-squared distribution, 89, 243

Constant term in model, 50, 90, 95, 109, 116, 142, 146, 158, 189, 192, 200, 209, 212
Contours, 131, 137
Correlation coefficient, 30
Critical value, 89
Cumulative periodogram, 88, 100
Cyclical pattern, 7
Cyclicality, 4

Data requirements, 5, 8
Decision making, 2
Decomposition, 4, 7–11
Dependent variable, 4
Deterministic process, 23
Deviations, 50
Diagnostic checking, 78, 86, 212
Differences, first regular, 132
    second regular, 133
    seasonal, 179
Differencing, 34, 86, 130, 179, 212
Discontinuities, 16

Econometrics, 5, 7–12
Elementary outcomes, 19
Estimated standard error, 86
Estimation of parameters, 49, 78, 83–86
Event, 20
    dependent, 28
    independent, 28
Expected value, 21
Exponential smoothing, simple, 4, 7–10, 140

Forecasts, minimum mean square error, 47–48
    point, 2
    prediction interval, 2, 49
    short term, ix, 3, 7–8
    updating, 212
Forecast control, 13
Forecast error, 47–48
    one step ahead, 52, 57, 67, 72, 83, 87
Forecast function, 47
Forecast profile, 47
Forecasting, ix, 79
Forecasting method, qualitative, 3
    quantitative, 1, 3, 7

Grid search, 85, 97, 109, 116

Holt–Winters, 4, 7–10
Horizontal pattern, 7, 16

Identification, ix, 11, 78–83
    multiplicative seasonal models, 188
IMA(1, 1) model, 139, 155, 267
    forecasts for, 140
IMA(1, 1) model, 134, 267
IMA(d, q) model, 139
Information at origin t, 48
Integrated moving average models, 139
Intervention analysis, 19
Invertibility, 64, 85–86

Kalman filtering, 4

Lead time, 2, 5, 47
Least squares estimates, 58, 84
Linear trend, 131, 137

MA(1) model, 62–69, 91, 108, 184, 267
    ACF for, 65, 73–74, 79
    estimated standard error for, 86
    forecasts for, 67, 75, 140
    invertibility condition for, 65, 73, 110
    mean of, 64, 74
    PACF for, 66, 73–74, 79
    starting value problem for, 68, 109
    sum of squares for, 109
    variance of, 64, 74
    variance of forecast error for, 69, 75
MA(2) model, 70, 122, 267
    ACF for, 70, 73–74, 79
    estimated standard error, 86
    forecasts for, 70, 75
    invertibility condition for, 70, 73
    mean of, 70, 74
    PACF for, 70, 73–74, 79
    variance of, 70, 74
    variance of forecast error for, 75
MA(q) model, 79
    ACF for, 81
Markov process, 53
Mean, of random variable, 22
    of time series, 23, 25
Mean square error of forecast, 48, 91

Method of least squares, 212
Model, integrated, 153
   linear regression, 53
   moving average, 62–70
   multiplicative seasonal, 185
   non-multiplicative, 187
   non-stationary, 78, 87
   seasonal, 78, 89
   time series, 3, 77
   tentative, 78–79, 86
Moving average coefficient, 64, 70
Moving average term, 109
Multiple regression, 5, 7–12

Noise, 50
Non-linear least squares, 114
Non-stationarity, in the mean, 26, 77,
   129
   in the seasonal pattern, 180
   in the variance, 26, 35, 78, 88, 129
Normal curve, 21
Normal probabability distribution, 21,
   23, 49, 242
Normal probability plot, 88, 100
Normal variable, 81

Operator, backward shift, 134, 142,
   180, 186
   regular autoregressive, 187–189, 233
   regular moving average, 187-189,
   233
   seasonal autoregressive, 187–189,
   233
   seasonal moving average, 187–189,
   233
Origin for forecast, 47
Outlier, 19
Overdifferencing, 136
Overfitting, 90, 101, 212

PACF, 38
Parameters, 23, 58
   redundant, 71
Partial autocorrelation function, 37–38
Period of seasonal pattern, 179
Plots of means and standard deviations,
   26
Portmanteau lack of fit test, 90
Prediction limits, 49, 58
Preliminary estimates, 85

Principle of least squares, 84
Principle of parsimonious parameteriza-
   tion, 80, 91, 115
Probability, 19
Probability density function, 20
Probability distribution, 20
Probability mass function, 20, 30
Process, stochastic, 23, 77
   white noise, 50
Purely random model, 50

Quadratic trend, 132

Random experiment, 19
Random shock, 50
Random variables, continuous, 20
   dependent, 30
   discrete, 20
   independent, 30
Random walk model, 136–137, 142,
   267
   forecasts for, 137
   variance of forecast error for, 137
Randomness, 4
Realization, 24
Regression equation, 5
Residual, 87
   mean, 90
   sum of squares, 88
   variance, 90. 212
Rule of thumb, 81

Sample ACF of the residuals, 100, 212
Sample autocorrelation coefficient of
   the residuals, 89
Sample PACF of the residuals, 212
Sample space, 39
SAR(1) model, 182–183, 192
Seasonal autoregressive and moving
   average models, 182–185
Seasonal autoregressive model, 182
Seasonal moving average model, 184
Seasonal pattern, 7
Seasonality, 4, 16, 35
SMA(1) model, 184
Spikes, satellite, 188
Standard deviation, of random variable,
   23
   of time series, 23, 25
Starting value problems, 85

Stationarity, 24, 31
Stationarity conditions, 85–86
Stationarity, in the mean, 212
  in the mean and variance, 24
  in the variance, 212
Stock market prices, 136, 142
Sum of squared residuals, 88
Sum of squares, 84
Sum of squares function, 84
Systematic changes, in mean level, 132
  in slope, 132

Testing for fit, 52
Tests for significance, 80
  for a sample autocorrelation
    coefficient, 81
  for a sample partial autocorrelation
    coefficient, 82
  for parameter estimates, 87
Time series, ix, 15
  accumulated, 16
  aggregated, 16
  continuous, 15
  deterministic, 131–132
  discrete, 15
  homogeneous, 135
  homogeneously non-stationary in the
    mean, 135
  non-stationary, x, 19, 129–177
  observed, 24, 77
  sampled, 15

  seasonal, x, 179
  stationary, x, 18, 47, 77
Time series models, 8, 12
Transfer functions, 5
Transformations, 26, 129–131, 190,
  212
  fourth root, 267
  logarithmic, 26, 129, 203, 267
  square root, 130
t-ratio, 81–82
Trend, 4, 7, 16, 34
TSERIES, x, 40, 82, 83, 85, 87, 90, 97,
  109, 121, 130, 135, 142, 160,
  189, 212–213, 269, 278

Variables, dependent, 31
  independent, 4, 31
Variance, of forecast error, 49
  of random variable, 22
  of time series, 25
Visual examination, 16, 19, 35, 179

White noise model, 49, 267
  ACF for, 50, 73–74, 79, 88
  forecasts for, 52, 75
  mean of, 51, 74
  PACF for, 50, 73–74, 79, 88
  variance of, 51–74
  variance of forecast error for, 52, 75
White noise process, 52, 88
Working series, 94, 142